P9-CCU-461

The Natural Formula Book for Home & Yard

edited by Dan Wallace

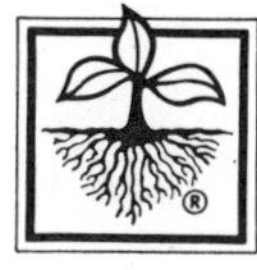

Rodale Press, Emmaus, Pennsylvania

The formulas in *The Natural Formula Book for Home and Yard* have been chosen for their emphasis on readily available, natural substances, commonly known for their gentleness and effectiveness. We have attempted to include cautions and guidelines for using ingredients in this book wherever appropriate. Yet, we realize that it is impossible for us to anticipate every conceivable use of formulas and the possible problems any use could cause. Moreover, we cannot know just what kinds of physical reactions or allergies some of you might have to substances used in this book.

For this reason, we cannot assume responsibility for the effects of using the formulas or other information found here. We recommend that before you begin to use any formula or substance you read the directions carefully. If you have any questions concerning the safety or use of any formula, we urge you to consult first with a physician or other appropriate professional.

Printed in the United States of America on recycled paper containing a high percentage of de-inked fiber.

Library of Congress Cataloging in Publication Data

Main entry under title:

The Natural formula book for home and yard.

Bibliography: p.
Includes index.
1. Recipes. I. Wallace, Dan.
TX158.N37 640′.2 82-5212
ISBN 0-87857-399-2 hardcover AACR2

4 6 8 10 9 7 5 hardcover

Table of Contents

Introduction
Natural Formulas: Why and How

If you're accustomed to doing things for yourself and your family, or if you'd like to, you're aware of the satisfaction that self-sufficiency brings to you. It's hard not to feel great when you show off some prize vegetables or flowers that you grew or a finely tooled rocking chair that you made yourself from raw lumber. A fire in a stove that burns with wood that you cut adds another dimension to the pleasure of the warm flames. No doubt once you've become self-sufficient in one area, you'll be eager to try another.

Making your own household products can give you the same sense of accomplishment that you receive from doing other projects at home. Whipping together ingredients you have on hand to make just the right formula for a certain task can be lots of fun in itself. And seeing that product work exactly right can fill you with a sense of command over your household that you'll find elating. You decide what ingredients to bring into your home, you know just how to use and store them, and you can be sure that their disposal is safe for you, your family, and your neighbors—in short, for the entire environment. You can save quite a bit of money by using natural formulas, too. With homemade products you don't pay the extra costs of advertising and packaging for commercial products.

In the *Natural Formula Book for Home and Yard* you'll find instructions for making home products for a wide range of chores around your household and yard. We also put in many suggestions on sound practices for doing these chores, to make things easier over the long run. By following these tips, you'll find each task less of a job every time you do it.

We've divided the formulas into four parts: "Household Products," "Natural Hygiene and Remedies," "Natural Convenience Foods," and "Outdoor Formulas." We also included four special sections on home skills that require more involved operations. These are "Homemade Soap," "Dyeing Wools with Natural Dyes," "Making Candles," and "Homemade Paints." Since we expect this book ultimately to be used as a reference, we've made it easy for you to find your way around. To look up a broad subject, like floors, for example, see the Table of Contents. If you need to know about a particular material or surface and you are unsure what subject it might fall under, or to locate any formula by name (one you've used before, perhaps) check the Index. General points of information can be helpful, too, to get the most out of the formulas. These points introduce each part, and we're sure that you'll find reading them useful. Also, even common substances sometimes need to be handled with care, so we've included a table below, listing the most frequently used ingredients along with cautions that you should follow when using them.

Common Ingredients and Cautions for Their Use

The substances listed below are common household items that are used in many of the formulas throughout this book.

While they are readily available in grocery stores, drugstores, and hardware stores, they should be handled carefully and stored away from children and pets. This list of cautions will enable you to use these ingredients safely when mixing up your own formulas.

Alcohol	Flammable and toxic; can be fatal if swallowed. Wear rubber gloves and work away from heat and flames.
Ammonia, household	Can irritate skin and eyes and is caustic if swallowed. Use in a well-ventilated area, wear rubber gloves, and avoid spills and splashes. *Never mix products containing ammonia with chlorine bleach, toilet bowl cleaners, rust removers, or oven cleaners.* The combination releases powerful, pungent, poisonous gases called chloramines.
Bleach, liquid chlorine	Do not use on items that are not colorfast. Use in a well-ventilated area, and wear rubber gloves. *Never mix with ammonia or toilet bowl cleaners.*
Hydrogen peroxide	Sold in solutions of various strengths; concentrated solutions are highly toxic and strong irritants. Flammable—keep away from heat and flames. Wear rubber gloves and use in a well-ventilated area.

Kerosene	Flammable—keep away from heat and flames. Toxic if absorbed through the skin, and poisonous if swallowed. Use in a well-ventilated area, and wear rubber gloves. *When using kerosene in the kitchen, turn off the pilot light if you have a gas range.*
Linseed oil, boiled	May be toxic; may contain traces of lead, cobalt, and manganese substances.
Mineral oil	Flammable—keep away from heat and flames.
Mineral spirits (naphtha)	Vapors are irritating; substance is poisonous if swallowed. Flammable—use in a well-ventilated area and turn off pilot light of gas range.
Pine oil	Can irritate skin and mucous membranes; is moderately toxic if swallowed. Combustible—use in a well-ventilated area.
Shellac	Flammable and toxic; keep away from heat and flames.
Turpentine	Flammable—keep away from heat and flames. Toxic if absorbed through the skin; can be fatal if swallowed. Use in a well-ventilated area, and wear rubber gloves.
Washing soda	Moderately toxic; can irritate mucous membranes. Wear rubber gloves when handling, and work in a well-ventilated area.

Finally, we've put together some pertinent appendices—a list of chemicals and their uses, ingredient sources common in most localities, a list of mail-order suppliers and manufacturers for materials you can't find in stores, and a reading list. The most important of these is Appendix A, "Chemical Substances and Their Recommended Uses." In this reference you'll find ingredients listed in the formulas and also some other chemical agents that you might want to consider for your own products. We've listed chemical terms as well as popular names, the appearance of the substance, any cautions necessary, and recommendations for use—internal, external, household, or not at all. If you have a question on any substance in this book, either for experiments with your own formulas or just to clear up some point, refer to this appendix first.

You can roll up your sleeves now, and get ready to mix; it's time to work with some formulas.

Part I Household Products

Suzanne Ebbert and Deborah Wilson

Buying household products at the supermarket can really add to the total of your bill; various cleaners and polishes can account for 30 percent or more of the items on an average shopping list. Of course, we need these products to keep our homes clean and orderly, but often when we buy a commercial product we're merely paying for the convenience of having someone else mix some simple ingredients together and put them into a handy dispenser. As we mentioned, the cost of such commodities is increased by advertising and fancy packaging, as you can see just by comparing a nationally advertised brand with one less well known—usually the national brand is more expensive. (Whenever you do buy something at the supermarket, whether it's an ingredient for your own homemade product or a product itself, try to buy the generic or store brand, which should be cheaper without these extra expenses.)

Perhaps more significant than the high cost of commercial formulas is the guessing game consumers often have to play while trying to figure out the contents of products they're buying. Unless you're an avid label reader, you might be overlooking substances that you want to avoid. Some labels carry only a partial list of ingredients, and a few list none at all. Knowing what is in a product can help you to identify and prevent certain allergic reactions (such as respiratory ailments and skin irritations) that are caused by various household products. Since some of these conditions can appear without a hint as to their source (irritating residues of some laundry products remain even after the rinse cycle), it's better to skirt as many commercial commodities with unfamiliar contents as possible. One good way to do this is to make them at home from your own formulas.

By preparing your own household products, you'll also relearn that old, almost lost skill called improvisation. Often, more than one formula will work for the same job. If you're out of the ingredients you need for one product, you can substitute another formula without running into difficulties, or to the store, for that matter.

Many of the basic ingredients for our formulas are familiar household items, such as ammonia, bleach, salt, vinegar, and baking soda. Some of these work as multipurpose cleaning agents, and combinations of many of them broaden their cleaning power even further. The table "Basic Ingredients for All-Purpose Cleaning" (below) gives an idea of the versatility of these common agents.

You'll find that the products from these formulas work just as well as their commercial counterparts and that many of them out-perform the brand names. Homemade agents are especially effective, because you control the proportions of the formulas, and you can increase or decrease the amount of some ingredients to arm you with the strength of the cleaners you want for your way of cleaning. You can also eliminate unnecessary ingredients from your formulas (for example, the perfumes and blue coloring in commercial window cleaners) that only add to the cost of store-bought goods. For those of you who like a touch of color, however, we've included a formula for a blue window cleaner.

Before you begin to work with any formulas, you may want to familiarize yourself with the guidelines below, which will help you to operate safely and efficiently.

Always follow the directions carefully. Read the entire formula before you start mixing. Heed all cautions! These cautions are very important. Whether you plan to use these formulas or to continue to rely upon commercial preparations, keep the phone number of your local poison control center handy.

As you gain experience with making your own household products, you'll find that you may prefer to mix some products in large batches. This works well for items that you use frequently. On the other hand, you will want to mix some formulas, such as certain specialty cleaners, only as you need them.

Most times you'll find that the best storage containers for your homemade products are empty containers that were used for similar commercial preparations. Manufacturers put a lot of time and money into the design of packaging containers. Although most containers are intended to be disposable, they can last for years, so save them. Make sure they are sturdy, nonreactive, and have good lids. Always start with clean, dry containers. Wash old containers with soap or mild detergent and warm water, then rinse and dry well.

Clearly mark each container, using a label such as the one below, listing important information. For extra safety, draw a skull-and-crossbones picture on the label of these or any other poisonous preparations, and label them *Poison.* Some state and local poison control centers have standard labels available. See if yours does.

Safety and *caution!* These two words can't be stressed enough. Almost any substance

This bottle contains: ________________
Prepared by: ________________
Date: ________________
Ingredients: ________________
Cautions: ________________
Poison control center phone number: ________________

can represent a potential hazard. Always follow directions for formulas carefully. Read and heed warnings on all commercial preparations you buy.

Very volatile substances such as kerosene and gasoline require a small vent opening in the storage container—use only approved containers for these items.

Do not mix two or more substances unless you are sure the mixing will not result in a violent, uncontrollable reaction or produce an extremely toxic by-product.

For extra safety, wear safety glasses or goggles when preparing solutions that can splatter. A pair can be purchased at your hardware store.

Always store both homemade and commercial products high on a shelf in a locked closet where children and pets can't possibly get at them. When using any potentially poisonous substance, never leave children or pets alone with it—not even for a few seconds.

Basic Ingredients for All-Purpose Cleaning

Ingredient	What It Can Do
Ammonia, household	Clean carpets, copper, dishes, enamel, floors, Formica, garbage cans, glass, grout, jewelry, linoleum, ovens, porcelain, refrigerators, showers, stainless steel, stoves, tubs, windows, and woodwork (painted). Remove stains.
Baking soda	Clean, deodorize carpets, counter tops, drains, refrigerators, upholstery, and vinyl. Extinguish grease fires. Freshen fabrics. Remove stains. Scour and/or polish aluminum, chrome, grout, jewelry, plastic, porcelain, silver, stainless steel, and tin. Soften fabrics.

Ingredient	What It Can Do
Bleach, liquid chlorine	Clean, deodorize, and disinfect basins, concrete, grout, sinks, tiles, toilet bowls, and tubs. Remove mildew and stains from carpets, clothes, concrete, upholstery, and wood floors.
Borax	Clean wallpaper, walls, and floors. Deodorize. Improve detergent power. Remove stains.
Cornstarch	Clean windows. Polish furniture. Remove stains. Shampoo carpets and rugs. Starch clothes.
Lemon juice	Deodorize. Clean windows and other glass. Remove stains from aluminum, clothes, and porcelain.
Mineral oil	Polish furniture. Wax floors.
Soap and water	Clean cars, clothes, dishes, doors, floors, glass, jewelry, people, pets, sporting goods, tools, walls, windows, and woodwork.
Steel wool	Remove rust and rust stains and stubborn films. Scour barbecue grills and broiler pans.
Vinegar	Clean bricks, carpets, coffeepots, dishes, fireplaces, glass, grout, paint brushes, walls, and windows. Polish metals. Remove mildew, spots (hard-water), stains, and wax buildup. Soften fabrics.
Washing soda	Clean and cut grease on barbecue grills, broiler pans, concrete, drains, fireplaces, floors, ovens, and walls. Improve detergent power. Remove stains. Soften water.

Chapter 1 General Cleaning

Manufacturers spend a lot of money trying to convince us, through the media and fancy packaging, that we need one special product for each cleaning job. That advertising is paid for by the consumer, who spends several cents an ounce for a catchy name or nifty gimmick. Fortunately, the ingredients to make inexpensive and safe alternatives are probably already in your kitchen cabinets. You can use them straight or mix them together to make one solution that will clean everything, even the kitchen sink.

All-Purpose Cleaners

Why pay for water when you already pay a water bill? Most all-purpose cleaners on the grocery shelves contain up to 95 percent water. They also contain strong alkaline detergents and, in some cases, solvents or traces of ammonia to loosen dirt and grime. Because they are strong cleaners, the ingredients are caustic to the skin and can be harmful if swallowed. Cleaners containing phosphates also pollute our water systems. Many common household products can be used to clean a variety of surfaces just as effectively, maybe even more safely, and they cost less.

Liquid chlorine bleach, or household bleach, is a disinfecting, deodorizing liquid that also bleaches out stubborn stains. A solution of bleach and water will clean and sanitize tile, porcelain, and enameled surfaces in the kitchen and bathroom.

■ All-Purpose Bleach Cleaner

2 tablespoons liquid chlorine bleach
1 quart cold water

Mix the bleach and water in a bucket. Moisten a cloth with the solution and wipe on surface to be cleaned. Let the solution stand about 2 minutes, then rinse well. Do not use on items that are not colorfast. If doubtful, spot-test on a hidden area first.

Yield: about 1 quart

Household ammonia, a weak solution of ammonium hydroxide in water, is one of the best grease and grime fighters around. Used full strength, ammonia removes tough-to-remove lipstick, tar, and grease stains. Mixed with varying amounts of water, it is an excellent light- to heavy-duty cleaner that dissolves and loosens dirt on glass, tile, enamel, and Formica surfaces.

You can make your own household ammonia, but the ammonium hydroxide which is used is more concentrated and, thus, more caustic. Because commercial ammonia costs only about a penny per fluid ounce, buying the ready-made solution is probably cheaper and safer.

■ Multipurpose Ammonia Cleaner

½ cup household ammonia
1 gallon warm water

Thoroughly mix ammonia and water in a pail. Use to scrub appliances, bathroom fixtures, floors, tiles, and painted walls, and to deodorize drains and garbage disposals.

Yield: about 1 gallon

Sodium carbonate, also known as washing soda, sal soda, or soda ash, is an alkali used in detergents and laundry bleach powders. (The term *alkali* derives from the Arabian word *alqili*, which means ashes of the saltwort plant.) In ancient times, sodium carbonate was obtained from the ashes of sea plants; the plants contained common salt, or sodium chloride.

In the late 1700s, a French surgeon invented a method to mass-produce washing soda by using sulfuric acid and salt; this method was used for at least a century. Today, two commercial processes are used: the Solvay method, which produces both baking soda (sodium bicarbonate) and washing soda; and an electrolytic process used to manufacture bleach, which provides both sodas as by-products.

Washing soda acts as a water-softening chemical that combines with minerals in hard water; the resulting compounds won't stay dissolved in water or cling as scum to clothes or other surfaces. By itself, washing soda cuts grease and removes stubborn stains. Better yet, it costs only about 2 cents an ounce and is available in most grocery stores.

■ Multipurpose Washing Soda Cleaner

3 tablespoons washing soda
1 quart warm water

Stir washing soda into water in a bucket until the washing soda dissolves. Sponge this on heavy dirt, or scrub with a stiff brush. This solution is especially effective on heavily soiled objects such as broiler pans, ovens, and barbecue grills.

Yield: about 1 quart

The most effective all-purpose cleaner you can make contains the cleaning power of both household ammonia and washing soda. This alternative is cheaper but not necessarily safer than commercial products.

■ Ammonia/Washing Soda Cleaner

½ cup household ammonia
⅓ cup washing soda
1 gallon medium-warm (not hot) water

Mix the ammonia, washing soda, and water in a pail. After washing, rinse surfaces with clear water. You can store any leftover solution in a clean bottle.

Yield: about 1 gallon

Baking soda is especially versatile. It is a scratchless scouring powder that, in addition to extinguishing fires, cleans and deodorizes chrome, porcelain sinks and tubs, and many types of pots, pans, and metal objects. It's also relatively nontoxic and costs only about 2½ cents an ounce.

An excellent all-purpose cleaner can be concocted from household ammonia, baking soda, and vinegar. Vinegar is a product of natural fermentation. Any liquid containing sugar can be converted by certain yeasts to alcohol and carbon dioxide gas. Certain bacteria attack the alcohol in the presence of atmospheric oxygen, forming acetic acid and water. Ordinary distilled white vinegar that you use on salads is made from grain alcohol, and contains about 5 percent acetic acid. It's the acid content that makes vinegar an all-purpose household cleaner, one that has been used for centuries.

■ Triple-Action Multipurpose Cleaner

¼ cup baking soda
1 cup household ammonia
½ cup white vinegar
1 gallon warm water

Pour baking soda, ammonia, and vinegar into water in a large bucket. (A more dilute solution can be made by halving the amount of baking soda, ammonia, and vinegar.) Mix thoroughly. Store this cleaner in a clean bottle and use as needed.

Yield: about 1 gallon

Scouring Powders

Scouring powders or cleansers from stores contain abrasive minerals such as silica, feldspar, and volcanic ash; clay fillers; and soap or detergents. Some contain bleach and phosphate builders. The abrasive ingredients in scouring powders wear away not only the dirt, but also part of the surface you're cleaning. They produce scratches and crevices that are harder to clean and harbor bacteria, and they eventually decrease the lifetime of the surface on which they are used. Thus, never use abrasive scouring powders on new basins or bathtubs, or on any plastic, Formica, or enameled surfaces. Instead, use a plastic mesh pad plus an all-purpose cleaner (you may wish to try some of the formulas in the preceding section) and some elbow grease to clean basins, tubs, and tiled surfaces.

You can make your own homemade scouring cleanser with whiting, a mildly abrasive chalk powder that's available at hardware and paint stores. The solution will be cheaper than commercial cleansers, and you can control the amount of abrasive added to it, which will save wear on your surfaces.

■ Scouring Cleanser

¼ cup soap flakes
2 teaspoons borax
1½ cups boiling water
¼ cup whiting

Dissolve soap flakes and borax in boiling water by stirring mixture. Allow it to cool to room temperature. Add whiting and stir well. Store cleanser in a sealed plastic or glass container in a dry, cool place. (A squeeze-top plastic container allows for easy use.) This cleanser is mildly abrasive and can be used on bathroom fixtures, kitchen sinks, painted woodwork (rub gently so as not to harm paint), and walls. If you prefer the cleanser to be more abrasive, additional whiting can be added, one tablespoon at a time, until the desired consistency is obtained. Shake well before using.

Painted-Wall Cleaners

If your walls aren't too badly soiled with grease or a heavy buildup of dirt, periodic vacuuming with a brush attachment to sweep off the cobwebs is usually sufficient. Using an old-fashioned feather duster (or its modern equivalent) or a couple of old socks secured over the end of a yardstick with a rubber band will save electricity and allow you to reach otherwise inaccessible areas.

You can remove occasional smudges by rubbing them with an artist's gum eraser or chunks of stale bread. And you can take off transparent mending tape stuck on the wall without damaging the paint or wallpaper by lightly pressing the tip of a warm iron on just the tape until it loosens.

Here are two formulas that will make grease spots disappear. Talcum powder, cornstarch, and fuller's earth are highly absorbent powders that really go to work on grease.

■ Talcum Powder Spot Remover for Walls

clean powder puff
white talcum powder

Dip puff in a small amount of talcum powder, and rub lightly over grease spot. Repeat until all grease is absorbed.

■ Paste Spot Remover for Walls

water
cornstarch or fuller's earth

Mix just enough water with cornstarch or fuller's earth to form sufficient paste to cover stains. Brush the paste on the spot, and let it set for about an hour. Brush off the powder. If the spot remains, repeat the procedure.

If the walls are really dirty and need a thorough washing, remember to work from the bottom up, not from the top down. When dirty water runs down over the dry, soiled wall, it leaves hard-to-remove streaks; it won't, however, stain wet, clean walls. Use a soft, absorbent sponge or, for heavy dirt, a piece of burlap. Old nylon or other synthetic socks are good for textured walls, because these materials won't tear off in little pieces as easily as a sponge would. Here's a handy way to stop that annoying stream of water from running down your arms: Secure an old washcloth around your wrist with a rubber band, or wear an old wristband.

You can mix up homemade formulas that are especially effective and safe for washing painted walls. The following cleaner combines the cleaning powers of ammonia, washing soda, and vinegar.

■ Ammonia Wall Cleaner

½ cup household ammonia
¼ cup washing soda
¼ cup white vinegar
1 gallon warm water

Measure ammonia, washing soda, and vinegar into water in a bucket. Mix thoroughly. Clean walls by following general directions above. Leftover solution can be stored in a clean bottle.

Yield: about 1 gallon

Ammonium sulfate, an inexpensive, water-soluble, crystalline form of ammonia, is used in the following formula. This cleaner is safe to use on both shiny enameled surfaces and surfaces painted with flat oil- or water-based paint.

■ Ammonia Wall Cleaner Concentrate

1 tablespoon ammonium sulfate
1 cup washing soda

Mix ammonium sulfate and washing soda together in a plastic container with a loose-fitting lid. Because pressure may build up, pack the powder loosely and do not seal the container airtight. Store this mixture dry until ready for use.

When you are ready to clean your walls, add 2 tablespoons of concentrate to 1 gallon of water and stir until dissolved. Then wash walls, following general directions. For extra-dirty spots, increase the strength by adding another tablespoon or two of the mix.

Yield: about 1 gallon

Borax is another effective, all-purpose cleaning compound. It is an alkaline powder that dissolves in water to improve detergent power, remove stains, and deodorize.

■ Ammonia/Borax Wall Cleaner

½ cup borax
2 teaspoons household ammonia
1 gallon water

Dissolve borax and ammonia in water in a bucket. Apply to walls, following the general directions.

Yield: about 1 gallon

Two old-fashioned, all-purpose wall and woodwork cleaners are kerosene and turpentine. Both are hydrocarbon solvents: Kerosene is a petroleum distillate, and turpentine is made by distilling gum from the bark of pine trees. Both are good grease removers.

You can buy deodorized kerosene, that is, kerosene that has been treated chemically to remove the heavy odor. Applied undiluted, kerosene is great for removing crayon marks from wood trim, painted walls and woodwork, plastic, and linoleum. An emulsion of kerosene and water (the kerosene floats on the top) dissolves grease, oil, and water-soluble stains; if all these stains are on the wall, the emulsion will remove them better than kerosene or water used singly.

■ Kerosene Wall and Cabinet Cleaner

½ cup deodorized kerosene
1 gallon hot water

First, dust or wipe off surface dirt. Add kerosene to water in a bucket. Wipe off grease on walls, rinse thoroughly, and dry. A portable fan speeds up the drying if it's especially humid. This cleaner works well on really greasy kitchen cabinets, too.

Yield: about 1 gallon

■ Turpentine Wall Cleaner

This formula is best suited for small-scale cleaning jobs. The price of turpentine can be prohibitive, so if you have a lot of walls to clean, you may want to consider using one of the other formulas in this section.

2 tablespoons soap flakes
1 pint water
6 tablespoons turpentine

Dissolve soap flakes in water in a small pail or old jar. Add the turpentine and stir rapidly. Clean the walls (from the bottom up) with a sponge or brush.

Yield: about 2½ cups

Wallpaper Cleaners

Wallpapered walls have much more delicate surfaces than painted walls do; thus they require careful cleaning techniques and less elbow grease (unless, of course, you're trying to remove the paper). Newer varieties of plastic-coated or vinyl wallpaper are on the market for use in kitchens and bathrooms. Although expensive, they are stainproof and can be washed easily with a solution of soap or detergent and water. Use water sparingly, because it can get between the seams and loosen the paper. Wring out your sponge or cloth thoroughly to keep it as dry as possible, and wash from the bottom up to avoid hard-to-remove streaks.

You can buy puttylike cleaners for nonwashable wallpaper, but they contain poisonous petroleum distillates or alcohol solvents. The following alternatives are cheaper and safer. It is always wise to test a small, inconspicuous area first and to clean small areas at a time.

■ Grease/Food Removers

Try any of these methods.

artist's gum eraser
inside of a loaf of stale bread (preferably rye)
wheat bran sewn in an old sock

Carefully rub any of these items over grease spots; be sure to overlap strokes to avoid streaks.

clean white blotting paper or paper towels
warm iron

Hold the blotting paper or several layers of paper towels over the spot, and cautiously press with an iron set on medium heat. To avoid scorching the wallpaper, experiment first on an inconspicuous section of the wall to determine the length of time you can safely keep the iron in place.

talcum powder
borax

You can quickly and effectively remove grease spots by rubbing either of these powders over the soiled area. Brush the powder away, and repeat if necessary. Leave the powder on more resistant spots for an hour or so.

cornstarch *or* fuller's earth *or* chalk
water

Make an absorbent paste by mixing a small amount of any of the absorbent powders with water. Pat the paste on grease spots, and let it dry for a few minutes. Then brush off with a soft cloth or brush and watch the stain disappear. Repeat if necessary.

■ Crayon Remover

baking soda
dry fine-grade steel wool (No. 0 or 00)

This method works especially well on very resistant spots such as crayon and scuff marks. Sprinkle some baking soda on a damp cloth, and rub this gently over the mark. Then rub very lightly with steel wool.

■ Ink Remover

1 tablespoon liquid chlorine bleach
1 pint cold water

Make a weak solution of bleach in water. First test on a small, hidden area. Apply a small amount with the edge of a cloth, and then immediately dab off with cold water. Dry by blotting with a dry cloth.

Glass and Window Cleaners

There are almost as many homemade solutions for cleaning glass as there are windows in your house. Many formulas are equally effective on windows, mirrors, and glass-top tables. All use the same widely available ingredients that are found in commercial products, for a fraction of the cost. All you have to do is save old plastic or glass spray bottles to store the solutions—they are especially convenient.

First, a few tips on window washing. Never wash windows when the sun is shining on them. They will dry too fast, and you'll be plagued with streaks. Cheap chamois cloths, old nylon stockings, squeegees or an old windshield wiper, and newspaper are all good, lintfree polishers compared to old rags or paper towels. A chamois is ideal, because it can be washed out and used repeatedly. There is something in newsprint ink that really shines glass. Tear a sheet of newspaper in half, crumple it, saturate it with solution, and wring it out over a bucket just like a rag.

When polishing windows, use up-and-down strokes on one side and side-to-side strokes on the other. That way, you can tell which side needs extra polishing. You don't have to take down drapes or curtains to wash the windows. Keep them out of the way by draping the ends through clothes hangers and hanging them from the curtain rod.

■ Ammonia Window Cleaner

3 tablespoons household ammonia
¾ cup water

Pour ammonia into a clean spray bottle and add water. If you need a lot for a particularly big cleaning job, use 3 cups ammonia and 1 gallon water.

Yield: about 1 cup

■ Blue Window Cleaner

3 tablespoons household ammonia
1 tablespoon white vinegar
¾ cup water
1 or 2 drops blue (or other color) food coloring (optional)

Measure ammonia and vinegar into a clean spray bottle, and add water. Add food coloring, if desired, and shake well.

Yield: 1 cup

■ Light-Duty Ammonia Window Cleaner

1 tablespoon household ammonia
1 cup isopropyl alcohol (70%)
1 pint water

Combine ingredients in a clean 1-quart spray bottle and shake lightly to mix.

Yield: about 3 cups

■ Alcohol Window Cleaner

The addition of liquid detergent to this formula gives it more cleaning power for heavily soiled windows.

1 pint water
2 tablespoons liquid dishwashing detergent
1 pint isopropyl alcohol (70%)

Measure water and detergent into a clean spray bottle, large enough to permit shaking the contents. Add alcohol, close top, and shake to blend.

Yield: about 1 quart

■ Heavy-Duty Window Cleaner

¼ cup household ammonia
¼ cup isopropyl alcohol (70%)
1¼ cups water
1 teaspoon liquid dishwashing detergent

Combine ammonia, alcohol, and water in a clean 1-pint spray bottle, and shake until thoroughly mixed. Add detergent and shake gently until mixture is well blended.

Yield: about 1¾ cups

For a big cleaning job where you need lots of a less-concentrated solution, use the following formula. It saves a lot of money—it costs only about 15 cents a quart, compared to an average $1.50 for a quart of commercial window washer.

■ Economy-Size Window Cleaner

½ cup household ammonia
1 pint isopropyl alcohol (70%)
13½ cups water
1 teaspoon liquid dishwashing detergent

Combine ammonia, alcohol, and water in a large bucket; stir vigorously until thoroughly mixed. With a long-handled spoon, stir in detergent until well blended.

Yield: 1 gallon

■ Heavy-Duty, Grease-Cutting Window Cleaner

This formula is good on really dirty windows, such as kitchen windows that are covered with a layer of grease and oil from cooking.

1 tablespoon deodorized kerosene
1 quart water

Mix kerosene and water and rub over the glass. Polish with newspaper or chamois.

Yield: about 1 quart

■ Old-Fashioned Window Cleaner

Old-fashioned cornstarch was grandmother's secret formula for making windows glisten. This material is slightly abrasive and is good for removing heavy smudges.

2 tablespoons cornstarch
½ cup household ammonia
½ cup white vinegar
1 gallon warm water

Stir cornstarch, ammonia, and vinegar into water.

Yield: about 1 gallon

■ Vinegar Window Cleaner

White vinegar was another of grandma's standbys. This is a very good method, one which leaves glass squeaky clean.

½ cup white vinegar
1 gallon warm water

Mix the vinegar and water thoroughly in a pail.

Yield: about 1 gallon

To keep windows from frosting in the winter, or your bathroom mirror from steaming, wipe a little glycerin over the surface, then buff with a soft cloth. Or, you can use the following formula.

■ Defrosting Window Cleaner

½ cup isopropyl alcohol (70%)
1 quart water

Mix alcohol in water in a small bucket.

Yield: about 1 quart

Scratch Removers for Glass

Occasionally, you may find superficial scratches on windows, mirrors, or glass-topped furniture. There are ways to apply first aid that will make the scratches less noticeable by filling them in somewhat. Try these three formulas to see what works best for you.

■ Paste Scratch Remover

2 tablespoons glycerin
2 tablespoons jeweler's rouge
2 tablespoons water

In a glass or plastic jar, mix all ingredients into a paste. You can store this until you need it; be sure to keep jar tightly covered. To use, dab some paste on a clean cloth and rub the scratched area. Wash off with clear water. Deeper scratches will require repeated applications.

■ Stained Scratch Cleaner

This formula removes the discoloration and stains in scratches on glass and mirrors.

1 part dry mustard
1 part white vinegar

Blend small equal amounts of mustard and vinegar to make a paste. Apply to scratch mark with your finger, and rub until the stain disappears. Rinse well with clear water.

■ Toothpaste Scratch Remover

Rub a little toothpaste into the scratch. (The liquid polishes for smokers work well.) Polish with soft, clean cloth until the scratch disappears.

Fireplace and Woodstove Cleaners

A blazing fire is delightful on cold, winter nights, but each time you burn a fire, black gummy creosote deposits build up in the chimney and on the bricks or stone. If creosote is allowed to accumulate for too long, the chance of a fire occurring in your chimney or stovepipe greatly increases. Hard woods, such as ash or oak, deposit less creosote when burned than do soft woods, such as pine or poplar. Frequent hot fires will burn off much of the creosote buildup. Still, you will have to clean the creosote out of your chimney or stovepipe at least once a year to assure the safety and efficiency of your fireplace or stove. You can scrape or brush it out yourself, but it's a messy job and it might be worth your while to call in a professional chimney sweep. While your chimney or pipe is being cleaned, have it checked for any structural flaws, since such weaknesses raise the possibility of the occurrence of fire.

■ Easy Fireplace Cleaner

Full-strength white vinegar brushed on vigorously will clean the tiling around the fireplace. Sponge away moisture immediately.

■ Light-Duty Fireplace Cleaner

1 cup washing soda
2 gallons hot water

Add washing soda to water and mix thoroughly. Scrub the bricks and stone briskly with a stiff brush. Rinse off loosened dirt with clear water

■ Heavy-Duty Fireplace Cleaner

1 6½-ounce bar naphtha soap
3 pints hot water
¾ pound powdered pumice
¾ cup household ammonia

Shave naphtha soap into an old pot. Add water, and heat until soap dissolves. Remove the mixture from heat and let it cool. Then stir in pumice and ammonia until the solution is thoroughly mixed.

Brush the mixture over the smoked-up areas; a paint brush will work very well. Let the mixture remain on the area for about an hour. Then, using a stiff brush, scrub the solution off with hot water and soap or liquid detergent. Finally, rinse that off by sponging with clear water.

Woodstove Cleaning

The energy crisis sent thousands of people into the woods in search of firewood to keep their woodstoves fired. All that burning can make a woodstove dirty in no time. Actually, maintaining a woodstove is fairly easy. Wash the glass doors occasionally with one of the window cleaners. (See "Glass and Window Cleaners," page 16.) You may have to scrub out the firebox with a stiff wire brush or a scraper made specifically for that purpose. At the end of the heating season, soot and ash should be removed from the exhaust passageways by vacuuming with a vacuum rented for that purpose, or with an old, spare machine.

Steel or cast-iron surfaces really require only periodic dusting, since most dirt and grease burn off during use. Polishing will restore the black finish. Most stove polishes contain graphite. Finely powdered graphite can be mixed with a little water to make a paste to rub over the surface. Bone black and lampblack deepen the color of some polishes, but they burn off faster than the graphite does. Stay away from cleaners that contain turpentine, which is highly flammable.

Chapter 2 Kitchens

Dishwashing

Cooking is fun; cleaning up afterward isn't. Postponing the chore only makes it worse. What's more depressing than waking up to a sinkful of crusted-on remnants of last night's gourmet feast?

Washing Dishes by Hand

If you're not lucky enough to own one of those miracles of modern life, an automatic dishwasher, the dishes have to be washed by hand. Presoaking saves a lot of work, so soak sugary dishes in hot, soapy water; egg-, fish-, and dough-coated dishes in cold, soapy water; and greasy dishes, pots, and pans in warm, soapy water. To protect your hands, wear a rubber glove on one hand and use a vegetable brush or dish mop with the other. That way, neither hand turns into a "dishpan hand," and one hand will be dry to grasp glasses and dishes that might slip and break. Put the silverware into the dishpan first so that it soaks while you wash glassware and dishes. Clean the pots and pans last. Rinse thoroughly, and let the china air-dry. Towel-dry pots, pans, and silverware to prevent water spotting.

When you wash dishes by hand, you need a mild solution that removes food and grease without irritating your skin. Commercial dishwashing liquids are formulated to be mild to the hands, to cut grease and oils, to produce lots of suds, to be safe for all dishes and tableware, and to be convenient and appealing to use. The main ingredients are biodegradable surfactants or surface-active agents. Compounds with long names like linear alkyl aryl sulfonate (LAS), alcohol ether sulfate (ES), and alcohol sulfate (AS) are high-foaming anionic surfactants. They solubilize, emulsify, and disperse grease and oil (fats and lipids) that normally don't dissolve in water. (Everyone knows oil and water don't mix, right?) Well, these ingredients break the grease and oil into small globules that will float in the water (like milk fats suspended in milk), instead of sticking to the dishes. Nonionic surfactants (amides and amine oxides) are also added to boost the foam and maintain it.

In addition, sodium xylene sulfonate (SXS) and sodium toluene sulfonate (STS), alcohols, and salts are added to keep the mixture stable and free-flowing. Dyes and perfumes are added to "sell" the product, as are "mildness additives" like protein and lanolin, which are supposed to protect the skin.

Actually, dishwashing detergents are among the mildest household cleaners, but they can be somewhat toxic if swallowed, they will irritate the eyes, and they can irritate the skin, especially if you are particularly sensitive.

The major drawback of commercial products is their cost. The cheapest, yet still effective, dishwashing detergent is plain hot water, combined with a good soil-removing agent—"elbow grease." All that propaganda and competition over thick, rich, long-lasting suds is for naught. The suds don't really increase the cleaning power, and more suds just mean more bubbles to wash down the drain. That's why you can't use liquid detergents in your automatic dishwasher—the foam interferes with the machine's spray action, and it can make a terrific mess! If you are turned off by the idea of a dishpanful of hot, greasy water, here are some effective, money-saving alternatives to the pastel parade of products on the market shelves.

■ Old-Fashioned Dishwashing Detergent

1 pint grated hard bar soap (or soap ends) *or* soap flakes
1 gallon water

Place bar soap or soap flakes in a pot. (Rub salad oil on the grater before using, for easy cleaning.) Add water and stir to mix. Heat the mixture over medium heat until it boils, stirring occasionally until the soap dissolves. Lower heat and simmer 10 minutes, stirring occasionally. Remove pot from heat and let the liquid partially cool. Pour this into a clean container and cover tightly. To wash dishes, pour about 1 teaspoon of liquid into a dishpan of hot water.

Caution: Do not use in an automatic dishwasher.

Yield: about 1 gallon

Another trick to help cut grease and to make the dishes sparkle when washing dishes by hand is to add a few drops of household ammonia or a few tablespoons of white vinegar to the dishwater.

The following methods will remove stains, cloudiness, and mineral deposits from narrow-necked glassware and those "antique" bottles you found at the dump.

■ Ammonia Bottle Cleanser

water
1–2 teaspoons household ammonia

Fill bottle or decanter with water, and add ammonia. Let this solution stand for several hours or overnight. Then wash and rinse as usual.

■ Builder's Sand Bottle Cleanser

1 cup builder's sand
1 cup water

Mix sand and water in bottle. Place one hand over the opening, grasp the bottle with the other hand, and shake vigorously. The sand will abrade the stains, yet it won't harm even fine crystal.

Varnished wooden salad bowls sometimes get sticky and musty smelling as they age. Washing with water ruins the finish. After each use, drain bowls completely, dry with absorbent paper towels, and polish with a few drops of mineral oil. Store bowls in plastic or paper bags.

Unshellacked or nonvarnished wooden finishes can be washed, but they will become discolored. Sand the wood with fine-grade sandpaper (No. 0 or 00). To avoid roughening the fibers, rub in a circular motion in the direction of the grain. Rinse for just a second under cold water, and towel-dry. To protect the finish, apply a coat of waterproof spar varnish.

To clean and deodorize breadboards, cutting boards, and butcher blocks, rub half of a cut lemon or lime over the surface. Wash, dry with a cloth, and cover with salt to absorb any moisture. Treat the wood with mineral oil. A paste of baking soda and water also works.

Automatic Dishwashing

Although an automatic dishwashing device was first patented in 1850, it wasn't until after World War II that automatic dishwashers became household items. They've remained popular ever since for good reasons. They save a lot of time, they're great for hiding the dishes when you're in a hurry, and they do a more thorough job of sanitizing the dishes. And because dishes are generally handled less than when handwashing, fewer are broken.

The effectiveness of dishwashers depends on three things: the mechanical action of a water spray; the force and temperature of the water; and the chemical action of special detergents. Water is sprayed from arms or towers, dissolving the detergent and carrying it and rinse water over, under, and around the dishes with enough force to loosen and remove soil. The number of cycles run through dishwashers varies; some have prerinse cycles, 1 to 3 wash cycles, and a final rinse cycle. Since 2 to 3 gallons of water are used and recirculated for each cycle, wash or rinse, a complete load can use up to 15 gallons of water. That's as much water used as if you hand wash and rinse dishes under a steadily flowing stream of hot water for 15 minutes (at a flow rate of 1 gallon per minute).

Water temperature is important in using dishwashers; the usual recommended temperature for operation is 140°F, and never lower than 130°F. If you rinse your dishes to remove grease before loading, however, you can turn down the household water heater to 120°F, and sometimes even to 110°F without affecting your dishwasher's performance. Experiment by lowering your water heater temperature and observing how well your dishwasher cleans. If your dishwasher has a temperature booster to preheat water before operations, you can turn this off, too, if you prerinse your dishes by hand. Lowering the temperature of your water will save energy in laundering and bathing, too, and also heat lost through radiation from the pipes and storage tank. Insulating your pipes and tank will further reduce this heat loss and add to your energy savings.

Automatic dishwashing detergents are specially formulated with strong ingredients to dissolve the food on the dishes without producing a lot of suds and foam that inhibit the machine's action. They must make the water "wetter," so that it can penetrate and loosen the food; tie up hard-water minerals so they don't interfere with the detergent; emulsify grease and oil; suppress foam caused by protein foods like egg and milk (you've seen the bubbles when you beat them); prevent the water from clinging to the dishes and forming water spots; and protect the dishes from the harsh effects of the hot water.

Nonionic surfactants are the most critical ingredient in dishwashing detergents; they have low sudsing characteristics, reduce the surface tension, and remove and emulsify hard-to-remove fats, like butter and cooking oils. Complex phosphate builders, like sodium tripolyphosphate, hold hard-water minerals (calcium and magnesium) in solution, so they won't leave water spots. They're also alkaline, which means they help remove dirt. Sodium silicate is used to inhibit corrosion; it protects machine parts, china, and aluminum. It's also a source of alkalinity. Sodium carbonate (washing soda) is often used to aid in breaking down greasy foods. Chlorine compounds are added to sanitize, to solubilize protein soils, and to remove stains. The detergents may also contain perfumes and colorings.

The alkalis in these products are so caustic that they can severely burn internal tissue if swallowed. In one extreme case we know of, an automatic dishwashing detergent burned right through the stomach wall. Obviously, the ingredients can also irritate the skin, eyes, and, if inhaled, the respiratory tract.

All products on the market contain phosphates, in varying amounts. There are limitations on the use of phosphates in New York, Michigan, Wisconsin, and Minnesota, because they harm the environment. They are the perfect food for marine plants such as algae, and when phosphates enter lakes and streams, algae start feeding, then multiplying rapidly, eventually choking out all other forms of life.

Unfortunately, formulas for homemade solutions without phosphate ingredients are currently unavailable. You should *never* substitute regular dishwashing liquids; they won't clean and the suds can be disastrous.

To get the best results from dishwashing detergents, always follow the dishwasher manufacturer's operating instructions. Before loading, remove large food particles. Don't waste energy by running a lot of hot water for prerinsing. Instead, load dishes and turn on the wash cycle for a few minutes without detergent. Don't run the full dishwashing cycle until you have a full load. And turn off the dishwasher right before the dry cycle. The dishes are already sterile by this time, and the retained heat will dry them.

Iron skillets should not be washed with automatic dishwasher detergents, because the detergent will remove the protective coating. It also may form hard-to-remove black spots on aluminum, stainless steel, and silver.

Never put wooden objects in the dishwasher. They may warp, crack, or lose their finish.

Commercial dishwasher detergents can leave water spots on the glasses. This formula will remove them. The scummy film on the inside walls of the dishwasher will also disappear.

■ Water-Spot Remover

1 cup liquid chlorine bleach
1 cup white vinegar

Load the dishwasher with water-spotted glasses and porcelain china. Do *not* put in anything made of silver, aluminum, or brass—everything will turn black! Pour bleach into a small bowl and place in the bottom rack. Close the door carefully, so that the bleach doesn't spill.

Run the washer through the wash cycle, but turn it off before the dry cycle. Then pour vinegar into the bowl, and run the washer through entire cycle. Everything will sparkle.

Tips for Washing Specific Materials

Ceramic Dinnerware Strong, hard ceramic materials are becoming very popular for everyday dinnerware. They can be safely washed in the dishwasher or by hand, but are especially prone to hard-to-remove gray marks caused by knives or forks. The marks can be removed with a plastic scouring pad and baking soda. Don't use steel wool pads; you'll only have more marks!

China Most modern china can be safely washed in the dishwasher. Fine china with decorative borders is protected from the force of hot water by sodium silicate, a buffering agent in automatic detergents. If you're not sure whether your pattern is dishwasher-safe, test a small item by including it in every load. If it doesn't show any changes after considerable washings when compared to the rest of the set, you should be able to wash all your pieces safely.

Chinaware that's discolored by tea or coffee can be cleaned by hand by first wetting the stain with vinegar, then rubbing it with a damp cloth dipped in salt. Baking soda is also effective, especially on old cups with cracked glaze. Rub a paste of baking soda and water over the stains; let the paste soak in for about an hour. Baking soda is safe to use on gold and silver decorative borders. It will also remove nicotine stains.

Crystal Except for thin-walled, delicate crystal that might break in very hot water, or glasses with precious metal trim, most undecorated glassware is safe in the dishwasher. Load glasses carefully, so they won't fall out. When washing glassware by hand, use a plastic dishpan or place a towel on the bottom of the sink to cushion it. When washing stemware, hold the bowl in your palm and the stem between your fingers. Rinse thoroughly with the following formula.

■ Crystal Rinse

1 part white vinegar
3 parts warm water

Mix vinegar and water and use to rinse glassware.

In soft-water areas, lime or soda-lime glass may become cloudy or etched by the silicates in automatic dishwasher detergents. Once there, this etching can't be removed, but you can slow down its formation by using water temperatures no higher than 140°F, using the minimum amount of detergent, slightly underloading the dishwasher to ensure thorough rinsing, and unloading immediately and drying thoroughly.

Enamelware Some cookware is made of iron, steel, or aluminum coated with an enamel or porcelain finish. The finish is hard, like glass, and can be cleaned easily by hand or in the dishwasher. It can be scratched, so abrasive cleaners should not be used. If your pots and pans have annoying stains, remove them with a paste of salt and vinegar, or try the stain remover below.

■ Enamelware Stain Remover

1 tablespoon liquid chlorine bleach
1 cup water

Mix ingredients in the stained utensil. Boil mixture in the utensil for about 10 minutes, until the stains disappear.

Oven-Proof Glassware (Glass Ceramic) Glassware that's safe for use from the refrigerator to the oven is made from borosilicate glass, which contains at least 5 percent boric oxide. You can wash these items by hand or in the dishwasher. Soak burned-on or baked-on food. Metal utensils or steel wool will leave marks on these objects; use a plastic scouring pad, with a little baking soda or scouring cleanser, to remove the marks.

Plasticware Everyday plastic (melamine) dishes and utensils can be washed automatically or by hand. The bleach in automatic detergents safely removes stains without removing the color. However, plastic items must be kept away from the heating element in the dishwasher.

As plastic cups age, stains sometimes penetrate to the point that you might decide to toss them out with the garbage. Don't! Rescue them instead by using silicone carbide paper. (It looks like fine, black sandpaper.) Wet the paper and rub away the stains. Instead of marring the finish, this sanding makes it as smooth as glass. Tea- or coffee-stained plastic cups are also brightened by scouring with a baking soda and water paste. Plasticware that doesn't respond to regular washing should be soaked in the following:

■ Plasticware Soaking Solution

1 cup liquid chlorine bleach
1 gallon warm water

Mix bleach and water together and soak plasticware in mixture for about 30 minutes, then wipe with a dishcloth and wash as usual.

Pots and Pans As soon as you finish cooking, fill pots and pans with hot water and let them soak until you do the dishes. That way, the food won't harden. If food is burned and crusted on the utensils, pour in some water and liquid dishwashing detergent. Boil this for about 15 minutes. The heat and detergent loosen burned-on food so that it's easier to wash off. Or sprinkle baking soda all over the surface and moisten that with a little water. After several hours, the burned-on food will lift right out.

Greasy, cooked-on crusts can be soaked off by filling the pot with hot water and adding 2 tablespoons of washing soda. Let the pot sit for a couple of hours and then wash. Because washing soda discolors aluminum, do not use this on aluminum utensils.

Deposits of lime sediment that accumulate in teakettles can be difficult to remove, especially considering the relatively small opening that makes them hard to scrub. The following formula will loosen the lime so that you can wash out your kettle with ease.

■ Lime Sediment Remover for Teakettles

1½ cups apple cider vinegar
1½ cups water
3 tablespoons salt

Mix together ingredients in teakettle, and boil for 15 minutes. Allow mixture to sit in kettle overnight, then wash out with clear water.

For formulas for cleaning pots and pans of specific metals, see "Metal Cleaners and Polishes" below.

Silverstone and Teflon These plastic-coated pots and pans are, of course, extremely easy to keep clean. They should be thoroughly scrubbed with a cloth or plastic scouring pad and hot water to which a detergent has been added; rinsed, and dried thoroughly. They're also dishwasher-safe, but they must be reseasoned with salad oil if washed in the dishwasher.

If not cleaned thoroughly, even Silverstone and Teflon can become stained by the buildup of grease and oil. These stains will make the nonstick surface ineffective. Try these inexpensive, simple formulas to remove the buildup, rather than the expensive, caustic, and corrosive products on the market.

■ Silverstone/Teflon Baking Soda Soak

2 tablespoons baking soda
½ cup white vinegar
1 cup water

Measure ingredients into utensil, place on stove, and boil 10 minutes. Wash as usual. Rub some salad oil over the surface to reseason the coating.

■ Silverstone/Teflon Bleach Soak

1 tablespoon liquid chlorine bleach
1 tablespoon white vinegar
1 cup water

Pour ingredients into stained pot. Allow to stand for at least 10 minutes, until the stain lightens. Wash thoroughly with liquid dishwashing detergent. If chlorine odor lingers, scrub with baking soda and water. Recondition the pan with salad oil.

Metal Cleaners and Polishes

Metals tarnish or discolor after constant exposure to the atmosphere and moisture. All-purpose metal cleaners that you buy contain abrasives (silica), acids (oxalic acid), ammonia, alcohols, and water. These chemicals are eye and skin irritants and are toxic if ingested. Ammonia vapors are harmful if inhaled. All-purpose cleaners are always more economical than specialized polishes. However, harsh abrasives should not be used on any metals.

The following homemade polishes are gentle enough for any metal object except silver, silver plate, and fine jewelry. Consult a professional before using any of these on valuable antiques.

■ Quick and Easy Metal Polish

Rub some soft-grade blackboard chalk onto a damp, coarse-textured cloth and polish the surface. The chalk removes dirt and grease and leaves a glossy finish, yet it won't scratch.

■ Ash Metal Polish

½ cup cigar ashes *or* wood ashes *or* diatomaceous earth
1 tablespoon baking soda
water

Mix ingredients into a smooth paste, and rub on with a soft cloth.

■ All-Purpose Metal Polish

½ cup isopropyl alcohol (70%)
¼ cup household ammonia
1 cup diatomaceous earth
¼ cup water

Blend alcohol and ammonia in a clean bottle or jar. Add diatomaceous earth and stir constantly until smooth and well blended. Slowly add water and stir until the consistency is that of thick cream. Blend well. *Caution:* Because silver is a soft metal that scratches easily, this polish should not be used on silver or other soft metals.

Shake or stir well before using. Apply with a soft cloth, rubbing in well. Let dry and then rinse thoroughly with water. Polish until dry.

Yield: about 2 cups

Aluminum Pots and pans are frequently made of aluminum. It's moderately priced, heats evenly and quickly, and does not tarnish. However, it does darken and discolor, especially after contacting alkaline foods such as rice and beans, egg shells, water, strong scouring powders, automatic dishwashing detergents, bleach, ammonia, oven cleaners, and baking soda. When cooking an alkaline food, add a few drops of vinegar or lemon juice to the water. (This won't change the taste of the food.) Rubbing regularly with plain, fine-grade steel wool or a steel-wool scouring pad keeps brushed- or smooth-finish pans shiny. Rub in one direction only, not in a circular motion. All-Purpose Metal Polish (above) will also shine aluminum.

Any acid foods will remove stains on aluminum. Slowly stew rhubarb or tomatoes or boil grapefruit rinds, lemon rinds, or apple parings in stained pots. Rubbing the stain with a cut lemon also works.

Caution: Never store foods in aluminum cookware, since certain food chemicals (especially those in acidic foods like tomatoes) will cause pitting of aluminum if left in the pan. Badly pitted or dented aluminum cookware should be discarded.

■ Aluminum Cleaner

1 pint water
3 tablespoons white vinegar *or* 2 teaspoons cream of tartar

Measure ingredients into pot and bring to a boil. Let the solution boil until stains disappear and pot brightens. Finish by polishing gently with fine-grade steel wool. This method is especially effective in removing lime scale that builds up in the bottom of aluminum teakettles. Wash utensils thoroughly before using.

■ Aluminum Polish

½ cup powdered alum
½ cup talc
¾ cup whiting

Mix ingredients in a clean jar. Use a damp cloth to dab mixture onto aluminum, and rub well. Rinse off with water, dry, and then polish with a soft cloth. Store leftover mixture tightly covered, away from children.

Yield: 1¾ cups

Cast Iron Most cast-iron cookware is preseasoned by the manufacturer to prevent rusting and to keep food from sticking. Clean it only with soap or a soap-filled steel wool pad. Detergents remove the oil seasoning, but you can reseason by rubbing with odorless salad oil. *Never* wash cast-iron cookware in a dishwasher. Steel wool pads should remove any rust caused by exposure of the iron to moisture and air.

Chrome Chrome items are coated with chromium, an element that resists tarnish and corrosion. Stainless steel is steel alloyed with chromium.

Remove water spots and stains from chrome with lemon juice. Polish with a soft cloth saturated with 70 percent isopropyl alcohol, dampened with a few drops of household ammonia diluted with water, or with a dry cloth and some baking soda. Applying paste wax to chrome fixtures prevents water spotting.

Copper Copper is used for many things in the household, including decorative objects, cookware, wiring, and piping. It is popular, not only because of its beauty, but because it is a great conductor of heat and electricity. Unlacquered copper tarnishes easily, and must be polished regularly to look its best. Brass Cleaner/Polish (see Index) is a good polish for unlacquered copper.

Some copper articles are lacquered to prevent tarnishing. Never use cleaners or polishes on lacquered articles; instead, dust them regularly, and occasionally wipe them with a damp sponge and dry with a soft cloth. If necessary, lacquered articles can be washed in warm, soapy water. (Never use hot water—the lacquer will crack and peel.)

Some copper cookware comes with a protective layer that must be removed before using cookware. Follow the manufacturer's directions for removal.

Copper cookware must be kept clean to prevent formation of a green deposit, a toxic copper salt known as copper carbonate or, more commonly, as verdigris. This forms because of a reaction between certain acidic foods and the copper. This is why copper cookware is frequently lined with other metals, such as stainless steel, chromium, and tin. To remove verdigris, try a soap and household ammonia solution, or the formula below.

■ Copper Verdigris Remover

1 tablespoon baking soda
1 tablespoon deodorized kerosene

Mix baking soda and kerosene. Scour the utensil with the mixture, then rinse and dry.

Commercial copper cleaners are usually less abrasive than all-purpose metal cleaners, although most do contain silica (sand) and acids to remove copper oxide and other chemicals that form the tarnish. The ingredients can irritate the skin and are mildly toxic if swallowed.

If you've been hiding your copper-bottom pots and pans because of their dull appearance, try one of these safe and effective remedies to restore the shine. They can be used for aluminum, brass, bronze, and stainless steel as well as for copper.

Acidic foods, including Worcestershire sauce, ketchup, and yogurt, remove tarnish, but must be washed away quickly to prevent green discoloration. You might try washing copper or brass objects in the water left after boiling potatoes or onions. Polishing with crumpled sheets of newspaper removes stains and restores luster, and combinations of acid and salt, as in the formula below, will remove tarnish. Also, try All-Purpose Metal Polish (page 30).

■ Quick Copper and Brass Cleaner

white vinegar *or* half a lemon
salt

Pour vinegar over the surface or rub with lemon. Sprinkle salt over the acid and rub in the mixture. Wash well and rinse with warm water. Polish dry.

■ Copper and Brass Spray Cleaner

white vinegar
3 tablespoons salt

Fill a small spray bottle with vinegar and add salt. Liberally spray the solution on copper utensils, let set for a while, and then rub clean. Leftover cleaner can be left in spray bottle for storage.

■ Copper and Brass Polish

2 cups water
½ cup soap flakes
3 tablespoons whiting
2 tablespoons white vinegar

Boil water in a medium-size pot and remove from heat. Pour in soap flakes and stir mixture until soap flakes are dissolved. Stirring constantly, add whiting and vinegar. Beat by hand or with an electric mixer until well blended. Store in a clean jar with a tight lid. To use, shake mixture well and rub on with a damp cloth or sponge. Rinse and wipe dry.

Yield: about 2 cups

■ Copper Polish and Cleaner

hot water
1 pint soap flakes
¼ cup precipitated chalk
2 tablespoons jeweler's rouge
2 tablespoons cream of tartar
2 tablespoons magnesium carbonate

Add enough hot water to the soap flakes to dissolve them. Then stir in the other ingredients until a smooth paste forms. Store this in a wide-mouthed, tightly covered glass jar. To use, apply paste with a cloth or sponge. Rinse off thoroughly with warm water.

Silver In spite of inflated prices, items made of sterling silver (92.5 percent pure silver) or silver plate (a layer of silver electroplated to a base metal) are still popular wedding gifts and common household items. Silver is popular because it acquires a patina or natural sheen that enhances its beauty and value. A soft and lustrous metal, silver is relatively inactive; that is, it doesn't react with the oxygen in the air. However, traces of hydrogen sulfide in the air cause a brownish black coating of silver sulfide to form on the surface of silver. Therefore, foods such as mustard and eggs, which contain certain sulfur compounds, cause silver to tarnish. Certain acids also react with silver, so don't store food in silver containers.

Normally, sterling silver only requires washing in soap and very hot water after each use to maintain it. Thorough rinsing and vigorous polishing to dry it are also necessary. Because soapy residues hasten tarnishing, careful rinsing is crucial. You can also wash sterling silverware in the dishwasher, but don't crowd the pieces. Don't put in old, hollow-handle knives (the cleaner may dissolve the cement that holds the handles and blades together) or pieces with ornate patterns, because the oxidation used to highlight the pattern may be removed.

Silver plate can wear away more quickly than sterling silver in the dishwasher, so it is best to wash worn silver-plated items by hand. Silver-plate finishes are soft and should be polished very gently. Silver-leaf finishes, thin coatings of silver, should not be polished at all because the silver may flake off. Dust regularly with a soft shaving brush to avoid tearing. If tarnished, silver-leaf items should be resilvered by a professional.

Store silver items in those special gray or blue Pacific cloth bags. Pacific cloth is cotton flannel impregnated with sulfur-filtering particles. If you don't have any, wrap the silver tightly in heavy plastic bags or plastic wrap. Don't use rubber bands to close the bags—rubber contains sulfur and it will tarnish the silver right through the plastic.

Moisture will accelerate tarnishing, so be sure that silver objects and packing materials are completely dry. Small muslin bags filled with absorbent silica gel (the kind that comes with cameras) are good to include when storing.

Commercial silver polishes from the store come in three types. Simple cleaners (dip-in or wipe-on liquids) contain acid, ammonia derivatives, and surfactants to remove dirt and tarnish. Cleaner/polishes contain ammonia compounds to remove dirt and tarnish, and mild abrasives (like diatomaceous earth) to bring out the shine. Antitarnish cleaners contain cleaners, polishes, and antitarnish ingredients such as polyethylene glycol or wax. All of these ingredients can irritate sensitive skin and eye tissue. Cleaners containing acids give off headache-causing, irritating fumes; some vapors are flammable. All are harmful if swallowed; they will upset the gastric system and burn tissue and are toxic.

Fortunately, numerous home remedies are available, most of them a good deal safer. All can be used on any silver or silver-plate objects, including tableware, candlestick holders, trays, or jewelry. However, always test any polish first on small, inconspicuous areas. Some may be too strong or abrasive for antique silver or satin-finish pieces.

■ Baking Soda Silver Polish

Sprinkle baking soda on a damp sponge or cloth and rub silver until clean. Cover persistent stains with a paste of baking soda and water and let this dry. Rinse until clean with warm water and polish dry.

■ General Silver Cleaner

This formula is good for both immersible and nonimmersible articles.

2 tablespoons whiting
sweet oil *or* olive oil

Moisten whiting with sweet oil or olive oil. Apply to silver and allow to dry. Rub off with a soft cloth. Polish with chamois. Store excess cleaner in a metal or glass container with a lid.

■ Immersible Silver Cleaner

This formula is to be used for immersible items only. *It should not be used on silver jewelry studded with precious gems or costume stones, or damage may occur. It should not be used on silver-plated items either. The plating may flake off.*

1 quart hot soapy water (not detergent)
2 teaspoons household ammonia

Place silver items in solution and wash, using an old nailbrush or toothbrush. Do not allow items to soak for prolonged periods of time.

■ Grandma's Favorite Silver Polish

Place tarnished silver in a pan and cover with sour milk or buttermilk. Let silver soak in this overnight, then rinse clean with cold water and polish dry. If you don't have any sour milk or buttermilk on hand, use regular whole milk.

■ Whole Milk Silver Polish

1 cup whole milk
2 teaspoons cream of tartar *or* 1 tablespoon white vinegar *or* lemon juice

Mix milk and cream of tartar, vinegar, or lemon juice. Soak tarnished silver overnight in mixture. Rinse with cold water, and polish dry.

■ Quick 'n' Easy Silver Polish

This cleaner is only slightly abrasive, and is good for delicate items.

Dab a little toothpaste on surface and rub with a damp cloth. Old, clean toothbrushes are especially good for getting into small, intricate areas and tiny cracks. Shoestring, or string, works well on the tines of silver forks discolored from eggs; roll the center in paste and loop around each tine to polish inner edges. Wash off the toothpaste, rinse, and buff well with a dry cloth.

■ Liquid Silver Polish

2 cups water
¼ cup soap flakes
½ cup whiting
1½ teaspoons household ammonia

Boil water in medium-size saucepan (do not use aluminum) and then remove from heat. Add soap flakes and dissolve thoroughly in hot water. Stirring constantly, add whiting. Beat mixture vigorously until blended and all lumps are dissolved. Cool completely. Stir in ammonia and blend well. Store in a clean bottle, covered tightly. To use, shake bottle well. Apply with a damp applicator, rubbing gently. Rinse and polish dry.

Yield: about 2 cups

■ Paste Silver Polish

1 cup water
¼ cup soap flakes
2½ tablespoons whiting
1 tablespoon isopropyl alcohol (70%)

Boil water in a medium-size pot, then remove from heat. Add soap flakes and stir to dissolve. Beat mixture with electric mixer at medium speed, or by hand, until it is foamy. Slowly add whiting and alcohol while beating constantly at low speed, or by hand, until it is smooth and creamy. Rub on gently with a damp sponge, rinse well, and wipe dry. Store mixture in a clean jar with lid.

Yield: about 1 cup

An alternative to liquid or paste polishes is electrolytic cleaning. Don't use this method on flatware with hollow handles—the hot water may dissolve the glue holding the handles in place. A chemical reaction between aluminum, salt, and baking soda loosens the tarnish.

■ Electrolytic Cleaning

water
1 teaspoon baking soda
1 teaspoon salt

Pour water into an aluminum pan, or an enameled pan with a piece of aluminum foil on the bottom, to a depth of 2 to 3 inches (enough to cover the amount of silver to be cleaned). Add baking soda and salt and heat until water boils. Carefully add tarnished silver, and boil 2 to 3 minutes. Remove silver, wash in warm, soapy water, rinse well, and polish dry. The silver will be shiny and clean, and all the tarnish will have settled at the bottom of the pan.

Stainless Steel Stainless steel flatware and cookware are made of steel alloyed with at least 11½ percent chromium. Stainless steel with a high nickel content (nonmagnetic-type) is often used for flatware. It is resistant to corrosion by detergents, salts, and acids. Magnetic stainless steel has a bluish cast, contains no nickel, and is generally resistant to tarnish, stain, and rust, although it can be pitted or rusted by prolonged contact with salty or acid foods.

Stainless steel is a poor conductor of heat, and many cookware manufacturers sell stainless steel pots with copper bottoms for better cooking performance. Copper bottoms should be cleaned using copper cleaners (see "Copper," page 32). Ordinary stainless steel is extremely durable and easy to clean, either by hand or machine. Don't use abrasive cleaners. Instead, wash with warm, soapy water, or try the following:

■ Stainless Steel Cleaner

1 tablespoon household ammonia
1 pint water

Mix ammonia and water, and use to clean stainless steel.

To keep stainless steel shiny and prevent water spots, always dry it completely. Rubbing with white vinegar, club soda, lemon juice, or 70 percent isopropyl alcohol will remove water spots.

Excessive heat and certain foods and detergents can cause a purplish or rainbow discoloration on stainless steel. To remove this from stainless steel, use a nonscratching scouring pad. For extra-tough stains, add a little borax to the water.

Borax is good for the occasional cleaning of stainless steel sinks, which often become dull in hard-water areas. Such discolorations can also be removed with All-Purpose Metal Polish (page 30) or Copper and Brass Polish (page 34). Be sure to test a hidden area first. Or, try rubbing with a damp sponge sprinkled with dry baking soda. Rinse with a clean, damp sponge and polish dry. This also works well on stainless steel toasters, coffeemakers, pots, pans, and the bottoms of electric irons.

Tin Tin is a naturally occurring, corrosion-resistant element, often used to coat other metals and to form alloys such as pewter and bronze. It's a lightweight, malleable metal with either a bright, shiny finish, or a dark tint for better heat retention. Avoid abrasive cleaners; the thin coating of tin may be scratched off and the metal underneath will rust. It also dents easily, so handle it carefully.

To clean, wash off with soapy water, and dry thoroughly. To polish, rub with a freshly sliced onion. Wash, then dry with a soft, clean cloth. If tin cake and pie pans are rusty, dip a raw potato into baking soda and scrub. Baking soda and water alone clean effectively, too. For very tough stains and stuck-on food, use a nonscratching scouring pad.

Zinc Zinc is a metallic element used in brass, bronze, and nickel-silver alloys. It is used to galvanize iron for coatings on buckets and garbage pails.

Clean with hot water and liquid dishwashing detergent. Remove stubborn stains with a mildly abrasive metal polish such as All-Purpose Metal Polish (page 30). Rub away tarnish with a solution of one part white vinegar or lemon juice and one part water. Leave solution on stains for 5 minutes. Then rinse, dry, and buff.

Sink Cleaners

Most kitchen sinks are made of porcelain enamel or stainless steel. Both are easy-to-clean materials, so that regular maintenance keeps them shining.

Greasy sinks will become clean quickly with Multipurpose Ammonia Cleaner (see Index). After washing stainless steel sinks, apply a little baby oil or mineral oil with a soft cloth and wipe away the excess. This prevents spotting and removes tiny scratches.

The following formula removes yellow rust stains caused by leaking faucets. Rubber sink pads and drain stoppers will also brighten before your eyes when soaked in this solution.

■ Stain Remover for Porcelain Sinks

1 teaspoon liquid dishwashing detergent
½ cup liquid chlorine bleach
½ cup white vinegar

Close the drain and fill the sink with a few inches of warm water. Add detergent, bleach, and vinegar. Let this solution stand in the sink overnight. In the morning, the stains will be gone. Rinse out sink with hot water.

For other tips on cleaning kitchen sinks and fixtures, see porcelain cleaners (see Index) and chrome and stainless steel cleaners listed under "Metal Cleaners and Polishes" (page 30).

Drain Cleaners

Caustic drain cleaners are the most dangerous products used in the home. They contain lye (potassium hydroxide or sodium hydroxide) which, when mixed with water, will burn through everything it touches. If swallowed, the effects are catastrophic, and there is no known antidote. In one case, a young boy swallowed lye; his mother gave him vinegar as the package directed. Vinegar neutralizes the sodium hydroxide, but the reaction also produces a lot of carbon dioxide. The resulting reaction between the two in this case was so violent that the child's stomach exploded. Frightening? You bet.

Most drain stoppages can be prevented. Do not wash grease, lint, hair, coffee grounds, or garbage down the drain. Once or twice a week, pour a teakettle of boiling water and some salt down the drain. This will dissolve grease and eliminate odors. Or, use a noncorrosive drain cleaner once a week.

■ Washing Soda Drain Cleaner

Pour 3 tablespoons of washing soda down the drain, then run a slow stream of very hot water from the tap to dissolve the crystals. Used regularly, this should keep the drains open.

■ Baking Soda/Cream of Tartar Drain Cleaner

1 cup baking soda
¼ cup cream of tartar
1 cup salt

Thoroughly mix ingredients together in a small glass container; store the powder tightly covered. Once a week, put ¼ cup of the mixture down the drain and immediately add 1 cup of boiling water. Wait a minute or so, and flush drain with cold water.

Yield: 2¼ cups

What should you do if the drain is clogged? First, try a plumber's helper or plunger. If that won't open the drain, try this, especially on grease clogs in kitchen sinks.

■ Noncaustic Drain Opener

1 cup baking soda
1 cup salt
½ cup white vinegar
1 kettle boiling water

Pour baking soda, salt, and vinegar into drain. Wait about 15 minutes, as these dissolve organic matter and grease. Flush drain thoroughly with boiling water. If this doesn't work, call a plumber or find someone who can operate an electric snake. Although not the cheapest solution, it certainly is the safest. Then use Noncaustic Drain Opener weekly.

Stove and Oven Cleaners

Follow the manufacturer's instructions for general cleaning of your stove or oven. Always wipe away grease after each meal and clean more thoroughly each week. The wires on electric ranges that furnish heat must not be touched with any metal while the current is on—an electric shock, blown fuse, short circuit, or burned-out coil may result. Also, don't touch coils with salt, soda, soap, or sugar. They may burn out the wires. If food should spill over, let it char. After the unit is cool, brush off particles with a nonmetallic bristle brush.

Cast-iron burners on gas stoves can be cleaned easily with the following procedure.

■ Cleaner for Cast-Iron Burners

3 quarts water
3 tablespoons washing soda

Pour water and washing soda into nonaluminum pan. Submerge burners in water and boil for a few minutes. Then wash as you would dishes, rinse, and let dry thoroughly before replacing on stove.

If you're not lucky enough to own a self-cleaning oven, cleaning it yourself has got to be one of the most-dreaded, messiest tasks around the house. Procrastinating only makes the job harder. That's probably why commercial oven cleaners have to be so strong. And strong they are. Lye (also known as sodium hydroxide, potassium hydroxide, or caustic soda) is the active ingredient. That's the same powerful, dangerous, caustic poison used in drain openers. Aerosol cleaners have added dangers: The cans can explode if heated or punctured, and the fine mist from aerosol cans might be inhaled.

What can you do? First, try to keep your oven as clean as possible. Put a sheet of aluminum foil on the floor of the oven, underneath but not touching the heating element. Although this may slightly affect the browning of some foods, the foil can be easily replaced when soiled.

Place pies or other foods that might spill over on a baking sheet. If there is a spill, sprinkle it immediately with salt to avoid the possibility of a fire. The food will char and can be wiped off with a sponge.

Scrub oven with Multipurpose Ammonia Cleaner or Scouring Cleanser (see Index). Wipe on, let it soak in, and then scrub with a plastic or nylon pad. Wash away baked-on dirt on the oven-door windows with a damp sponge and baking soda.

Here's the best solution yet; although not entirely without danger, it really works.

■ Oven Cleaner

1 cup household ammonia
3 cups boiling water

Warm oven at 200°F for about 20 minutes and then turn off. Open windows and doors to ventilate ammonia vapors. Pour ammonia in small dish and place that on the top shelf. Fill broiler pan with boiling water and set that on the bottom shelf. Leave them overnight.

The next morning, open the doors and windows again and stand back as you open oven. Leave the room and let this air until all the strong vapors disappear.

Wash off the inside of the oven with liquid detergent and water. Even hard, baked-on grease should be loosened enough to clean easily. If not, you may have to repeat the procedure.

Here's a nifty, nonmessy way to clean all the removable parts of the stove and oven (including racks, broiler pans, and chrome rings). This also works on barbecue grills.

■ Easy Cleaner for Removable Oven Parts

Carry all removable parts outdoors and place them in a plastic garbage bag. Pour in 1 to 2 cups household ammonia. Seal the bag with a tie, and leave outside for a couple of hours. Remove parts from bag and rinse clean with a garden hose.

Fire Extinguishers

While on the subject of stoves and ovens, some mention of fire extinguishers is in order. Fires are classified by three types: Class A—wood, paper, textiles, plastic, rubber, and other nonliquid combustibles; Class B—grease, oil, paint and gasoline (combustible liquids); Class C—live electrical equipment (appliances connected to household wiring).

Different kinds of commercial extinguishers are manufactured for each class. Any water-based extinguishers (soda/acid, pump-tank, gas-cartridge, and foam) should *not* be used on electric, gasoline, or oil fires. Electricity may be conducted up the stream of water into your body. Gasoline and oil, which are lighter than water, will float on top and continue to burn. Special dry-chemical, vaporizing-liquid, and carbon dioxide extinguishers are sold for electrical fires. All homes should have at least one approved fire extinguisher.

When food spills or cooks over in the oven, sprinkle salt on it immediately. If flames flare up, immediately shut the door and turn off the oven. The lack of oxygen and loss of heat should smother the flames.

To reduce the chance of fat catching on fire when broiling meat on a rack, place a piece of bread in the broiler pan to soak up dripping fat. This also eliminates smoking.

For grease fires, throw baking soda over the blaze to snuff it out quickly. Baking soda is one of the ingredients in some commercial fire extinguishers. Always keep a box handy by the stove. After using baking soda to put out a fire on a broiling steak, you can even salvage the meat by rinsing it with water.

For putting out outdoor cooking fires, use Flame Extinguisher (see Index).

■ Liquid Fire Extinguisher

This extinguisher is for use on Class A fires. Caution: *Do* not *use this on grease, oil, petroleum-product, or electrical fires.*

2 cups washing soda
1 cup potassium alum
¾ cup borax
¼ cup potash
1½ quarts water glass
2 gallons water

Caution: Both potash and water glass are caustic to the skin and toxic upon ingestion. Wear rubber gloves and handle carefully.

Thoroughly mix washing soda, potassium alum, borax, and potash in a large container. Pour water glass into a large, clean garden pump sprayer that delivers a coarse, high-volume spray. Slowly pour the dry mixture into the sprayer. Stir until all ingredients are dissolved. Add water and blend well. Cover the sprayer tightly, label *Poison*, and store away from children. To use, direct liquid at base of fire, using a coarse, high-volume spray.

Yield: about 2 gallons

■ Dry Fire Extinguisher

This extinguisher is suitable for use on Class B fires.

2 pounds baking soda
6 pounds fine-grade mason's sand

Mix ingredients thoroughly and store in eight 1-pound glass, metal, or impervious plastic containers. Locate them strategically around the house, especially in the kitchen, garage, and workshop. In case of fire, sprinkle the mixture directly on fire, smothering the flame.

Yield: 8 pounds

Refrigerator Cleaners and Deodorizers

Refrigerator spills will come up easily if you periodically wipe over the sides and shelves with a cloth dampened with glycerin. Don't use harsh, abrasive cleansers; try Multipurpose Washing Soda Cleaner (see Index) or white vinegar to prevent mildew.

Clean the condenser at *least* once a year, preferably once a month. This is important, and may save a visit from the repairman. When the dirt builds up, the motor may overheat and shut off automatically. The condenser is located at the back or bottom of the refrigerator. Always disconnect electricity before you remove the grille, then vacuum or brush off.

To mask refrigerator odors, pour vanilla on a piece of cotton and place inside the refrigerator. Or try one of the following methods.

■ Baking Soda Deodorizer

Remove top from a box of baking soda, and label the box with the date 2 months away. Place the opened box on refrigerator shelf to absorb odors, and replace on indicated date. Pour the contents of the used box down the drain to remove odors and keep open.

■ Charcoal Deodorizer

Fill a small bowl with powdered charcoal (the kind used for potted plants or aquariums) or charcoal barbecue briquettes. Place on shelf of refrigerator to absorb odors rapidly. If you have really horrendous, spoiled-food odors, set pans filled with briquettes on several shelves.

■ Absorbent Block Deodorizers

¼ cup chalk
1 cup portland cement
¼ cup silica gel
1 cup vermiculite
water

Mix chalk, cement, silica gel, and vermiculite together in container. Gradually add water until you have a thick, creamy paste. Pour into matchboxes, paperclip boxes, or small cans. Air-dry blocks 2 to 3 days, then place in 350°F oven for 2 hours. Remove blocks from boxes or cans and place 1 or 2 in refrigerator. These blocks will last up to 2 weeks. They can be reactivated several times (until they crumble) by putting in a 350°F oven for 2 hours.

Kitchen Cabinet and Counter Top Cleaners

Cooking grease, oil, and soot build up into a greasy layer on kitchen cabinets. The following formulas will cut through that.

■ Grease Remover for Wooden Cabinets

½ cup deodorized kerosene
2 gallons water

Add kerosene to water, and use with paper towels or old rags to wipe off grease. Rinse thoroughly with clear water and dry.

■ Grease and Wax Buildup Remover for Wooden Cabinets

Apply mineral spirits with fine-grade steel wool (No. 0000), using long, sweeping strokes. Follow the grain of wood, working on one small area at a time. Wash off each area with soapy water and dry thoroughly.

Grease Remover for Painted Cabinets

¼ cup baking soda
1 cup household ammonia
½ cup white vinegar
1 gallon warm water

Before using the formula, press a hot, damp cloth against any grease deposits until they soften. Thoroughly mix all ingredients in a large bucket. Wash cabinets with sponge and solution. Rinse off with a clean sponge and water. Wipe cabinets completely dry.

Wipe off kitchen counter tops frequently with one of our all-purpose cleaners (see Index). Never use abrasive scouring powders, steel wool, or bleach on Formica counter tops; they will ruin the finish. Stains on counter tops made from materials other than Formica can be wiped away with a paste of baking soda and a little water. If stains are persistent, leave the paste on 30 minutes.

Bleach Stain Remover

This method works on purple food-pricing marks that stain counter tops. Wear rubber gloves, and test this first on an inconspicuous spot. If the color bleaches out, don't use it. Soak a cotton ball in liquid chlorine bleach and place over stain for only 1 minute. Then wipe clean with a damp cloth.

Butcher-block counter tops can be wiped with a cloth or sponge slightly dampened with soapy water. Dry immediately. Every few weeks, oil the surface with mineral oil. Do not use vegetable oil, as it will turn rancid in a few days.

Multipurpose Kitchen Deodorizer

This mixture cleans as well as deodorizes.

4 tablespoons baking soda
1 quart water

Mix solution, or use baking soda on a damp sponge. This will clean and deodorize refrigerators, sinks, cutting boards, counter tops, and all other kitchen surfaces.

Chapter 3 Bathrooms

For most people, cleaning the bathroom is the least-favorite household chore. Sprays, foams, bubbles, and little men serenading you from rafts might make the job seem more like fun, but they also make it more expensive. The formulas that follow will save you money, are probably safer, and make the work as effortless as possible—some consolation, anyway, for a job that must be done.

Toilet-Bowl Cleaners

Toilet bowls are made of vitreous china, a glassy-coated, acid-resistant porcelain or ceramic. Commercial toilet-bowl cleaners contain acids (hydrochloric acid, or sodium bisulfate, an ingredient in granular cleaners which turns to sulfuric acid when mixed with water), plus detergents, surfactants, sometimes alkalis and dyes, and perfumes. The powerful acids loosen and dissolve scum that collects on the bowl, but do not damage the porcelain or ceramic surface.

Acids are dangerous poisons—they can burn your skin and eyes on contact and are corrosive and potentially lethal if swallowed. If mixed with chlorine bleach, they will release irritating, potentially lethal chloramine gases.

Fortunately, there are a number of effective and cheaper alternatives for both general cleaning and stubborn stain removal. The bleaches in these formulas will sanitize, deodorize, and clean your toilet. Because they are mild acids, the surface can be soaked with them without damaging the enamel. Scouring powders or liquids should never be used on toilet bowls; they may create tiny nicks and crevices that will harbor bacteria.

For especially resistant rings, try plain fine-grade sandpaper (No. 0 or 00) or fine steel wool. Dip some water out of the bowl to lower the waterline and expose the entire ring. Then rub away the stain very gently.

■ Bleach Toilet Bowl Cleaner

For a simple cleaner, pour ½ cup of liquid chlorine bleach into the toilet bowl and let it stand for at least 30 minutes. Then scrub with a long-handled toilet brush, and flush. *Caution:* Make sure pets and children stay away from the area.

■ Ammonia/Peroxide Toilet Bowl Cleaner

1 teaspoon household ammonia
1 cup hydrogen peroxide
2 quarts water

Mix ammonia, water, and peroxide in a bucket and pour mixture into toilet. Allow mixture to stand for 30 minutes, then scrub inside of toilet bowl with a long-handled brush and flush. If toilet is badly stained, allow mixture to remain in bowl for several hours.

If there are stubborn, difficult-to-reach stains under the rim of the bowl, soak a clean rag in the mixture and wedge under the rim. Then pour cleaner into bowl and let stand for several hours. Remove rag and flush (the rag can be washed and used again). The stains will disappear as clean water flows around rim.

Ring around the collar—ring around the toilet bowl. Rusty rings and stains from minerals in hard water make even antiseptically clean toilets look dirty.

■ Light-Duty Stain Remover

borax
lemon juice

Mix sufficient borax and lemon juice to make enough paste to clean entire ring. Flush the toilet to wet the sides. Then rub on paste and let set for about 2 hours. Scrub thoroughly.

Tub, Basin, and Tile Cleaners

Plan to clean the bathroom right after someone has finished their bath or shower, shut the doors and windows and run the shower. The steam helps loosen dirt, and everything will wipe clean more easily. A sponge mop makes it easy to reach the ceiling and upper walls.

Porcelain Cleaners

Porcelain enamel coats many bathtubs and basins with an impervious, hard, glass-like finish. It is easy to clean but porous enough to trap bacteria. Because the surface will scratch, strong, abrasive cleaners should be avoided. Usually, a nylon scouring pad works well enough with household ammonia or any other all-purpose cleaner.

Another liquid that saves time and money and makes sinks, tubs, and showers shine, is old-fashioned kerosene. Use it with caution.

■ Kerosene Liquid Porcelain Cleaner

1 cup deodorized kerosene
1 cup mineral oil

Buy the least-expensive mineral oil you can find. Mix the kerosene and mineral oil together, and store it in an impervious plastic or glass container with a lid. To use, dampen an old cloth with the solution and run it over the surface. Polish briskly and then rinse well with water. The soap scum will disappear like magic. To remove any kerosene residue from the surface, wash with soap and water, then rinse well.

Yield: 2 cups

Really scratched or stained surfaces may require a stronger cleanser and more concentrated elbow grease. Try using the scouring pad with Scouring Cleanser (see Index), or with ordinary baking soda. Baking soda works on any porcelain, enamel, marbleized, or fiberglass surface, and does not scratch or leave a gritty residue.

■ Baking Soda Porcelain Cleaner

Dip a damp cloth into some baking soda and rub over stains and scum until clean. Rinse off well with clear water. You also can make a paste with water and apply that to textured or especially stained surfaces. Allow to set a few minutes before rubbing clean and rinsing.

■ Bleach Stain Remover

Stubborn rust spots from leaky faucets and rusty pipes respond especially well to ordinary liquid chlorine bleach.

Saturate a paper towel with liquid chlorine bleach, and leave it on the stain for several hours. Rinse well. Or, fill the tub or sink with water to cover the stains. Add several cups of liquid chlorine bleach and let this solution stand overnight.

Rubbing with a cut lemon removes light stains. The following pastes bleach out the darker stains such as rust spots. One of the ingredients, cream of tartar, is effective when sprinkled on a damp cloth and rubbed on full strength. Use Heavy-Duty Porcelain Cleaner only on old, persistent porcelain stains that don't respond to other methods.

■ Borax Stain Remover

3 tablespoons borax
1 tablespoon lemon juice

Mix the ingredients to form a paste. Scrub stain with a nylon pad or a brush and rinse with clear water. If the stains persist, add a drop or two of household ammonia to the paste and reapply. Let this set for about 2 hours before you scrub well, then rinse.

■ Cream of Tartar Stain Remover

3 tablespoons cream of tartar
1 tablespoon hydrogen peroxide

Mix the ingredients to form a paste. Using a nylon pad or a brush, scrub stain, then rinse with clear water.

■ Heavy-Duty Porcelain Cleaner

1 6½-ounce bar naphtha soap
2 gallons hot water
½ cup mineral spirits

Shave naphtha soap into water. Add mineral spirits, and stir until the soap dissolves. Briskly brush this mixture on stains. Then rinse thoroughly.

Ceramic Tile Cleaner

Glazed or unglazed ceramic tiles, often used on bathroom floors and walls, are easy to keep clean. Abrasive cleaners should be avoided because they fade colors and destroy the glossy finish.

The following two all-purpose ceramic tile cleaners are good for weekly cleaning.

■ General Ceramic Tile Cleaner

¼ cup baking soda
½ cup white vinegar
1 cup household ammonia
1 gallon warm water

Measure baking soda into a scrub bucket, and add vinegar and ammonia. Pour in water and stir until the baking soda dissolves. Scrub the solution on the tile with a brush, nylon pad, or sponge. Rinse surface well with clean water.

Yield: about 1 gallon

■ Light-Duty Ceramic Tile Cleaner

¼ cup washing soda
½ cup white vinegar
½ cup household ammonia
1 gallon warm water

Mix washing soda, vinegar, and ammonia in a scrub bucket. Add the water and stir. Scrub surface well with solution.

Yield: about 1 gallon

In hard-water localities, soap scum frequently dulls the surface of ceramic tile. The insoluble film that forms from the reaction of soap with mineral salts in the water is hard to remove. An old-time solution is to dip a cloth into deodorized kerosene and then wipe over the walls. The scum disappears like magic.

Excessively coated surfaces will respond to the following treatment. Use plain, dry fine-grade steel wool (No. 0 or 00), but not the soapy kind of pad. Work on a completely dry surface. Test a small patch first before doing the whole area. Scour lightly; the dirty scum will come right off and then can be washed down the drain.

■ Light-Duty Ceramic Tile Stain Remover

Hard-to-remove rust stains on ceramic tiles can also be treated with paste solutions.

3 tablespoons baking soda
1 tablespoon liquid chlorine bleach

Mix the baking soda and bleach into a paste. Scrub stain with a small brush and rinse thoroughly.

■ Heavy-Duty Ceramic Tile Stain Remover

1 part sodium citrate
6 parts glycerin
water
whiting

Dissolve sodium citrate (a white powder used as a water softener or detergent) in the glycerin by stirring. Add sufficient water to thin this mixture to a milklike consistency, and then mix in enough whiting to form a paste. Spread a thick coating on stains and let stand. Rinse off with clear water.

If you are really energetic, you can "starch" freshly washed ceramic tile. Cover tile with a thin coat of laundry starch or use our formula for Starch (see Index). After this dries, polish to a rich, glossy finish with a soft, dry cloth.

Grout Cleaners

The grout that binds ceramic tiles usually contains portland cement, water, and very fine sand. The mortared joints can become dingy and mildewed if neglected. Mildew is a mold that lives and grows in warm, damp places. Cleaners work by removing and killing the mold, which prevents further growth (and new stains). A cloth moistened in white vinegar or deodorized kerosene and rubbed over the grout effectively cleans away dirt, kills mildew, and restores whiteness. An old toothbrush is ideally sized for scrubbing grout. Use it with one of the following cleaners.

■ Baking Soda Grout Cleaner

3 cups baking soda
1 cup warm water

Prepare this mixture fresh each time. Mix the baking soda and warm water into a smooth paste. Scrub into grout and rinse well with clear water.

Yield: about 1 cup

■ Chlorine Bleach Grout Cleaner

¼ cup liquid chlorine bleach
1 quart warm water

Pour bleach into scrub bucket, add water, and stir until blended. Scrub grout with a small brush.

Yield: about 1 quart

■ Ammonia Grout Cleaner

1 teaspoon household ammonia
¼ cup hydrogen peroxide
¾ cup water

Blend ingredients in a small jar or bowl. Saturate stained areas and scrub vigorously with a stiff brush; let soak for several minutes. Rinse well and repeat if necessary.

Yield: about 1 cup

Disinfectants

Bathroom odors, like most odors, are caused by bacteria. An arsenal of germ-fighting weapons is stocked on the grocery shelf, but these products also contain phosphate detergents and are expensive. Their strong odors are due to the disinfectants they contain—often phenol compounds or pine oil. Any kind of disinfectant kills bacteria and mold, but the effects are only temporary. Thorough, frequent cleaning is most beneficial. Keeping surfaces dry also helps to prevent the growth of mildew and fungi, including the one that causes athlete's foot.

■ Chlorine Disinfectant

This is an effective, inexpensive homemade disinfectant.

¼ cup liquid chlorine bleach
1 quart warm water

Mix bleach with water in a bucket. Scrub all surfaces to be disinfected and cleaned. Then rinse completely.

Yield: about 1 quart

Another homemade solution that is very similar to commercial products contains pine oil, which has (what else?) a strong, piney odor. It is a good disinfectant, and is convenient, because it can be stored.

■ Pine Oil Disinfectant

1 pint soap flakes
6 cups hot water
1 pint pine oil

Slowly stir soap flakes into water in a large, clean glass jar, and mix until the soap dissolves. Remove any suds from the surface, or stop stirring until the foam disappears. Then pour in the pine oil very slowly, and stir until the mixture is thoroughly blended. Store tightly covered. For general cleaning and disinfecting, dilute with water. To disinfect areas that harbor intense concentrations of bacteria, such as toilet bowls, apply full strength.

Yield: ½ gallon

Cleaners for Other Bathroom Surfaces

Shower-Curtain Cleaners

Do you clean your shower curtain once a year like many people do? The easiest method is to let your washing machine do the work for you. However you do it, an ounce of prevention is worth a pound of cure (that often calls for a lot of hard scrubbing). Before you hang the curtain, soak it in a solution of salt and water in the bathtub. This should prevent mildew formation. If you still get around to it only once a year, here are some mixes that will get rid of that unattractive, moldy scum.

■ Light-Duty Shower-Curtain Cleaners

white vinegar
baking soda
lemon juice *or* fresh lemon

First, try removing the mold by rubbing the curtain with vinegar. If that fails, apply baking soda. Dip a damp sponge, nylon pad, or small brush in baking soda and briskly rub surface. If your curtain is still moldy, rub half a lemon or some lemon juice on the reverse side of the curtain, or all over on light-colored curtains. *Caution:* Before applying lemon or juice, test a small, inconspicuous area. The lemon can discolor dark-colored curtains, or fade printed ones.

■ Cleaning Shower Curtains in the Washing Machine

½ cup laundry detergent *or* soap flakes
½ cup baking soda
1 cup white vinegar
mineral oil

Fill washing machine with warm water and throw in 2 bath towels and the shower curtain. Measure in the detergent and baking soda. Run through the entire wash cycle. Then add vinegar and a few drops of mineral oil to the rinse water. Mineral oil will keep the plastic soft and flexible. Do not spin-dry or wash out the vinegar.

Remove curtain from the machine and hang it immediately. After the curtain dries, the wrinkles will disappear. Afterward, try to clean the curtain regularly; getting in the habit of wiping the moisture away after your shower helps. Also, occasionally wiping with warm water and mineral oil keeps the curtain soft.

Shower-Head Cleaners

"Clogs" are in on feet, but not in shower heads. If you live in a hard-water area, the shower head may get clogged with mineral deposits. To remove this buildup, periodically detach the shower head and clean it with one of the following formulas.

■ Metal Shower-Head Cleaner

½ cup white vinegar
1 quart water

Pour vinegar and water in a pot and completely submerge the shower head. Boil 15 minutes.

■ Plastic Shower-Head Cleaner

1 pint white vinegar
1 pint hot water

Pour vinegar and water into a pot to cover shower head. Soak about 1 hour.

Homemade Soap

Diana Branch McMasters

Just one ingredient in commercial detergents—phosphates—starts us off with three good reasons to consider making our own soap at home. Phosphates are (1) a petroleum-based product. That makes them (2) expensive. And they cause (3) water pollution in a very subtle form. Algae feed on phosphates, multiply, and eventually choke out other life forms.

And making your own soap lets you custom-make your recipe. You can add scents, color, even texture, and leave out ingredients to which you may be allergic. Lanolin, a common ingredient in commercial soaps, causes allergic reactions in some people. Vegetarians and others who prefer not to use animal products can avoid the use of animal fat—the basic ingredient in commercial soap—by using vegetable fats in their recipe. And making soap at home does help you economize. Savings aren't readily apparent with bar soap, since it lasts a long time and is relatively cheap, but laundry and dish detergents disappear fast and are expensive. Real savings can be made here.

Making simple soap is an easy process involving just three basic ingredients—lye, fat, and water. Lye is an emulsifying agent that lifts dirt and grease from the item being washed. Fat acts as a medium for holding caustic lye in a diluted state and provides the lather of suds which picks up dirt and holds it in suspension until it can be rinsed away with clear water. The water is used to dissolve the lye, which comes in a crystalline form.

Years ago, lye was leached from wood ashes in a backyard ash pit. Now it can be found at any grocery store tucked in among the drain cleaners. *Caution:* Lye is toxic. Lye will burn as it reacts with moisture on the skin and can be fatal if swallowed. If it comes in contact with skin, flush with water for 15 minutes; flush eyes for 20 minutes. If swallowed, drink large quantities of water or, preferably, milk, and contact a physician. Keep out of children's reach during use and storage. In fact, it might be wise to dispose of any leftover lye by pouring it down a drain immediately after you've finished making a batch of soap. Otherwise, store lye in a sealed can or a jar with a tight lid. Be sure to keep the lye dry, since moisture causes it to cake.

Until you get involved with exotic oils, scents, and colors, fat will be the one ingredient that leads to the most variation in the character of your soap. Tallow is freshly rendered beef fat, while lard is from pork. Tallow yields a harder, longer-lasting soap that is preferable to that made from lard. Leftover drippings from bacon, hamburger, and the like can be saved and used to produce a soap that cleans well. But it is the old-fat smell of this same yellow-colored soap that has given homemade soap a bad name. To get milder-smelling soap, you can wash and deodorize fats after rendering.

For white, sweet-smelling soap that needs no deodorizing, use fat trimmings either fresh from the butcher or kept fresh by freezing. To save on trimming time, ask the butcher for solid hunks of fat, such as those that come from around the kidney, rather than meat trimmings. To render it pure, fat must be separated as much as possible from meat, blood, veins, and any nonfat tissues connected to it. Then it should be cut into small chunks and melted down over a low heat. This is called rendering, and it separates impurities from the fat as it melts. You can then strain the impurities away, using either an old sheet or several layers of cheesecloth.

To wash leftover fats, melt them down and boil in an equal amount of water with 1 teaspoon of alum or baking powder added per quart. Boil for about 10 minutes. Once cooled, the fat can be skimmed off the top of the water. Any fat found on the underside of the fat block that has not congealed should be discarded. If odors persist, cooking potatoes in the fat will help remove them. *Caution:* Fats are extremely flammable and should not be melted down over high heat or left unattended.

Tools of the Trade

Lye is not only good at eating through dirt, it will eat right into pots and pans as well. One of your most challenging jobs involves finding the right tools. Never use tin or aluminum to make soap. Only enamel, stainless steel, glass, porcelain, pottery, or wood should be used. Even then, it is best to set these utensils aside and use them solely for soapmaking. In time, even glass will show signs of corrosion, and your wooden broom handle stirrer will become noticeably shorter after years of use.

A complete arsenal of soapmaking tools includes:

large pot (any type) for melting fat
1-quart, lye-resistant pot or jar for mixing lye and water
large porcelain pot for mixing fat and lye
an old broom handle (or long wooden stick) for stirring
cloth for straining fat and lining soap mold
soap mold (shoe box, wooden box, or glass baking dish)
glass measuring cup
rubber spatula or wooden spoon
thermometer
rubber gloves
surgical mask
safety goggles

Mixing the Ingredients

Once all of your tools have been collected and ingredients prepared, the process of bringing the ingredients together to make soap involves the following five steps: (1) preparing the lye and water mixture; (2) melting the fat; (3) allowing both to cool to their respective proper temperatures; (4) mixing and stirring; and (5) pouring the soap into a mold.

[*Continued on next page*]

Caution: This step is safest when done outside or in a well-ventilated area to avoid irritation to eyes and throat. Mixing lye with water creates a chemical reaction that generates heat and gives off harsh fumes. Also, be sure to put on your gloves, surgical mask, and safety goggles before you begin. Because of the quick rise in temperature, it is best not to use a glass container for this step unless it is specifically made to withstand heat. Measure water first (or herbal tea, for scent), then add the lye, stirring constantly with a long stick with your head turned away until the lye is dissolved. Soft water yields better results.

The temperatures desired for mixing the lye and water mixture with the fat depends upon the kind of fat used.

tallow: cool lye mixture to 93°F; tallow to 125°F
lard: cool lye mixture to 77°F; lard to 98°F

Old hands at making soap can tell by feeling the outside of the containers when temperatures are just right. Beginners should use a thermometer.

When temperatures are right, slowly pour the lye and water mixture into the fat in a thin stream. Then stir slowly but constantly for 10 to 30 minutes, sometimes even up to an hour, until the soap has turned thick and creamy, almost like honey. You will know it is ready for the mold when you can drop a thin stream from your spoon back into the bowl and it holds its shape on top of the batch.

At this point you can add oil-based scents and colorings, such as those used in making candles. Shavings from crayons can be introduced, either stirred in just enough to leave streaks in the soap or fully melted and stirred in to make a solid-colored soap. Yellow food coloring is fairly stable in soap, but other colors are not recommended. Add more coloring than seems necessary. Soap will harden to a much lighter color than it appears in its liquid state.

You can scent your soap with fragrant oils just before the soap goes into its mold, or use a strong herbal tea for the portion of water used to mix with lye at the beginning of the recipe. Alcohol-based extracts and perfumes are not recommended, since they can affect the chemical nature of the soap and also because they are not as potent as oils. A recommended amount to start with is 1 teaspoon of scented oil for every 1 to 2 cups of liquid soap, or about an ounce for every gallon.

If a batch won't thicken, it is likely that temperatures were too high; if so, setting the pan in cold water may bring on thickening. Set the batch aside and stir every once in a while. It may eventually thicken on its own. *Never* discard a bad batch down the sink or you'll be calling the plumber to get things running again. Put it in a glass jar with a tight lid, and set it out for the trash, or bury it.

The mold should be prepared ahead of time. It need be nothing fancier than an old shoe box, but whatever the container, it must either be lined with a damp cloth or thoroughly greased. Pour the soap into the mold as high as 4 to 6 inches if you have enough liquid soap. Liquid soap won't swell or shrink—you'll have as much hard soap as liquid. Let it set for a few hours, then score the firm-but-not-yet-hard soap with a stainless steel knife along lines where you want the soap to break into bars later.

At this point the soap is still caustic. Let it set for at least three weeks in a dry place, such as a cupboard, before using. Storing the cut-up bars in paper wrappers will hold in scents and color. During this time the harshness will dissipate and the soap will gradually turn from its present manila color to a crispy white. Once hard, the bars can be pried apart with a knife. Carving the squared-off edges round with a knife will make the bars easier to handle.

This soap can be used for all purposes—left in bar form for the bathroom or shaved into a powder with a vegetable grater for washing dishes or the laundry. If you're not satisfied with the way it lathers, remember that homemade soap lathers better in soft water. It could easily be the water and not the soap recipe that is responsible.

Soap Recipes

Here is a recipe with which to practice. It will produce a nice, hard white bar that doesn't lather as well as the commercial brands you're used to, but which will last longer and get things good and clean.

■ Simple Soap

6 cups freshly rendered tallow
¾ cup lye
2½ cups cold soft water

Follow the general directions (above) for mixing and molding the soap. Cut it into bars for bathing, or grate it into shavings for doing dishes or laundry. For more soap, double the recipe.

Yield: 6 to 8 bars

■ Mary Weaver's Household Soap

Mary Weaver, of New Tripoli, Pennsylvania, has been using this soap recipe for her family for over 20 years. It isn't as harsh as the simple soap recipe and cleans just as well. She usually makes two batches a year. Mary says that adding the sugar was her grandmother's way of adding a little love, but we've found that a little sugar also helps make a better lather.

[*Continued on next page*]

5 pounds freshly rendered tallow
1 pound lye
1 quart cold soft water
½ cup borax
2 teaspoons sugar
½ cup household ammonia

Follow the general directions (above) for making soap, but incorporate this additional step. Dissolve borax and sugar in ammonia and add to recipe as soon as the lye and fat are mixed.

Yield: 15 to 20 bars

■ Vegetarian Soap

An all-vegetable shortening, such as Crisco, can be substituted for animal fat in any recipe to make a soap that's free of animal by-products. It is a relatively expensive soap to make, because you can't render your own fats from inexpensive scraps as you can with tallow. It is also a soft soap that doesn't last long, although it does lather well.

6 cups solid vegetable shortening
¾ cup lye
2½ cups cold soft water

Follow the general directions (above). This soap will take longer than usual to thicken. Stir constantly for the first 15 minutes and intermittently thereafter until thick. It may also take up to a few weeks to harden.

Yield: 6 to 8 bars

■ Herbal Complexion Soap

The oatmeal and baking soda in this recipe stimulate as they cleanse, while the oils soften the soap and the skin. The soap will have an earthy tone and fragrance from the herbs and a mottled appearance from the oatmeal. Any flour, such as whole wheat or rice, can be substituted for the oatmeal, which is included in the formula for its mildly abrasive texture.

2½ cups herbal tea
5 cups freshly rendered tallow
1 cup coconut oil
¾ cup lye
¼ cup baking soda
1 cup oatmeal
2 teaspoons vitamin E oil
1 teaspoon fragrant oil (optional)

Allow the herbs for the herbal tea to set overnight before straining. Prepare and mix the tallow, oil, and lye according to the general directions (above), using the herbal tea in place of water. Dissolve the baking soda in as little boiling water as possible and allow it to cool before adding to the soap. Add the baking soda, oatmeal, vitamin E oil, and fragrant oil as soon as the mixture is ready to pour into its mold. Mix well before pouring.

Yield: 6 to 8 bars

■ Soap Shampoo

You can concoct your own shampoo recipe using soap. The scent of lemon is a favorite for feeling fresh and we include baking soda in the recipe to help reduce hair oiliness.

2 cups freshly rendered tallow
1 cup vegetable oil
⅓ cup lye
1¼ cups cold soft water *or* herbal tea
1¼ cups lukewarm water
½ cup vegetable oil
up to ¼ cup baking soda (optional for oily hair)
2 teaspoons lemon oil
1 teaspoon yellow food coloring (optional)

Prepare the tallow, vegetable oil, lye, and cold water as though making bar soap, following the general directions (above). When the soap mixture has thickened, add the lukewarm water and the second portion of oil, baking soda (dissolved in as little boiling water as possible and allowed to cool), lemon oil, and coloring, if desired. Store in a glass jar with a lid. (For other shampoo formulas, see Index.)

Yield: about 1½ quarts

Either of the last two recipes can be made from powdered soap bought at the store or by shaving bars of simple soap you already have on hand. Simply grate the soap into a powder with a vegetable grater and melt in a double boiler over a low heat. Then add the extras.

Chapter 4 Laundry

Doing the laundry has become progressively more complex, because we have so many different kinds of fabrics to wash these days. In addition to natural fibers, such as wool, silk, cotton, and linen, we have an array of various kinds of synthetics, such as dacron, rayon, nylon, polyester, acetate, and acrylic, to name just a few. And different fabrics must be cared for in different ways. The type of washing agent, the water temperature, whether to hand- or machine-wash—all these factors must be considered. Some items can't even be immersed in water and must be dry-cleaned.

Prior to the 1940s, soap and water, javelle water (an old-fashioned bleaching agent), bluing, and starch were about the only things required for each wash day. Today, we can use a variety of soaps, bleaches, laundry boosters, heavy-duty detergents, all-purpose detergents, and cold-water detergents, plus a host of specialty cleaning agents. To complicate things even more, many of these are available in different concentrations and in both liquid and powder forms. All this adds up to a lot of wash-day confusion and a lot of money. The truth of the matter is that most of these commercially available items contain various mixtures of some very basic ingredients—all camouflaged by fancy packaging and some fancy prices. As you'll see later in this section, you can formulate many of these products yourself; you'll then have control over which ingredients are included and which are eliminated.

In caring for any fabric, follow the instructions on the label, especially if you're not sure about its fiber content. Don't exceed the amount of laundry product recommended by the manufacturer of your machine. You can use less, though, and save money. Also, use the mildest technique possible that will still get the job done. Result—the laundry will be sufficiently clean and the articles will last longer. Use of harsh laundry agents and excessive heat removes colors and weakens fabrics, which means you'll have to replace clothes more frequently.

Detergents

In the broadest sense, the word *detergent* means anything that acts as a cleaning agent. In other words, anything that has detergency or cleaning power. Both soap formulations and synthetic detergents fall into this category. Synthetic detergents (commonly called simply detergents) are different from the soap formulations in that they contain a petrochemical or other synthetically derived surfactant. In soap formulations, the surfactant is the soap itself, which is made by the action of the alkali (usually lye) on fat or fatty acids. Tallow is the major fat used, although certain vegetable oils are often employed. A surfactant is nothing more than a surface-active agent that decreases the surface tension of water, making the water "wetter" and better able to penetrate fabrics. Also, it combines with grease and dirt to form an emulsion or suspension that floats off the clothes in the wash water. The surfactant provides most of the cleaning power.

Synthetic Detergents

Synthetic detergents may contain more than one surfactant in order to serve as all-purpose cleaning agents that will work on most kinds of materials. In addition to surfactants, a synthetic detergent can contain "builders" that tie up the hard water ions (calcium and magnesium) and make the water more alkaline or basic (that is, a higher pH) so that surfactants can be more effective. Synthetic detergents may also contain bleaching and brightening ingredients, enzymes,* corrosion inhibitors (sodium silicate) to protect the washing machine and plumbing, and perfume.

A detergent's surfactants are determined on the basis of the washing conditions (water temperature and water hardness) and the type of fabric to be washed. Hydrophilic (water-attracting) fibers such as cotton, wool, silk, and linen require anionic surfactants. These are high-sudsing agents and are mostly the linear alkylate sulfonate type (LAS). Others include alkane sulfonate, alkyl ethoxylate sulfate, alkyl glycerl sulfonate, and alkyl sulfate.

Hydrophobic (water-repelling) fibers such as permanent-press polyamide and polyester are cleaned more easily by a nonionic surfactant. As the name suggests, these do not ionize (form ions) in water. They are particularly effective in removing oils. Many are low sudsing and include ethoxylated alcohols and alkyl amine oxides. There is another type of surfactant, called cationic. These are generally more expensive than the other two types but are also germicidal and have fabric-softening properties. The best known of these are the quarternary ammonium compounds, such as alkyl

*Enzymes act as biochemical catalysts to break down certain soils and stains to simpler forms which can then be removed. Amylase is used to break down starches and other carbohydrates; protease breaks down proteins. Enzymes are contained in many presoaking products.

dimethyl benzyl ammonium chloride. Some are widely used in disinfecting/sanitizing cleaners and in wash/rinse/dryer fabric softeners.

Builders are contained in detergents because of the hardness factor associated with the washing process. Calcium and magnesium present in the water, dirt, soil, and chemical residues from textiles all contribute to the total hardness. The most common and most controversial builders are the polyphosphates, with sodium tripolyphosphate and trisodium phosphate being the most frequently used.

Both the builders and the surfactants have been implicated in water pollution. The problem first emerged in the late 1950s and early 1960s because of the use of low biodegradable surfactants, called ABS surfactants (alkyl benzene sulfonate). The chemicals in these surfactants did not decompose into simpler substances and ended up as poisons in our water systems. This problem was alleviated, though, by the industry's switch to LAS surfactants, which are biodegradable and nonpolluting.

The builders present a different problem. Phosphates, the most popular builders, happen to be basic nutrients for algae and other marine plants. The input of large amounts of phosphates leads to an overgrowth of plant life in rivers, lakes, and streams, a process known as eutrophication. This can then lead to oxygen depletion and the choking off of fish and animal life, resulting in the aging and death of a lake or pond.

Some substitutes for the phosphate builders now being used are sodium carbonate (washing soda), sodium citrate (used particularly in liquid laundry detergents), and aluminum silicate. Sodium carbonate is the one predominantly used in heavy-duty detergents. It is corrosive to washing machines and plumbing; therefore, a corrosion inhibitor (often sodium silicate) is usually added. Sodium carbonate is also somewhat harsh and should not be used on delicate fibers. Furthermore, it masks and therefore lessens the effectiveness of flame-retardant products. You can formulate your own synthetic detergents, but the ingredients are available only in industrial-size quantities and, even if you can find someone who will sell you smaller quantities, the price is very high. The most practical thing to do is to shop for the best price for commercial synthetic detergents.

Soap Detergents

With the growing concern over phosphate-containing detergents, more people are asking, "Why not go back to soap?" Today, consumers have almost completely substituted detergents for soap. The primary disadvantage of soap is that, in hard water, soap leaves on clothes a greasy, grayish film known as soap curd. If the water in your area is soft or only slightly hard, you could return to using soap for most of your laundry purposes. If you live in an area where the water is moderately hard to very hard, you can still use soap if you add a water softener such as washing soda to the wash load. The clothes may not be as bright, because modern automatic washers have not been designed for use with soap. Old-fashioned wringer washers squeeze some of the soap curd out of the clothes. In automatic washers, however, the spin-cycle water is forced through clothes by centrifugal force. This traps the soap curd among the cloth fibers.

To substitute soap for detergent, you must first strip your clothes of any remaining detergent residues. Do this by washing your clothes in your machine with hot water and ¼ cup washing soda. You need to do this only once for all clothes that you wash in your machine. Then you can wash loads normally, using the following instead of detergent.

■ Soap for Your Automatic Washer

1 cup pure soap flakes or powder
2–4 tablespoons washing soda

Add ingredients to washing machine as you would detergent, and wash. The amount of washing soda you use will depend upon the hardness of your water—for very hard water, use 4 tablespoons.

■ Soft Soap

This is a basic formula for a jellied soap that has hundreds of uses around the house.

¼ cup pure soap flakes *or* grated soap ends
1 cup water

Place ingredients in a saucepan. Heat on low setting, stirring until soap is melted. Strain into a jar or other handy container and cover. This formula has many uses—washing hands and fine washables and light-duty cleaning. You can use any type of soap you wish—a delicate cosmetic soap or a spot-removing naphtha one. *Caution:* Do not use this soap in your dishwasher.

■ Soft Soap for Delicate Washables

This soap is excellent for fabrics that cannot be machine-washed, and even machine-washable items will stay new looking and will wear longer if washed by hand with this soap.

¼ cup soap flakes *or* grated soap ends
1 cup water
¼ cup borax

Place ingredients in a saucepan. Simmer, stirring, until mixture reaches a uniform consistency. Strain into jar or other handy container. Cover and store. Wash most items in hot water with a small amount of soft soap. For wool, use the soft soap and cold water.

Bleaching

A bleaching agent is an oxidizing or reducing chemical, such as sodium hypochlorite, sodium perborate, sulfur dioxide, sodium acid sulfite, or hydrogen peroxide. Different bleaching agents have different chemical properties and will have different effects on various fabrics.

The most widely known laundry bleach is chlorine bleach, which usually contains sodium hypochlorite. Powder bleaches often contain what is known as chloride of lime or chlorinated lime—this is actually a mixture of calcium hydroxide, calcium chloride, and calcium hypochlorite. These chlorine-type bleaches are very effective. Since chlorine is a good oxidizing agent, it also destroys bacteria and is, therefore, a good disinfectant.

Chlorine bleach does have some drawbacks. It must *never* be mixed with ammonia or any ammonia-containing products, since a toxic gas will form. It should be used sparingly because of its environmental impact. (After disposal, it reportedly combines with other substances to form carcinogens.) It can weaken cloth fibers, causing clothes to wear out more quickly, so use bleach only when you must. Chlorine bleach should never be used on silk, wool, elasticized fabrics, rayon, leather, and items that are not colorfast. If in doubt, spot-test the fabric to make sure. Using an eyedropperful of a dilute solution of bleach, apply a few drops to an inconspicuous part of the garment. Allow it to dry, then examine area for fading. Remember—when in doubt, don't use chlorine bleach.

In this section, we have included four bleaching formulas—two chlorine-type* plus two nonchlorine-type bleaches. The nonchlorine-type bleaches are not as strong as the chlorine type and, therefore, are not as harsh on clothes.

■ Heavy-Duty Bleach

1 gallon water
2 cups chlorinated lime
3 cups washing soda

Mix ingredients in an old plastic bucket. Stir well. Allow to stand, uncovered, for 24 hours. Strain into storage containers—plastic bleach bottles or glass bottles with lids. Use as any commercial liquid bleach. *Caution:* Be careful of fumes during mixing and avoid contact with skin. Keep away from children and pets.

*You may wish to buy ready-made chlorine bleach at the supermarket, since, in comparison to fancy cleaners, it is one of the least expensive laundry products available. We include these bleach formulas for those people who really want to do it *all* by themselves.

■ Liquid Chlorine Bleach

This, too, is a heavy-duty bleach. Put 6 ounces of sodium hypochlorite in a 1-gallon glass or plastic container (not metal), and add sufficient water to fill container. Store covered tightly. *Caution:* Avoid contact with skin and eyes. Keep away from children.

■ Hydrogen Peroxide Bleach

This is a very gentle bleaching agent and is good for bleaching even washable white silk.

1 part hydrogen peroxide
8 parts water

In a dishpan or sink, mix a sufficient amount of the ingredients to cover garment to be bleached. Immerse garment for 5 to 30 minutes, as necessary, to remove stains or lighten garment. Rinse garment in clear water and discard bleach mix.

■ Oxygen Bleach

Some fabrics, such as wool, silk, and those with delicate colors, can't be exposed to chlorine bleaches. For these (or for any fabrics if you prefer not to use chlorine bleach at all) the following formula is suitable. This formula relies on the bleaching action of the oxygen released by mixing sodium perborate and water.

2 tablespoons sodium perborate
1 cup water

Dissolve sodium perborate in water. Soak article of clothing in this solution, or add ¼ cup of solution to washing cycle. This bleaching formula is safe for all fabrics, but use cold water for very fine washables and wool.

Fabric Softeners

Fabric softeners add softness and fullness to fabrics. They reduce static electricity on synthetics so that garments will not cling. Fabric softeners also reduce linting and make ironing easier. Here is one that's simple to make.

■ Fabric Softener

1 quart lauryl pyridinium chloride
1 cup isopropyl alcohol (70%)
⅓ cup water

Mix and store in convenient container. Use 2 to 3 tablespoons to each load of wash during the rinse cycle. Do not pour softener directly onto clothes, for this can stain them. Do not use any other laundry product in the rinse cycle with the softener. Also, do not overuse the softener. This is especially important for items such as towels and diapers; excessive softeners can create a waterproof coating on their surfaces and reduce their absorbency.

■ Baking Soda Fabric Softener

This one can be used whether you're using a synthetic or soap detergent. Add ¼ cup baking soda to the wash load. Clothes will feel soft and smell fresh.

■ Vinegar Fabric Softener

This is a good softener to use if you're using soap in your automatic washer. Add ¼ cup white vinegar to the final rinse cycle. This will help to remove any soap curd that's trapped.

Miscellaneous Laundry Formulas

■ Spray and Wash

This formula is great for removing built-up soil and dirt in those hard-to-clean areas such as collars and cuffs.

2 tablespoons household ammonia
1 teaspoon liquid soap or detergent
1 pint warm water

Mix well and store in a convenient spray container. Spray mixture on tough spots and let set about 15 minutes. Then wash as usual, in an automatic washer or by hand.

■ Deyellowing Formula

This formula is especially for silk and wool items, which often yellow.

1 tablespoon white vinegar
1 pint water

Mix ingredients. Sponge article with solution and rinse. Wash items as usual, or use the formula for Soft Soap for Delicate Washables (page 67).

With the advent of synthetic fabrics, the words *starch* and *ironing* have become almost foreign to our vocabulary. Because many synthetic fabrics are made from petroleum, a nonrenewable source, there may be a movement away from the "miracle" synthetics back to the natural fabrics—cotton, wool, linen, and silk. These are made from renewable sources and are biodegradable. They do have one disadvantage—they require ironing, but starch makes ironing easier.

■ Starch

1 tablespoon cornstarch
1 pint cold water

Mix and stir to dissolve the cornstarch. This mixture can be used as any starch—it can even be used in a spray bottle. Remember, shake or stir before using.

■ Fabric Freshener

Add ¼ cup baking soda to the washing load.

For items that require a stronger freshener, such as diapers, soak for several hours in the following solution before washing:

½ cup baking soda
1 gallon water

A baking soda solution is also great if you've had a close encounter with one of those small, furry, black and white animals, skunk for short. Don't bury your clothes—soak them in a baking soda solution.

Cleaning the Washing Machine

Periodically, your washer needs some attention, too. The use of corrosive laundry detergents causes a buildup of mineral and chemical deposits. To minimize this problem, use the following procedure.

■ Automatic Washing Machine Cleaner

Fill the washer with warm water. Add 1 cup of white vinegar and run through entire cycle. Do this about once every month.

The outside porcelain surface of your washer can also get crusty-looking after a while. To keep it new-looking longer and prevent rust from forming, use regular car wax on it about twice a year.

Stain Removal

Removing stains from a garment or upholstery fabric can be one of the most frustrating chores, simply because when the method used doesn't work, it *really* doesn't work. In some instances, whatever you've tried may make the stain set and then removal becomes even more difficult. This is especially true with substances that contain protein, such as milk, cream, and blood. Using hot water on such stains causes the protein in these substances to denature. (Heating or adding strong acids or alkalines to protein causes its chemical structure, and therefore its solubility properties, to change.) Then the stain becomes very difficult to remove completely. Cold water is the rule with protein-containing stains. Stain removal can be tricky, but there are some very basic rules of thumb which can make the job easier.

1. Timing is very important. Remove the stain as soon as possible.
2. Always keep the fabric content and color in mind when removing a stain. You want to remove the stain without ruining or discoloring the fabric.
3. Use a step-by-step approach. First, try the simplest, mildest technique. If it works—great! If not, try a stronger method and then an even stronger one, until the stain is lifted from the fabric.
4. A stain must be soluble (that is, able to be dissolved) in the stain remover applied in order to be successfully removed. This concept of solubility is very important. We must think in the terms of solvent and solute. A solvent is any substance that will draw another substance, called a solute, into solution. For many stains, plain water is an excellent solvent; for others, only a petroleum-based solvent, such as kerosene or gasoline, will work. Alcohol is another familiar solvent. It is often described as an in-between type of solvent, sharing certain solvent properties common to both water and petroleum-based solvents. All alcohols have solvent capabilities. The one used here, isopropyl alcohol, is the most readily obtainable.

Stain Remover Formulas

Table 4.1 presents step-by-step methods for removing stains; that is, if the first one doesn't work, try the next. This technique will minimize damage to the fabric.

Table 4.1 Specific Laundry Stains and Their Removal

Blood and Meat Juice
Rinse with cold water, soaking and swishing if necessary.
Use mild soap and cold water.
Use starch paste (cornstarch and water) and cold water.
Use club soda and cold water.

Chocolate and Cocoa
Rinse with cold water, soaking if necessary.
Use mild soap and cold water.
Use borax and cold water.
Use bleach and cold water only if recommended for fabric. See "Bleaching," page 68.

Coffee and Tea (with milk or cream)
Use cold water, then use hot water.

Cream and Milk
Rinse with cold water.
Use mild soap and cold water.

Egg
Rinse with cold water, soaking if necessary.

Fruit and Fruit Juices
Use boiling water, soaking if necessary.
Use bleach and hot water if recommended for fabric. See "Bleaching," page 68.

Grass
Use cold water.
Use soap and cold water.
Use naphtha soap and cold water.
Use 70% isopropyl alcohol.
Use turpentine, then wash thoroughly in cold water.

[*Continued on next page*]

Table 4.1—*Continued*

Grease and Oils
Use French chalk, blotting paper, or other absorbent if it is a spill, then:
Use warm water and soap.
Try 70% isopropyl alcohol.
Try turpentine.

Ink
Use cold water.
Try lemon juice.
Try bleach if recommended for fabric. See "Bleaching," page 68.

Iodine
Use soap and warm water.
Try 70% isopropyl alcohol.
Try bleach if recommended for fabric. See "Bleaching," page 68.

Medicine
Use 70% isopropyl alcohol.
Use warm water and soap.

Mildew
Use cold water.
Try bleach if recommended for fabric. See "Bleaching," page 68.

Paint and Varnish
For water-based products:
Use warm water and soap.
For oil-based products:
Use 70% isopropyl alcohol.
Try turpentine.

Perspiration
Use soap and warm water.
Bleach in the sun or with one of our bleach formulas. See "Bleaching," page 68.

Table 4.1—*Continued*

Rust
Use lemon juice mixed with salt.

Wax
Scrape off as much as possible, then:
   Use French chalk, blotting paper, or other absorbent with a warm iron.
If residue remains:
   Use 70% isopropyl alcohol and then bleach if necessary and if recommended for fabric. See "Bleaching," page 68.

Dyeing Wool with Natural Dyes

Nancy Moore Arobone

Commercial dye preparations do not come close to the muted, rich hues found in nature, where the subtle colors seem to enhance each other's beauty so that "clashes" are virtually impossible. Naturally dyed wool gets more lustrous and fuller in color with the passage of time. Wool is ideally suited for natural dyes because it is very porous, which permits the color to penetrate the fibers fully.

One of the most enjoyable aspects of using natural dyes is that each batch is an experiment in color. Because so many elements can affect the color you will get from your dyestuff, it is very difficult to get the same color twice. The age of the plants at the time of harvesting, the season in which the plant is picked, and even the type and quality of wool affect the color. Generally, mature plants will produce deeper color than young plants, and plants gathered in autumn will be stronger-hued than those gathered in the spring.

Many common garden plants and flowers produce vibrant dyes. But you may find that you want to expand your garden somewhat to include varieties known specificially for their dyeing properties. If you decide to collect your dyestuffs from the countryside, keep in mind that many plant species are endangered. Take care not to clean out an area completely; leave enough plants to insure that propagation will occur and your supply will be replenished.

You won't need to invest in any expensive equipment. In fact, you probably have what you need in your kitchen. Since some dye plants are poisonous, it is important to keep your dyeing utensils separate from your kitchen things, and *never* use dyeing implements for food preparation. For the best results, use enameled pots, making sure that there are no chips or cracks, because the exposed metal may react with the dye and drastically alter its color. An enameled cauldron, nonmetallic measuring spoons and cups, a glass cooking thermometer, rubber gloves, and a scale for weighing your wool are useful. For stirring, a glass rod, a painted wooden stick or broom handle, or wooden dowels or spoons can be used. If you use unfinished wooden implements for stirring, be aware that the dye will be absorbed into them; have several on hand if you are working with different colors.

Always work with clean wool, as any dirt or residues will show through the dyes. For optimum results use soft water—preferably rainwater, but tap water with softener added may also be used—for all treatments and for rinsing wool.

Preparing the Dye Bath

When you extract color from plant materials, soaking them in soft water prior to the cooking stage will produce a stronger dye and can save energy by reducing the cooking time. Freshly picked plants generally yield more potent dyes, but dried plants can be used. Mashing or pulverizing the material also aids in the extraction process.

The tender plant parts, comprised of the more delicate leaves and stems, ripe berries, and flowers, do not require soaking. Fibrous materials, such as the tougher leaves and stems, should be soaked for at least three days. Woody materials, such as bark, twigs, and branches, should be soaked for at least one week. And for the richest color, soak nut hulls for at least two weeks. Some people leave the plant material in the dye bath while the wool is being colored, called simultaneous dyeing, which intensifies the effect, while others strain off the plant material. If you decide to use the simultaneous method, keep in mind that some of the plant fibers and particles may become lodged in the wool.

Working with Wool

When working with wool, care must be taken to prevent matting, hardening, or shrinking. Never subject wool to drastic changes in temperature, either hot or cold. Wool can withstand high temperatures if it is brought to them gradually, but wool should *never* be boiled. Too much stirring will cause matting and shrinking. Gently bobbing the wool under the water surface is the safest way to distribute the dye evenly.

Since wool can absorb more than half of its weight in water, never hold it dripping over the water. To avoid weakening and stretching the fibers, place wool in an enamel colander or strainer immediately after removing it from hot water. When working with cold water, gradually squeeze the excess water from the wool while lifting it. Never twist or wring wool. Squeeze or press it with your hands, or use a towel to blot out water.

Wool may be dyed in the fleece, skein, or as fabric. If you are dyeing skeins (loosely wound yarn on reels), tie them with a cotton string, because a piece of yarn will stretch when it becomes wet. Also, wool must be totally saturated with soft water, and immersed entirely, not in stages, for even distribution of solutions. Always weigh wool when it is dry, not after it is saturated with water.

Mordants

Before wool will properly take most dyes, it is necessary to apply a mordant. This is a substance that acts as a binding agent and fixes the color to the wool. Without the use of a mordant, most dyes will fade with exposure to light or water.

Many chemicals can be used as mordants. For our purposes, only two ingredients are necessary. Alum is available at pharmacies, botanical supply stores, and some supermarkets. It can have the effect of making the wool feel sticky or hard. If this happens, rinse the wool well following mordanting. Cream of tartar is available at most grocery stores. Keep these ingredients out of the reach of children.

[*Continued on next page*]

■ Alum Mordant

2 tablespoons powdered alum
1 gallon soft water
4 ounces clean wool, moistened

Stir alum into water over heat. Add wool. Gradually increase the temperature of the mixture until it reaches the simmering point. This should take about an hour. Stirring wool occasionally, simmer another hour. Turn off heat and allow mixture to cool to about room temperature. Proceed with dyeing when wool has cooled, or dry treated wool (see "Rinsing and Drying," below) and store in plastic bags for future use.

■ Alum-Cream of Tartar Mordant

2 tablespoons powdered alum
1 teaspoon cream of tartar
1 gallon soft water
4 ounces clean wool, moistened

Follow the instructions for Alum Mordant (above). Add cream of tartar with alum.

Direct Dyeing

There are some dyes that will take to the wool rather well without the use of mordants. This technique is known as direct dyeing. Always add water to the dyepot to replace that which has boiled away.

■ Green Butternut Hull Dye (brown to black)

1 quart butternut hulls
2 quarts soft water
2 ounces clean wool, moistened

Cover butternut hulls with water. Soak about two weeks. Boil mixture until desired color is reached. Cool to room temperature. Strain hulls from mixture, if desired. Immerse wool in the solution, place over low heat, and gradually increase temperature until it is just simmering. Simmer about 30 minutes or until the desired color is reached. Remove from heat. Rinse and dry wool (see "Rinsing and Drying," below).

■ Walnut Hull Dye (brown)

1 quart dried or fresh walnut hulls
2 quarts soft water
2 ounces clean wool, moistened

Cover walnut hulls with water and soak at least 2 weeks. Boil mixture until desired color is reached. Cool to room temperature. Strain hulls from mixture if desired. Immerse wool in solution, place over low heat, and gradually increase temperature until it is just simmering. Simmer until desired color is reached. Remove from heat. Rinse and dry wool (see "Rinsing and Drying," below).

Dyeing Mordanted Wool

Due to the variable results natural dyes give, it is impossible to predict exactly the shade a dye will produce. It's best to have a flexible attitude when you are dyeing—imagine that you are conducting a unique experiment, one you may never be able to reproduce again.

The intensity of the color can be heightened by altering the amount of the dyestuff or by keeping the wool immersed for a longer period of time. Be sure to check on the wool from time to time while it is in the dye bath to make sure that it doesn't get too dark. Bear in mind that when the wool dries, it will be somewhat lighter than it is while wet. Also, be sure to replace any water that has cooked away during the dyeing process.

■ Carrot Top Dye (greenish yellow)

2 quarts soft water
1 quart carrot tops
2 ounces clean wool treated with Alum-Cream of Tartar Mordant (above), moistened

Pour water over carrot tops. Simmer mixture for about an hour. Strain carrot tops from mixture, if desired, then cool to room temperature. Add wool. Place over low heat, and gradually increase temperature of mixture until it is just simmering. Simmer from 30 minutes to an hour, gently bobbing wool just under the surface of the water until desired shade is reached. Rinse and dry wool (see "Rinsing and Drying," below).

[*Continued on next page*]

■ Elderberry Dye (lavender to blue)

2 quarts soft water
1 quart mashed elderberries
salt (if you want a lavender tint) *or* baking soda (if you want a blue tint)
2 ounces clean wool treated with Alum Mordant (above), moistened

Pour water over elderberries. Add salt or baking soda, depending on the tint desired. Simmer mixture about 10 minutes or until desired shade is reached. Strain berries from mixture, if desired, then cool to room temperature. Add wool. Place over low heat, and gradually increase temperature of mixture until it is just simmering. Simmer until desired shade is reached. Rinse and dry wool (see "Rinsing and Drying," below).

■ Goldenrod Dye (yellow)

1 quart goldenrod flowers
2 quarts soft water
2 ounces clean wool, moistened

Gather goldenrod flowers before all the flower heads have opened fully. Cover the flower heads (no leaves) with water. Bring water to a boil and simmer 30 minutes to an hour, until desired color is obtained. Strain goldenrod flowers from mixture, if desired, then cool to room temperature. Immerse wool in the solution, place over low heat, and gradually increase temperature until it is just simmering. Simmer about 30 minutes or until desired color is reached. Allow wool to remain in the bath an additional 2 hours before washing and rinsing. Rinse and dry wool (see "Rinsing and Drying," below).

■ Marigold Dye (buffed yellow)

2 quarts soft water
1 quart marigold flowers
2 ounces clean wool treated with Alum-Cream of Tartar Mordant (above), moistened

Pour water over marigold flowers. Simmer mixture 15 to 30 minutes. Strain marigold flowers from the mixture, if desired, then cool to room temperature. Add wool. Place over low heat and gradually increase temperature of mixture until it is just simmering. Simmer from 30 minutes to an hour, gently bobbing wool just under the surface of the water until desired color is reached. Rinse and dry wool (see "Rinsing and Drying," below).

■ Onion Skin Dye (burnt orange)

2 quarts soft water
1 quart brown onion skins
2 ounces clean wool treated with Alum Mordant (above), moistened

Pour water over onion skins. Simmer mixture about an hour. Strain onion skins from mixture, if desired, then cool to room temperature. Add wool. Place over low heat, and gradually increase temperature of mixture until it is just simmering. Simmer from 30 minutes to an hour, gently bobbing wool just under the surface of the water until desired color is reached. Rinse and dry wool (see "Rinsing and Drying," below).

■ Sumac Dye (beige)

1 quart red sumac berries
2 quarts soft water
2 ounces clean wool, moistened

Crush berries in water and soak 12 hours. Boil mixture about 30 minutes or until desired color is reached. Cool to room temperature. Strain berries from mixture, if desired. Immerse wool in solution, place over low heat, and gradually increase temperature until it is just simmering. Simmer about 40 minutes or until desired color is reached. Remove from heat. Rinse and dry wool (see "Rinsing and Drying," below).

Caution: Sumac berries used for dyeing are red in color. White sumac berries are poisonous to some people and can cause a severe skin rash. Use *only* the red berries.

These are just a few possibilities. Do your own experimentation with any flowers or plants that strike your fancy. The ratio is basically one part plant material to two parts water. Time of processing and the type of mordant can really change your results. Have fun!

Rinsing and Drying

After the wool has reached the desired color, the remaining dye must be removed from the wool. After you remove the wool from the dyepot, immediately place it in a pot of water that is nearly as hot as the dye bath. Rinse again in a pot full of water that is just a bit cooler. Continue immersing the wool in gradually cooler pots of water until the water is clear after the wool is immersed in it and the wool is only slightly warm. Remove excess water by gently pushing the wool with your hands, then blot the wool with a clean towel.

Drying takes much less time if it is done outdoors. Naturally, the weather must be conducive to this type of activity. Dry the wool on flat screens or on towels, in the shade. If you are not entirely satisfied with the color of your wool, you may choose to place it in the sun to dry. This will either cause the dye to fade or will brighten the color considerably, depending on the dye. When the wool is completely dry, it is ready to use.

Chapter 5 Furniture

No matter what it's made of, furniture eventually loses that "showroom glow." Here are some methods to restore the new look to all your furniture.

Wooden Furniture

Wooden furniture is usually finished with varnish or lacquer, or sometimes shellac, and rubbed to a rich, shiny polish. To maintain this luster, it should be dusted regularly with a clean, dry cloth. Oiled and treated cloths should be used only on oil-polished furniture; don't use them on waxed furniture, because the oil will gum the finish. Polish or wax the furniture every two to three months to protect and preserve it. Once a year, waxed furniture should be carefully washed before coating with a fresh layer of wax.

Apply polishes and waxes with clean cloths, or try an old, clean powder puff. Old pieces of velvet are also good, lint-free polishing cloths. If you wear an old pair of socks like a pair of gloves, the job will be finished in half the time. Apply a liquid or paste wax in a thin coat on a clean surface. Allow that to dry, then buff with a clean cloth, following the grain of the wood. All excess wax should be removed so that the surface is dry to the touch. After you've polished your furniture, sprinkle on a little cornstarch and rub to a high gloss. The cornstarch absorbs any excess oil and leaves a highly polished surface free of fingerprints.

There is a variety of commercial waxes and polishes for wooden furniture available. All-purpose polishes are sold as liquids, aerosols, or pump sprays. They are meant for use on wood protected with varnish, resin, or plastic (urethane) coatings. They can also be used on vinyl, ceramic or plastic tiles, Formica counters, and marble. These polishes contain water, petroleum distillate solvents, wax, silicone fluid, emulsifiers, and, more often than not, a lemon fragrance. The solvents dissolve previous coats of polish (and thus shouldn't be used on wood treated with waxes), anchor dust so that it can be easily wiped away, and preserve the finish by spreading a protective layer of wax.

Even though they are easy to use, these products are expensive and, if mishandled, can be hazardous. The petroleum distillate solvents are flammable (as are the propellant gases in aerosols), and dangerous if swallowed or inhaled. If the solvents get into your lungs, they can cause a fatal form of chemical pneumonia (aspiration of as little as a drop or two can be fatal for a small child). The ingredients can also irritate your skin and eyes.

Fortunately, you can make a number of solutions that are a lot safer and cheaper, too. The oils keep the wood from drying out and cracking and leave a polished finish. The polishes give a greater gloss than waxes, but they also attract dirt and dust more easily.

If not applied properly, oil-based polishes can build up to a thick layer that won't harden and will attract dirt. A brown, gummy residue may come off on the polishing cloth, and the finish will look dull and streaked. Oils should be applied sparingly; use only as much as will penetrate and be absorbed by the wood. Any excess should be wiped off, and the finish should be polished again only when the last layer has been removed.

Water is the basic ingredient of the following two polishes, which should be used on furniture that's been varnished, lacquered, or shellacked. Water-based polishes should not be used on fine, waxed furniture that's not protected with a lacquer finish or other waterproof sealant.

■ Multipurpose Furniture Polish

2 tablespoons olive oil
1 tablespoon white vinegar
1 quart warm water

Add olive oil and vinegar to water and mix well. The solution can be stored in a glass bottle or jar; a spray bottle makes it especially convenient. It works best if kept warm while using; place the bottle in a pan of hot water for a while. The solution will wash off dirt and dust and leave a light oil film. After applying, rub dry with a soft, clean cloth.

Yield: about 1 quart

■ Pine Oil Furniture Polish

The detergent in this formula acts as a wetting agent that allows the water to mix with the oil, thus forming an emulsion.

1¼ cups mineral oil
1 tablespoon pine oil
¼ cup liquid dishwashing detergent
1½ cups water

Mix mineral oil, pine oil, and detergent in a clean jar. Stir until the solution is clear. Add water very slowly, while stirring mixture constantly. Apply with a soft cloth and polish dry. Leftover solution can be stored in the jar.

Yield: about 3 cups

The following oil and wax wood polishes are meant for furniture that does not have a protective coating of varnish or lacquer. With one exception, they do not contain water, because it can damage the wood.

■ Lemon Oil Furniture Polish

1 tablespoon lemon oil
1 quart mineral oil

Mix lemon oil into mineral oil in a clean spray bottle. Spray on, rub in, and wipe clean.

Yield: about 1 quart

■ Silicone Oil Furniture Polish

1 tablespoon silicone oil
1 pint mineral oil

Mix silicone oil and mineral oil in a clean bottle or jar. Apply with a cloth, let dry, and wipe to a smooth, glossy finish with a clean cloth. Store the excess, tightly capped, in the bottle or jar.

Yield: about 2 cups

■ Furniture Wax

Carnauba wax is a nontoxic, hard wax made from the leaves of a palm tree that grows primarily in Brazil.

1 tablespoon carnauba wax
1 pint mineral oil
3–4 drops lemon oil (optional)

Place wax and mineral oil in the top of a double boiler. (A double boiler *must* be used to avoid the possibility of the wax catching on fire if placed directly on burner.) Heat mixture, stirring occasionally, until the wax is completely melted. Add lemon oil and stir until well blended. Cool the mixture, then store it in clean metal or glass containers. Apply wax with a soft cloth, then buff to a sheen with a clean cloth.

Yield: about 2 cups

The effectiveness of the following polish depends upon the petroleum distillate solvent, mineral spirits, but if you handle this substance with the care suggested in the table "Common Ingredients and Cautions for Their Use," on page 2, you can eliminate its potential dangers.

■ Mineral Spirits Wood Polish

3 parts mineral spirits
2 parts mineral oil

Measure ingredients into a wide-mouth jar and mix well. Apply with a soft cloth and wipe off excess. Store leftover polish away from heat.

Use this polish on less-than-top-quality furniture. The mineral spirits in this polish might remove more of the wood's natural oils than can be replaced by the mineral oils.

■ Once-a-Year Polish for Fine Wood Furniture

Although this formula does contain water, this relatively small amount will not affect your unsealed wood furniture if the polish is used only once yearly. The water creates an emulsion in the mixture that produces a whipped-cream consistency, allowing the polish to flow easily when applied.

3 parts boiled linseed oil
3 parts turpentine
3 parts white vinegar
1 part water

Mix linseed oil, turpentine, and vinegar in an old container. Pour in water and stir thoroughly.

Apply this to unsealed items or furniture, but do not use on varnished, lacquered, or shellacked finishes. It is a very rich polish, good for yearly polishing of very fine and antique pieces. Excess polish should be stored covered and away from heat.

If your furniture has accumulated a lot of dirt and polish, this dirt and polish must be removed before repolishing. To do this, use soap or one of the formulas below, or try Grease and Wax Build-Up Remover (see Index).

To clean finished furniture with soap, make a rich, foamy suds with pure white soap or soap flakes and warm water. Dip a cloth into just the suds, wring dry, and wash a small area. Rinse right away with another cloth, wrung out of clear, warm water, and wipe dry. Repeat over entire surface. When thoroughly dry, polish.

■ Polish Build-Up Remover

1 part water
1 part white vinegar

Mix ingredients in a bowl. Moisten a soft cloth with the solution, wring out, and rub gently over surface. Dry immediately with a clean, soft cloth.

■ Combination Wood Cleaner and Polish

10 tablespoons white beeswax
2½ cups turpentine
1 tablespoon soap flakes
2½ cups water

Carefully melt beeswax in a double boiler over low heat. (You must use a double boiler to prevent the wax from catching on fire.) Remove from heat and let partially cool. Slowly add turpentine, stirring constantly until well blended. In a separate container, dissolve soap flakes in water. Slowly add this to turpentine mixture. Stir continuously until the mixture is smooth. When cool, the mixture can be stored in clean, wide-mouth, screw-cap jars. To use, apply with a soft cloth, then buff to a sheen with a clean cloth.

Yield: about 5¼ cups

Cleaners for Special Problems

Alcohol Stains Spilled drinks, medicines, skin lotions, and perfumes dissolve many finishes. Wipe up spills immediately, and rub spots vigorously with an oil polish.

For old stains, mix rottenstone or powdered pumice with raw or boiled linseed oil to make a paste. Rub stain lightly in the direction of the grain with the paste. Wipe repeatedly with a cloth dampened with linseed oil, then polish.

Burn Marks Light burn marks will usually disappear with a little furniture polish or mayonnaise—let it set before wiping off with a soft cloth.

A paste made from rottenstone or powdered pumice and salad oil is also effective. Rub paste into burned spot in the direction of the grain. Wipe paste off with a cloth dampened slightly in oil, and wipe dry.

Candle Wax First, scrape away as much wax as you can with a plastic credit card or a dull knife. Wash off the remainder with soap suds, then polish.

Heat Marks A cloth dampened with camphor oil, peppermint oil, or turpentine will remove the white heat marks left when you forgot to use a trivet. Or, use a paste of rottenstone, powdered pumice, or cigar ashes, mixed with lemon oil or linseed oil.

Another method is to rub the mark with a piece of hard paraffin or candle. Cover this with blotting paper or paper towels and press with a warm iron. Repeat, if necessary. Then rub well with a soft cloth.

Paint Splatters Wipe up fresh spots with a cloth dampened with liquid wax or turpentine or with soap and water, then polish.

Soften old spots first with linseed oil, let it set, then scrape away carefully. Rub off traces with paste made from rottenstone and linseed oil, then polish.

Paper and Decals If paper is stuck to a table, you can remove it without ruining the finish by pouring on salad oil or mineral oil. After the paper soaks overnight, rubbing with a soft cloth will safely remove it.

Decals on painted furniture can be removed by soaking with white vinegar in the same manner.

Scratch Marks Always rub with the grain of wood when applying any scratch-repairing solutions. Mineral oil or white petroleum jelly work well on minor, superficial scratches. Cover scratches and let stand for about 24 hours. Then rub into wood, wipe off excess, and polish.

Deeper scratches may require the use of a shellac wax stick, available in a variety of colors at paint and hardware stores, or a crayon that matches the shade of the wood. Heat a knife blade and melt the stick or crayon against the blade, and let it drip into the scratch. Smooth over damaged area with your finger, and let this cool for 5 to 10 minutes until the wax solidifies. Use a plastic credit card or dull knife to scrape away the excess, and polish until it blends in well.

Try any of the following techniques for individual types of wood.

Ebony: Apply black shoe polish, eyebrow pencil, or crayon to the scratch. Wipe with a soft cloth.

Mahogany: Rub with a dark brown crayon or buff with brown shoe polish.

Maple: Mix a few drops each of denatured alcohol and iodine. Apply to scratch with a cotton swab. After the mixture is dry, wax and buff to polish.

Red mahogany: Paint scratches with iodine, using a cotton swab or a fine-grade artist's paint brush.

Teakwood: Rub scratch gently with fine-grade steel wool (No. 0000), then rub in Once-a-Year Polish for Fine Wood Furniture (page 85).

Walnut: Break a fresh, unsalted walnut or pecan in half, and rub the scratch with the broken side of the nut. The oil from the nut will remove any discoloration.

White Water Spots and Rings White, light hazy marks or rings sometimes form when you forget to use a coaster. The spot can usually be removed by regular polishing, or by rubbing with a paste made from a mild abrasive and oil. Abrasives include cigar, cigarette, or fireplace ashes; salt; baking soda; or pumice. Mix one of these with olive oil, mineral oil, salad oil, white petroleum jelly, vegetable shortening, butter, or mayonnaise, to form a paste. Apply gently only to the spot, let stand a few minutes, and buff dry.

Often, just a coat of mayonnaise or white petroleum jelly left for 24 to 48 hours will remove the spots. This is especially effective on mahogany furniture. After stains are removed, wash the surface and rewax.

If these remedies don't work, try rubbing with a little 70 percent isopropyl alcohol, and dry immediately with a clean, dry cloth. Or, use 1 or 2 drops of household ammonia on a damp cloth.

Finally, toothpastes containing extra whitening ingredients are a very mild, effective abrasive. Spread on marks and rub well for a few minutes. If this dulls the surface, restore the luster with one of the polishes or waxes.

■ French Polishing Technique for Damaged Areas

The following technique works well to restore damaged or worn areas on furniture, or to remove nail-polish remover or alcohol stains.

1 part shellac
1 part denatured alcohol

Mix shellac and alcohol thoroughly. Saturate a lint-free cloth with the mixture. Roll the cloth into a ball that fits into your palm. Then apply another tablespoon of the solution to the surface. Using the cloth, work the solution into the damaged area, rubbing with a back-and-forth motion. Keep reapplying the mixture to the cloth as needed, until the spot blends in with surrounding area. This technique may take up to 30 minutes to produce satisfactory results.

Upholstered Furniture

Cloth Upholstery

Upholstery should be vacuumed regularly. Don't forget the crevices, where all those crumbs, coins, and keys seem to hide. Many of the commercial upholstery (and carpet) shampoos are very foamy aerosols or liquids. They contain detergents, surfactants, dyes or fluorescent brighteners, and water to lift the dirt and grime. Foamy solutions should be used for upholstery, to avoid saturating the cloth. Always test first on a small, inconspicuous area. Don't use foamy solutions on pile fabrics such as imitation fur or velvet.

■ Foamy Upholstery Shampoo

6 tablespoons soap flakes
1 pint boiling water
2 teaspoons household ammonia *or* 2 tablespoons borax

Mix ingredients together. Allow mixture to cool until it gels, then whip into a stiff foam with a hand eggbeater or an electric mixer. Immediately brush the dry suds onto the upholstery, applying them to a small area at a time. Use *only* the suds; don't soak the fabric with water. If the suds start to disappear, beat the solution again. Quickly wipe the soiled suds off each section with a damp cloth. An electric fan will speed the drying process.

For specific stains on upholstery, try the following methods. Always test the formula on an inconspicuous area before using. Wait 15 minutes. If upholstery fabric is damaged, consult a professional. Never overwet fabric or rub too hard. Always work from the outside of the stain toward the middle. Table 5.1 lists stain remover mixtures referred to in the section that follows it.

Table 5.1 Upholstery Stain Removers

Name	Ingredients
Absorbent powder	Cornstarch, talcum powder, fuller's earth, or cat-box litter
Ammonia solution	1 tablespoon ammonia 1 pint water
Baking soda paste	Baking soda blended with enough water to form a paste
Borax solution	1 tablespoon borax 1 pint water

[*Continued on next page*]

Table 5.1—*Continued*

Name	**Ingredients**
Chlorine bleach solution	1 tablespoon liquid chlorine bleach 1 pint cold water
Cornstarch paste	Cornstarch blended with enough cold water to form a paste
Glycerin solution	1 part glycerin 1 part warm water
Sodium perborate solution	½ teaspoon sodium perborate ½ cup water
White vinegar solution	1 part white vinegar 1 part water

Beer Sponge gently with cold water, or try Foamy Upholstery Shampoo (above). Dried stains should be sponged with white vinegar solution.

Blood Cover immediately with cornstarch paste. Rub lightly, and place the cushion or furniture in the sun to dry, if possible, to draw the blood out into the cornstarch. Brush off. Repeat as necessary.

Chewing Gum Chill with an ice cube to harden, then scrape off carefully.

Coffee or Tea Sponge with borax solution, or loosen the stain with glycerin solution. You can also use chlorine bleach solution.

Grease Sprinkle a small amount of absorbent powder on fresh spots. Brush in well, and let stand until the stain is absorbed. Brush off, and remove any excess with a slightly dampened cloth. Salt, applied the same way, also absorbs grease and prevents staining. Or, rub baking soda paste on spotted areas. Allow to dry and then brush or vacuum away.

Ink Try rubbing 70 percent isopropyl alcohol on ball-point ink. You can also try sponging with amyl acetate (banana oil), but this is a flammable, volatile liquid, toxic if inhaled or swallowed. Fountain-pen ink can be removed with a sodium perborate solution. Sponge onto spot, then rinse off with a cloth and clean water.

Mildew Cut a lemon in half, dip into some salt, and rub the spot. Then place cushion or furniture in the sun. Brush off mildew with a stiff brush. Sponge with Foamy Upholstery Shampoo (above).

Shoe Polish Try 70 percent isopropyl alcohol or glycerin solution, followed by Foamy Upholstery Shampoo (above).

Leather Upholstery

Leather-topped furniture or leather upholstery should be dusted regularly with a soft, dry cloth. Never use furniture polish, furniture oils, or varnish; the solvents they contain may soften the finish and cause it to become sticky.

Clean soiled leather with a damp cloth and Saddle Soap (see Index), or with Foamy Upholstery Shampoo (above). Wipe off all traces of soap with a damp, clean cloth, and polish with a soft cloth. Stale beer also works.

Leather should be polished and preserved to keep it soft and to prevent cracking. Rub it occasionally with castor oil or lemon oil. Use white petroleum jelly on light-colored leathers, because most oils tend to darken leather. Wax buildup can be removed with white vinegar solution. The following treatments will also polish leather.

Apply white vinegar very sparingly, on a wrung-out cloth.
Brush furniture with skim milk, and polish with a soft cloth. (This will also remove ball-point ink stains.)
Mix 1 pint linseed oil and 1 cup water or white vinegar; shake well, rub in, and polish dry.

■ Leather Cleaner/Polish

This solution will clean and polish leather simultaneously.

¾ cup isopropyl alcohol (70%)
½ cup white vinegar
1½ cups water

Mix ingredients together thoroughly. To use, dampen cloth with mixture and rub into leather until clean. Mixture can be stored in a clean, covered bottle or jar.

Yield: 2¾ cups

Vinyl Upholstery

Vinyl (upholstery) should not be oiled. Body oils, polishes, and even oils from cooking harden the vinyl. It will crack and become impossible to soften. You can apply white petroleum jelly to vinyl furniture to prevent cracking and peeling.

Fortunately, vinyl is highly impervious, so it is easy to remove any oil buildup. Use baking soda paste or white vinegar solution (see Table 5.1). Clean with a rough, dampened cloth. Or, you can rub with a mild soap and water solution or 2 teaspoons of liquid dishwashing detergent mixed with 2 cups of water. Or try the following solution:

■ Vinyl Cleaner

3 cups baking soda
1 cup chalk

Mix ingredients. Sprinkle on a damp sponge or a rough-textured cloth. Rub over surface, concentrating on headrests, arms, and seats. Remove with clear water and wipe dry.

Yield: about 4 cups

Miscellaneous Furniture Materials

Bamboo, Cane, Rattan, Reed, and Wicker

Dust or vacuum regularly furniture made of any woven natural materials, or wipe it with a cloth dampened with water. To prevent yellowing, scrub with a stiff brush that's been moistened with salt water. To prevent it from drying and cracking, rub furniture occasionally with lemon oil. Or, once a year, place outside and wet thoroughly with fine spray from a garden hose, or wash off under shower. Especially dirty furniture can be washed with pure soap suds plus a splash of household ammonia. Rinse with clear water and dry. Once a year, coat furniture with shellac.

Gold Leaf Furniture and Frames

■ Gold Leaf Cleaner

1 cup denatured alcohol
1 pint water

Mix ingredients together in a container. Saturate a clean cloth in mixture and rub lightly over area. Wipe dry immediately.

Yield: 3 cups

Chapter 6 Floors

Grandma and Grandpa may not have had to worry about soaring fuel costs and nuclear arms races, but they did have to contend with some problems that modern life has alleviated. Isn't it comforting to know that we can clean our soft, plush carpets by vacuuming them with a machine, rather than by sweeping them with tea leaves or grass clippings that have been scattered about? And after a hard week at work, at least we don't have to roll up the carpet, drag it outside, hang it over the clothesline, and beat it with a carpet beater.

No matter what's covering the floor, it will get dirty. Unless we adopt the Japanese custom of removing our shoes upon entering, we will continue to track dirt throughout the house. Compound that with everyday spills and the contributions of Morris and Fido, and you have a mess! Fortunately, with regular maintenance, your floors can be kept like new.

Wooden Floors

Wooden floors are expensive and require special care. Think of them as fine wood furniture, and treat them with the same respect. Vacuum or sweep them regularly to prevent dirt from being ground in.

Cleaning methods depend on the finish on your floors and the degree of abuse that they've suffered. Floors sealed with shellac or nonwaterproof varnish generally should not be scrubbed with water or any cleaner containing water unless absolutely necessary. Water-based polishes or waxes should not be used; instead, use a solvent-based product such as turpentine. Water raises the grain and, according to certain schools of thought, destroys the wood's beauty. Lacquered floors and those finished with waterproof sealants can be washed with mild soap and water and rinsed with clear water.

Unfinished floors can be waxed to protect the wood and to ensure easy cleaning. Untreated wood can be cleaned with some mild dishwashing detergent suds, made with as little water as possible. Oiled wood can be dusted with an oiled cloth or mop, and washed, only occasionally, with mild soapsuds. Rinse with clear water, as little as possible. Or, scrub away stains with Scouring Cleanser (see Index). Painted wooden floors should be washed with soapsuds made from a mild soap, a mild detergent and water solution, or the formula below.

■ Painted Wooden Floor Cleaner

1 teaspoon washing soda
1 gallon hot water

Mix ingredients together and wash floor with mixture, using a sponge, mop, or soft-bristle brush. Rinse floor with clear water. This solution also removes mildew.

■ Vegetable Oil Wooden Floor Cleaner

This formula, as well as the one that follows it, not only cleans the grime, but also restores some of the oil to wooden floors, which helps to preserve them.

2 tablespoons household ammonia
1 pint mineral oil
5 tablespoons turpentine
½ cup vegetable oil

Mix all ingredients in a clean, wide-mouth jar. To use, add 1 cup of mixture to 1 quart of warm water in a bucket, and following the grain, mop floor with solution. Wipe completely dry with a clean cloth.

Yield: about 2¾ cups

■ Oleic Acid Wooden Floor Cleaner

Oleic acid is a nontoxic fatty acid used in soaps.

2¼ cups mineral oil
¾ cup oleic acid
2 tablespoons household ammonia
5 tablespoons turpentine

Mix oil and oleic acid, then add household ammonia and turpentine. To use, add 1 cup of mixture to 2 quarts of warm water in a pail. Apply with a sponge mop or cloth. This doesn't require rinsing, unless the floor was really dirty.

Yield: about 3½ cups

If you're lucky enough to find a gem of an old house at a bargain price, the wooden floors in it may have seen better days. Don't despair—bleaching will remove the years of stains and ground-in dirt. First, prepare the surface by washing with one of the floor cleaners above. Then use either of the following solutions. Their bleaching power comes from strong alkaline ingredients. *Caution:* Sodium perborate is a caustic, systemic poison that may be fatal if swallowed, and water glass is corrosive to tissue.

■ Wooden Floor Bleach Paste

Mix ½ pound sodium perborate with enough water to form a paste, and spread on one section of the floor at a time. Leave it on about 30 minutes, then rinse off with clear water. Repeat on other sections, and apply as often as needed.

■ Liquid Wooden Floor Bleach

4½ quarts water glass
10 ounces sodium perborate
1 gallon very hot water

Dissolve water glass and sodium perborate in a bucket containing water. Mop solution over floor and leave for 30 minutes. Rinse this off with clear water. Reapply if necessary.

If heavily soiled, waxed floors can be washed with a mild detergent solution or, for troublesome areas, with a little turpentine on a soft cloth. The floors should then be rewaxed.

Commercially available waxes contain petroleum distillates that act as a solvent base to keep the other ingredients in solution and to help remove dirt, grime, and leftover polish. They also contain up to 25 percent wax, which coats the wood after the solvents evaporate and which can be polished into a shiny finish. You can mix up your own homemade floor waxes by using the following formulas.

■ Simple Liquid Floor Wax

2 tablespoons paraffin
1 quart mineral oil

Very carefully melt paraffin in the top of a double boiler. *Caution:* Do not melt over direct heat. Stir in mineral oil, cool, and store in glass bottles. To use, apply with a cloth, allow to dry, and polish lightly.

■ Hard-Finish Liquid Floor Wax

½ cup ceresin wax
2 tablespoons yellow beeswax
2⅛ cups turpentine
1 tablespoon pine oil

Melt both waxes in the top of a double boiler. *Caution:* Do not melt over direct heat. Remove from heat and slowly stir in turpentine and pine oil. Cool and store in glass containers. To use, apply with a cloth, allow to dry, and polish.

■ Paste Wax for Wooden Floors

9 tablespoons carnauba wax
5 tablespoons ceresin wax
2½ tablespoons montan wax
2 tablespoons yellow beeswax
1 tablespoon pine oil
1 pint mineral spirits
¼ cup turpentine

Melt all 4 waxes in top of a double boiler. *Caution:* Do not melt over direct heat. Add pine oil and blend well. Remove from heat and cool slightly. Slowly add mineral spirits and turpentine, stirring constantly until well blended. Store in a covered jar. Apply small amount to floor, allow to dry, and polish vigorously.

Yield: about 3½ cups

■ Nonslip Wooden Floor Polish

Gum arabic provides more friction to prevent slipping than wax does.

½ cup orange shellac
2 tablespoons gum arabic
2 tablespoons turpentine
1 pint denatured alcohol

Mix shellac, gum arabic, and turpentine into alcohol until gum arabic dissolves. Store this in covered bottles or jars. Apply mixture with a cloth, sponge, or mop, and allow it to dry for at least 30 minutes, then buff.

Yield: about 2½ cups

Finally, if some hot-rodder has been drag-racing on your good wooden floors, you can remove the black skid marks with very fine-grade steel wool (No. 0000) and a little cooking oil. Rub lightly until the marks disappear, and wipe away the excess oil.

Resilient Floor Coverings

Asphalt, rubber, vinyl, and vinyl-asbestos tiles and linoleum sheets are classified as resilient floor coverings. They are durable, washable materials that "bounce back" or regain their shape after pressure is applied. All are bonded to the floor with mastic, a pastelike cement, either directly or over a layer of felt. Sometimes a plywood subflooring is used to provide a smooth surface. If you're not sure what kind of floor you have, consult a professional.

Weekly floor-washing can be done with a solution of mild soap or detergent and warm water. Adding a splash of vinegar helps to break up grease particles that settle after cooking. Scrub heavily soiled floors with an all-purpose household cleaner such as Ammonia/Washing Soda Cleaner or Multipurpose Ammonia Cleaner (see Index). Or use the following multipurpose floor cleaner. It's safe for all tile and linoleum floors, but do not use it on cork or wooden floors.

■ Multipurpose Floor Cleaner

½ cup liquid chlorine bleach
¼ cup white vinegar
¼ cup washing soda
1 gallon warm water

Mix all ingredients in a pail. Mop small areas at a time with a minimum of liquid.

Be sure to wipe up moisture completely because both the backing and adhesive of resilient tile floors can be damaged by excessive water. Seepage of water between the tiles may loosen them from the subflooring, causing the tiles to curl. If this happens, place a piece of aluminum foil over the bulge and iron over this several times with the iron set on medium heat. The heat will soften and reactivate the adhesive. Put weight on the area until it is cool. Remember, when washing kitchen floors or other tile or linoleum floors, damp-mop. Do not flood the floor with water.

If stubborn black skid marks or crayon marks appear before you've had a chance to wax, dampen a soft cloth and rub over mark with a dab of toothpaste, or make a jelly out of mild soap and rub it carefully over the spots with a dry piece of fine-grade steel wool (No. 00). Wipe clean and wax. To avoid furniture marks, glue pieces of old carpeting or felt pads to the bottoms of chair legs.

To keep floors looking new, wipe up spills immediately, and wax your floors only when they need it. They'll need it less frequently if you use a self-polishing finish or wax. Most self-polishing floor finishes are water-based emulsions of natural or synthetic wax, acrylic or styrene copolymers that form a plastic film, solvents, emulsifiers, humectants, and fragrances. Before using these finishes or waxes, the floor should be stripped of the old wax with a commercial stripper/cleaner, or a solution of three parts water to one part 15 percent isopropyl alcohol. Then apply finish or wax sparingly, and spread it so thin that it's barely visible. Usually, two or three thin coats wear best. If you apply it too thick, the top layer hardens, but the wax underneath stays soft. It will collect a lot of dirt and won't offer much protection.

Asphalt

Asphalt tile is a mixture of asbestos fibers, lime rock, inert fillers, and colored pigments, bound together by asphalt or resin. The tile is very brittle. Grease softens asphalt, but alkalis won't harm it. Most soaps contain ingredients that form an emulsion upon contact with certain compounds in the tile, thus weakening it. Therefore, wash asphalt tiles with solutions of synthetic detergents, not soap-containing formulas. Water should be used sparingly and wiped up immediately. Solvents (turpentine and mineral spirits) and oils also attack and disintegrate asphalt tile. Never use solvent-based liquid waxes or cleaners. Use a water-emulsion, resin-finish formula instead.

Alcohol spills on asphalt tiles will form white spots. Remove them by rubbing with baby oil or olive oil. Resistant black marks and stains can be removed by rubbing with fine-grade steel wool (No. 00) and a little water and detergent.

Linoleum

Linoleum is a mixture of either linseed oil, resins, and ground cork pressed on a burlap or canvas backing or of linseed oil, resins, and wood fibers attached to a felt backing. Its life can be increased by regular waxing.

In contrast to asphalt tiles, strong alkali cleaners shouldn't be used on linoleum; they remove the linseed oil binders, which dries out the floor so that it becomes brittle and cracks. Instead, use a mild detergent and water solution, applied sparingly. Add a capful of baby oil to preserve the floor at the same time. Adding sour milk or skim milk to the rinse water will shine the floor without polishing.

Dull, greasy film on linoleum can be washed away with 1 cup of white vinegar mixed in 2 gallons of water. Dry thoroughly. Use Multipurpose Floor Cleaner (above) or an all-purpose cleaner on heavily soiled floors, and then wax with Linoleum Floor Wax (below).

Caution: Do not use these waxes on asphalt-, rubber-, or cork-tiled floors, or on wooden floors.

■ Simple Linoleum Polish

1 part thick boiled starch
1 part soapsuds

Make a mixture of equal parts of starch and soapsuds. Rub on floor and polish dry. This preserves and protects the finish.

■ Linoleum Polish

½ cup carnauba wax
2 tablespoons paraffin
¼ cup yellow beeswax
1 quart turpentine

Carefully melt carnauba wax, paraffin, and beeswax in top of double boiler over low heat. *Caution:* Do not melt over direct heat. Remove from heat and stir in turpentine. Let mixture cool, then pour into bottles. To use, apply sparingly to linoleum, allow to dry, then polish with a clean, dry cloth.

■ Linoleum Floor Wax

¾ cup carnauba wax
¾ cup ceresin wax
1 pint mineral spirits

Carefully melt both waxes in top of a double boiler over low heat, stirring well. *Caution:* Do not melt over direct heat. Remove from heat and let cool slightly. Stir in mineral spirits. Store wax in a jar. To use, apply small amount with soft cloth, let dry, and polish briskly.

Yield: about 3½ cups

No-Wax Floors

High-quality, no-wax floors have a thin surface layer of shiny, durable polyurethane. It requires minimal care and can be kept clean with a mild detergent solution. Special treatments are generally unnecessary; consult your dealer or the manufacturer.

Rubber Tiles

Rubber tiles sometimes contain asbestos fibers; they are colored by mineral pigments. Oils, solvents, strong soaps, and strong alkalis will harm the surface. Rubber has excellent rebound properties (bounces right back!). Wash with clear water, a mild detergent, and a clean mop.

Vinyl and Vinyl-Asbestos Tiles

Sheet vinyl and vinyl-asbestos tiles have largely replaced linoleum and asphalt tiles in new homes. Vinyl is a type of plastic that is tough, nonabsorbent, flexible, and shiny. It is resistant to damage by water, acids, alkalis, grease, and oil. Floors can, of course, still be damaged by excessive use of water.

Sheet vinyl is soft and can be damaged easily by abrasion and wear. Regular waxing will extend its life. Some vinyl-asbestos tiles can go without waxing for extended periods.

Use Multipurpose Floor Cleaner (page 98) or one of the linoleum solutions (above) on vinyl flooring. Remove wax buildup by pouring a small amount of club soda on a section. Scrub this in well, let it soak in a few minutes, and wipe clean.

Nonresilient Floors

Brick, stone, concrete, and tile are known as nonresilient floor materials because they yield only to the greatest of pressure. Although brick, stone, and concrete make durable floors, unless they are sealed or glazed like most tile, particular care must be taken in cleaning these relatively porous surfaces.

Brick and Stone

Because brick and stone are very absorbent, soap solutions should be avoided. You can wash off burn marks with straight vinegar. For general cleaning, use this formula:

■ Brick/Stone Cleaner

1 gallon water
1 cup white vinegar

Mix in a bucket. Scrub floor with a brush and this mixture, and rinse with clear water.

Concrete

Clean dirty or greasy concrete with an all-purpose detergent and warm water, or Concrete Cleaner, Heavy-Duty Concrete Cleaner, or Multipurpose Washing Soda Cleaner (see Index). Scrub thoroughly and then hose off cleaned areas.

For stubborn coffee, tea, and ink stains, use a bleach solution.

■ Concrete Bleach

1 tablespoon liquid chlorine bleach
1 pint warm water

Mix bleach and water in a bucket. Wash, rinse, and allow to dry. For tough stains, reapply mixture and let set 15 minutes before rinsing.

Ceramic and Terrazzo Tiles

Ceramic or terrazzo tile floors are easy to keep clean. Wash with a mild soap, Scouring Cleanser (see Index), or a synthetic detergent solution. Soap doesn't work well in hard-water areas; it leaves an insoluble film. Multipurpose Ammonia Cleaner (see Index) will renew the sparkle.

Wax freshly washed tile with a thin coat of Starch (see Index). Let this dry and polish to give a high gloss.

Rust spots can be removed with the following:

■ Tile Rust Remover

1 part sodium citrate
6 parts glycerin
water
whiting

Dissolve sodium citrate in glycerin. Thin this with a little water, then add enough whiting to form a paste. Spread the paste thickly over stains, then clean and rinse.

Carpets and Rugs

Wool Rugs

Expensive oriental, antique, or multicolor wool rugs should be cleaned professionally, to avoid shrinkage. Also, the dyes used on wool rugs may not be colorfast.

Synthetic Fiber Rugs

Regular vacuuming is necessary to keep carpets and rugs looking like new. Even so, they may occasionally need a more thorough cleaning, since the fibers can harbor bacteria, and the trapped dirt can trigger allergic reactions. Professional cleaning is expensive, but you can do the job yourself for a fraction of the cost—all it takes is a few, simple ingredients, time, and some elbow grease.

Carpet shampoos clean the surface of the rug. The detergents foam up, trapping the dirt and lifting it to the surface. When the shampoo dries, you can vacuum up the dirt and detergent residue. Some shampoos are liquids that you can scrub in with a sponge mop or an electric shampooer with rotary brushes; some are foams that you spray on.

Shampooing is a major chore. Furniture should be removed, or protective waxed-paper or foil "booties" or plastic bags should be slipped over furniture legs to prevent stains. It's best to shampoo on a dry, sunny day, not on a humid day when the carpet will take forever to dry. Don't soak the carpet, because it may mildew. Also, always test any shampoo first on an inconspicuous area. Use a white cloth and rub the solution on the rug. If the cloth remains white, go ahead with your shampooing.

The following formulas are suitable for all synthetic fibers. Again, always test the mixture first, especially if you have shag carpets; be sure all remnants of paste shampoos can be thoroughly removed before cleaning the entire carpet.

■ Carpet Vitalizer

2 gallons hot water
1–2 tablespoons household ammonia

Mix ingredients together and sponge a small area at a time with the solution. Rub each area at once with a dry, absorbent cloth to remove as much moisture as possible.

■ Carpet Color Restorer

1 cup white vinegar
½ teaspoon household ammonia
1 gallon hot water

Add vinegar and ammonia to the water and mix. Wring out a cloth in mixture and scrub over the rug. Wipe up excess moisture with a dry cloth.

■ Liquid Dishwashing Detergent Carpet Cleaner

½ cup mild liquid dishwashing detergent
1 pint boiling water

Mix detergent and boiling water. Then let this cool until it forms a jelly. Whip into a stiff foam with an eggbeater or electric mixer. Apply with a damp cloth or sponge to a small section of carpet and rub gently. Wipe off with a clean cloth. Allow to dry. Repeat if necessary.

■ Carpet Cleaner for Oil and Grease

3 cups whole wheat flour
1¾ cups water
1 tablespoon aluminum stearate
1 tablespoon salicylic acid
1¼ cups mineral oil

Mix flour and water into a paste. Blend in aluminum stearate and salicylic acid. Slowly add mineral oil to this paste, stirring constantly. Store this in a glass, metal, or impervious plastic container.

To clean, brush the paste into a small section and leave for a few minutes. Then wipe this off with a damp cloth or sponge. Repeat until the oil and grease are removed.

■ Soapless Carpet Cleaner

1 cup isopropyl alcohol (70%)
5 cups white vinegar
¼ teaspoon lauryl pyridinium chloride

Mix alcohol and vinegar in a jar. Stir in lauryl pyridinium chloride, until it dissolves. Brush mixture into rug surface and allow to dry. Vacuum the dried powder. Store the leftover solution in a tightly covered jar.

Caution: Lauryl pyridinium chloride is combustible.

Yield: about 6 cups

■ Heavy-Duty Carpet Cleaner

1 pint washing soda
1 cup fuller's earth
¼ cup turpentine
liquid dishwashing detergent

Blend washing soda and fuller's earth. Slowly stir in turpentine and mix vigorously until blended. Store in clean jar. To use, mix cleaner with a small amount of liquid dishwashing detergent to form a stiff paste. Brush this into the carpet, allow to dry, and vacuum the residue.

Some shampoos are powders, containing absorbents such as sawdust or diatomaceous earth, some detergents, and, sometimes, petroleum solvents. The absorbents pick up dirt and grease, which can then be vacuumed away. A simple, inexpensive alternative for lightly soiled carpets is cornstarch or salt. Sprinkle either one generously over the rug, leave for about an hour, and then vacuum, vacuum, vacuum.

Sisal Fiber Rugs

Sisal fiber rugs should be vacuumed regularly or scrubbed with a stiff brush on both sides. Be sure to remove dirt from underneath, because it can sift through the fibers. Wipe occasionally with a damp cloth. Badly soiled rugs should be sent to a professional cleaner.

To freshen or restore faded fiber rugs, try one of the following methods.

Paint with canvas dye paints.
Brush on color stain used for shingle siding—the fiber absorbs the stain and won't chip or flake off.
Thin your favorite color paint with turpentine—1 part turpentine to 3 parts paint. Work thoroughly into fibers with a stiff brush.
Use any dye meant for cottons. Dissolve dye in boiling water and apply to rug with a brush.

Throw Rugs

Scrub small throw rugs (like rag rugs) with one of our carpet shampoos or cleaners (above). It's easy if you throw the rugs into the bathtub and scrub them with a broom. Or put them into a bucket of soapy water and plunge the rug up and down with a plumber's helper. You can also clean small throw rugs in your automatic washer—just be careful not to overload, and keep the load balanced. Or you can wash them at the local Laundromat in one of the heavy-duty machines.

By the way, you can prevent them from curling by rinsing in thin starch water (see Starch in Index). Or seal the underside with a coat of shellac and then wipe on a thin solution of starch. Allow to dry completely before using. This will also keep them from slipping and sliding all over. Other skid preventions include an old rubber bath mat or dish-drain mat placed under each rug, or two or three rubber jar rings (the kind you use when making home preserves) wound together with thread and then sewn to each corner of the rug; they'll work like suction cups.

Carpet Stain Removers

Spills need not mean stains if you remember the "Ten Commandments."

1. Use paper towels to attack stains before they dry.
2. Be calm; blot the spot. Don't grind out your anger on those innocent little carpet fibers.
3. Blot from the outside toward the inside. You don't want to make matters worse.
4. Test the weakest of the stain removers below on an area under the sofa. Wait 15 minutes. If the carpet still looks okay, proceed.
5. If that fails, try the next-strongest stain remover.

6. Don't pour on the stain remover—you might end up ruining the latex or foam backing, and it'll take forever to dry.
7. Don't use soap or soap powder.
8. Squeeze on lukewarm water to rinse, and blot, blot, blot dry.
9. Weight down a dry towel with a heavy object to soak up all the moisture; replace with a dry towel when the first gets soggy.
10. Be patient.

The four stain removers below are in order by their strength; the weakest one is first—the strongest, last. To use any of them, first blot the stain with paper towels, then mix the ingredients together, dip a damp sponge or cloth into the mixture, and gently rub the stained area. (Don't forget to test stain remover first on a hidden area.) Rinse, then soak up moisture, following directions in the "Ten Commandments" above.

■ Detergent Carpet Stain Remover

1 teaspoon all-purpose detergent
1 cup lukewarm water

■ Vinegar Carpet Stain Remover

½ cup white vinegar
1½ cups lukewarm water

■ Detergent/Vinegar Carpet Stain Remover

1 tablespoon all-purpose detergent
1½ tablespoons white vinegar
1 pint warm water

■ Extra-Strength Carpet Stain Remover

Caution: This stain remover may fade or damage certain fibers, especially wool.

1 tablespoon household ammonia
¾ cup water

You might also try one of these instant stain removers: club soda, glass cleaner, shaving cream, or toothpaste; or see Table 6.1 for some specific stains and how to deal with them.

Table 6.1 Carpet Care—Removing Stains and Foreign Substances

Alcohol

Apply club soda with sponge; rub in gently until the stain is lifted.
Sponge with warm water or detergent and water.
Rub with solution of 1 part glycerin and 1 part water.
Sponge dried stains with turpentine substitute (available at hardware stores).

Blood

Act fast to get the stain out before it sets.
Apply club soda or *cold* water with sponge; rub in gently until the stain is lifted.
Sponge with a solution of 1 teaspoon household ammonia or salt in 1 cup cold water.

Burns

Trim burned fibers with scissors.
Repair burned area by shaving off some fuzz from an inconspicuous area of the rug. Roll fuzz into a ball. Apply cement glue or rubber cement to backing of rug in burned area; press fuzz down onto glue. Cover with tissue and weight with a book or small piece of wood until glue dries.

Candle Wax

Scrape off as much wax as you can with a dull knife. Then, place paper towels, napkins, brown paper bag, or blotter over the wax residue and press with a warm iron. Repeat as necessary.

Chewing Gum

Freeze with an ice cube to harden, then scrape off with a dull knife.

Chocolate

Massage glycerin into spot; rinse off with plain water.

Coffee and Tea

Apply club soda or cold water with sponge; rub in gently until stain is lifted.
Sponge off with one of our carpet shampoos.
Sponge with solution of 1 teaspoon borax and 1 cup water.

Grease or Gravy

Brush baking soda or cornmeal on lightly, leave overnight, and vacuum.

Mud

Allow to dry to a powder, then vacuum.
Use one of our carpet shampoos to remove any remaining stain.

[*Continued on next page*]

Table 6.1—*Continued*

Pet Stains

Act fast, so that fibers and dyes aren't harmed.

Sponge with any of the following; if the first remedy doesn't work, try the next one, and so on: clear, warm water; club soda; solution of 1 part vinegar or lemon juice and 1 part water; detergent and water.

Rub dried, cleaned cat stains with a cloth dampened in household ammonia. Takes away odor and prevents cat from doing it again—in the same spot, anyway.

To clean and sanitize feces- or urine-spotted rugs, try Rosemary Castile Soap (see Index).

Tar

Allow tar to harden.

Scrape away the solidified tar with a dull knife.

Rub with solution of 1 part glycerin and 1 part warm water.

Use one of our carpet shampoos.

Carpet Cleaner and Deodorizer

Baking soda, patented in the United States in 1878, is a cheap, excellent natural deodorizer, without any perfumes or dyes. It neutralizes most carpet odors caused by food, pets, cigarette smoke, and dampness. It's also a food additive (everyone has a box in their kitchen cabinet), so it's safe to use around children and pets.

Don't use baking soda on a wet carpet, and test first. Generously sprinkle baking soda over entire carpet. Wait at least 15 minutes (overnight if it's really bad). Vacuum away all the smell.

■ Carpet Deodorizer

2 cups cornmeal
1 cup borax

Mix cornmeal and borax, and sprinkle on carpet. Allow mixture to remain on carpet at least 15 minutes, and vacuum. Repeat if necessary.

Chapter 7 Special Materials

There are many items all around the house and workshop that you may not know how to clean. Perhaps you just ignore the problem, or maybe you rely upon those expensive, commercial specialty cleaning and polishing products. It's true that many special materials, such as leather, suede, gold, and brass, require a cleaning and/or polishing agent that is compatible with the special characteristics of that material. A cleaning agent for one material may not be effective on a different type of material. Worse yet, it may dull, scratch, or even ruin it. The difference between leather and suede is a perfect example. A good saddle soap is excellent for cleaning leather goods, but don't even think about using it on suede, as it will permanently damage suede.

Caring for special items doesn't have to be mystifying or expensive. All you need is a little know-how and some good formulas. You'll find that many can be whipped up right in your kitchen with ingredients that you have on hand or that may be easily purchased at the grocery or hardware store.

Metals

Aluminum

Aluminum comes either painted or unpainted. Painted items require gentler care so as not to damage the paint, which will flake off if abrasive cleaners are used. Also, pitting of the metal will occur if unpainted articles are subjected to abrasive treatment. Never use naval aluminum jelly or steel wool on aluminum.

Use a mild detergent solution or Multipurpose Aluminum Cleaner (below) to clean aluminum; harsh detergents can dull it. For extra protection, periodically give painted aluminum a coat of car paste wax.

■ Multipurpose Aluminum Cleaner

For both painted and unpainted items, such as screen doors and outdoor furniture, baking soda is the cheapest cleaner available. Use it straight from the box, applying it with a damp sponge, or add ¼ cup baking soda to a bucket of warm water. Then rinse with clear water and dry.

Brass and Bronze

Brass is an alloy of two parts copper to one part zinc. Some old pieces are made of copper and tin. Many brass items have been coated with a protective lacquer. Brass cleaners and polishes should not be used on lacquered items. Instead, dust them and occasionally wipe them with a damp sponge. If the lacquer peels or cracks, it will have to be removed. The article will then have to be cleaned and treated with a new coat of lacquer.

To relacquer brass, first remove all old lacquer by using Lacquer Remover for Brass (below). Then polish item with Brass Cleaner/Polish (below). Rub with acetone to remove every trace of residue. Spray or brush on transparent metal lacquer.

■ Lacquer Remover for Brass

½ cup baking soda
1 gallon boiling water

Mix a solution of baking soda and water. Put lacquered article into solution. Allow water to cool and then peel off lacquer.

If the lacquer has worn off completely, and the brass has tarnished, use the following remedy to restore the metal's shine, or try All-Purpose Metal Polish or one of the cleaners for copper (see Index).

■ Brass Cleaner/Polish

Caution: *This is not to be used on lacquered items.*

1 part salt
1 part flour
1 part white vinegar

Wash items in warm, soapy water. Rinse and dry, then mix salt, flour, and vinegar together to make a paste. Apply and rub vigorously. Rewash in soapy water, rinse, and dry.

Bronze is also an alloy, usually of copper and tin plus trace metals. Most bronze objects are lacquered and require only occasional dusting. Polish with paraffin oil, which is derived from paraffin distillate. *Caution:* Paraffin oil is flammable. Wipe on paraffin oil and then polish with a cloth or chamois. Unlacquered bronze can be washed with soap or liquid dishwashing detergent and water, or with heated white vinegar or buttermilk. Rinse off thoroughly and polish with Brass Cleaner/Polish (above). You may also use All-Purpose Metal Polish (see Index).

Occasionally, bronze objects become heavily tarnished with green spots, or verdigris, which also forms on copper and brass. Rub the spots with brown shoe polish and buff well, or use Copper Verdigris Remover (see Index).

Chrome

Here's a quick and inexpensive way to clean chrome: Dip a damp sponge in baking soda and rub onto surface. Allow to set for a minute or two. Rinse with clear water and dry with a soft cloth. For stubborn spots, apply the baking soda directly to the spots and rub with a damp, nonscratching scouring pad. For other chrome cleaners, see Index.

Gold

Gold is a soft metal that is very ductile and malleable, so much so that it can be hammered, rolled, or molded into almost any shape. Gold is not affected by exposure to air—it doesn't tarnish. In jewelry terminology, gold content is described in carats. Pure gold is 24 carats; it is used rarely for commercial items because it is too soft. A 12-carat item is, therefore, 50 percent gold combined with another metal (copper, silver, or nickel). Items can also be gold-filled, which means that the gold is fused to a base metal. Gold-plating is another commercial way of using gold—the article is coated with gold by an electrochemical process. Gold-plated items must be treated carefully, or the plating will rub off and replating will be required. Never use anything abrasive on any kind of gold, because it will scratch easily.

■ Gold Cleaner

1 teaspoon baking soda
¼ cup water

Mix baking soda and water together to make a paste. Using a very soft cloth, rub paste over surface. Rinse with clear water and buff dry with a very soft cloth.

Pewter

Pewter is a gray-colored alloy of several metals, mostly tin, with varying amounts of antimony, copper, and lead. If you're concerned about a pewter object's resale value, most collectors and dealers recommend occasional dusting or washing with soap and water, not polishing. Pewter can be cleaned by rubbing with fine-grade steel wool (No. 0000) and olive oil, a moist paste of wood ash and water, or with toothpaste and a damp cloth. An old-fashioned method of cleaning pewter is by rubbing moist cabbage leaves over the surface, then buffing with a soft cloth. You may also wish to try the following cleaning formulas.

■ Pewter Cleaner for Dull Finish

Make a paste out of rottenstone and olive oil. Apply with a soft cloth. Rub over surface. Wash with soapy water solution, rinse, and dry with a soft cloth.

■ Pewter Cleaner for Bright Finish

Make a paste from isopropyl alcohol (70%) and whiting. Apply paste to entire surface and allow to dry. Then polish with a soft cloth. Wash in a soapy water solution, rinse, and dry.

If you wish to polish your pewter, try fine-grade powdered pumice for dull-finish pewter, or jeweler's rouge for bright-finish pewter. Rub powder on surface with a sponge or cloth. Rinse off well and polish briskly with a soft, clean cloth.

Masonry

Brick and Stone

Brick and stone surfaces are generally porous and should not be cleaned with soap. Use Brick/Stone Cleaner (see Index) for these materials.

Concrete

Concrete can be cleaned with Multipurpose Washing Soda Cleaner (see Index). You can also use the following formulas.

■ Concrete Cleaner

¼ cup washing soda
2 gallons warm water

Mix washing soda and water in a scrub bucket. Wash concrete with this solution, rinse with clear water, and allow to dry.

■ Heavy-Duty Concrete Cleaner

1 pint liquid chlorine bleach
2 gallons warm water

Mix ingredients together in a bucket. Wash concrete with mixture, rinse with clear water, and allow to dry. For tough stains, allow mixture to set about 15 minutes before rinsing.

Marble

Marble is a form of crystallized limestone with a texture that ranges from granular to compact. It can take a high polish. Usually, a good polished piece of marble needs only to be washed with a damp sponge or, occasionally, a soap and water solution. Never use detergents or abrasive cleaners on marble. Sometimes marble will yellow naturally, or you may have tough spots that are difficult to remove. Try this cleaner.

■ Marble Cleaner

½ cup white vinegar
1 cup household ammonia
¼ cup baking soda
1 gallon hot water

Mix ingredients together in a bucket. Wash marble with solution, using a sponge. Rinse with clear water and wipe dry.

Slate

Slate is sometimes used in fireplaces and tabletops and is often used for flooring. Slate is porous and absorbent, so never use a soap solution to clean it.

■ Slate Cleaner

3 tablespoons washing soda
2 gallons warm water

Mix ingredients in a bucket and, using a sponge, wash the slate surface. Rinse with clear water and dry.

■ Slate Polish

Apply a thin layer of linseed oil. Rub in vigorously. Wipe up excess with absorbent toweling or cloth. This will clean the slate and give it a polished look.

Personal Items

Hairbrushes and Combs

Hairbrushes and combs should be cared for according to the type of material from which they are made. For plastic and rubber brushes and combs, fill the bathroom sink about half-full with warm, soapy water. Add about ¼ cup of baking soda. Allow items to soak for 15 to 20 minutes. For extremely dirty combs, go over the teeth with an old nailbrush. Natural bristle brushes can be cleaned the same way as plastic ones, except add ¼ cup ammonia to the water. After the brushes and combs are cleaned, rinse with clear water and allow to dry.

Jewelry

Taking care of your jewelry, whether antique heirlooms or costume items, requires a little common sense and a few working tips. First, remove your rings and bracelets before immersing your hands in hot water or cleaning solutions. Precious gems can be damaged, fake ones can become "unglued," and plated items may flake. If you prefer not to remove your jewelry, wear rubber gloves.

Many precious gems (including aquamarines, rubies, opals, sapphires, and emeralds, but never pearls) may be cleaned with lukewarm (never hot), soapy water and a soft nailbrush or toothbrush. Rinse and dry. For pearls, rub on a few drops of glycerin and shine with a very soft cloth. Wash diamonds in warm, soapy water with a few drops of ammonia added, rinse, and dip them into a small bowl of isopropyl alcohol and lay them on a soft tissue to dry.

Wash costume jewelry in soapy, lukewarm water. Do not soak. A soft nailbrush or toothbrush can be used, very gently, for cleaning details on jewelry. Buff dry with a soft cloth. Do not wash wooden items—just dust them off.

Leather

The problem with leather is that it dries out and cracks. The oil in leather must be replenished occasionally. Wash leather articles by hand with a solution of pure soap in warm water. Do not submerge items in the solution. Instead, use a soft cloth or sponge. Rinse with clear water and buff dry with a soft cloth. Never use synthetic detergents on leather. Instead of a soap solution, you can use Saddle Soap (below) to clean leather. Use it before any preserving oils have been applied. Never dry wet leather in direct heat, as this will stiffen the articles.

Caution: Do not use any formulas in this section on suede. Suede requires its own special care.

■ Saddle Soap

3½ cups water
¾ cup soap flakes (not detergent)
¼ cup neat's-foot oil
½ cup paraffin *or* beeswax

Heat water to boiling point in a sturdy pot, then lower to simmer. Slowly add soap flakes and stir gently. In the top of a double boiler* (not over direct heat), combine neat's-foot oil with paraffin or beeswax. Heat until paraffin or beeswax is melted, then stir. Turn off all heat and slowly add oil and wax mixture to the soap solution. Stir until thick. Pour into containers and cool. Old shoe polish tins are great as containers. To use, apply with a damp sponge over leather surface. Buff dry with a soft cloth.

Caution: Both neat's-foot oil and paraffin are flammable. Also, neat's-foot oil may darken some leathers, and items do not take a polish well after this oil has been applied.

■ Leather Preservative for Polished Leather

This formula will soften leather items, such as shoes, belts, bags, and luggage.

1 cup lanolin
1 cup castor oil

Mix ingredients together. Clean the leather surface first with a warm soap solution, or use Saddle Soap (above). Apply preservative with soft cloth every 3 months. Items may be polished as usual. Store preservative in metal or glass container with a lid.

*If you do not have a double boiler, you can use this alternative. Fill a large saucepan no more than half-full with warm water. Combine the neat's-foot oil with paraffin or beeswax in an old 1-pound coffee can. Place the coffee can inside the pan of water and heat over low heat until the wax is melted, then stir. Continue with the directions above.

■ Leather Preservative for Unpolished Leather

Neat's-foot oil is a great conditioner for leather. First, clean the surface with a warm soap solution as described earlier in this section, or use Saddle Soap (above). Surface should be slightly damp before applying neat's-foot oil. Apply the oil generously, rubbing it in with a soft cloth. Allow the oil to soak in. Reapply if the leather is very dry. Repeat every 3 months. (See cautions concerning neat's-foot oil in Saddle Soap, above.)

■ Leather Preservative for Light-Colored Leather

Clean the surface of either polished or unpolished leather by using a soap and warm water solution, or use Saddle Soap (above). Then generously apply white petroleum jelly. Allow to soak in for several hours. Remove excess with a soft cloth. Reapply every 3 months.

■ Spot Remover for Leather

This is a great little helper for removing grease spots from leathers. Beat up an egg white until stiff. Using a soft cloth, apply stiffened egg white to leather and rub until grease is gone. Unbelievable? Just try it! This one comes from an antique and classic car buff who uses it to remove stains from those luxurious leather interiors.

Suede

Suede is leather with a napped surface. Never use leather-cleaning products on suede unless they are specifically designed to clean suede as well. Suede spots easily and absorbs dirt readily. To clean, rub gently against the nap, and then with the nap, using a soft brush. For stubborn stains use the following:

■ Suede Cleaner

Make a paste of fuller's earth and water. Apply to suede and allow to dry. Brush clean with a soft brush.

Making Candles

Diana Branch McMasters

Making candles is a popular hobby-craft that is simple enough for children, yet has enough creative possibilities to intrigue the artisan. Since many books on candle-craft exist, we'll concentrate here on inexpensive formulas. Special candlemaking wax sold in craft shops is expensive, so we will show ways to stretch paraffin and how to use tallow and mutton fat. We'll also explain the best use of beeswax and where bayberry candles come from.

There are two candlemaking methods: molding and dipping. Molding is the most convenient method, but it requires, of course, a mold. Wax is melted, colored, and scented (if desired), poured into the mold, and set aside to harden.

You can make your own mold out of any container that has a seamless interior. Cans will not do, because they are creased on the inside. You can use bottles by cutting off the bottom with a bottle cutter, for access to remove the candle. (Since candles contract during cooling, removing them from molds usually presents few difficulties.) Commercial molds are not expensive, and, because they make such good-looking candles, they're usually worth buying.

Dipping requires more time and patience, but it is a pleasant task. Wicking hung from a rod is dipped in hot wax, allowed to harden, and dipped again. This process is repeated about 30 times; make sure the candle hangs straight as you dip. The level of wax must be kept high in the dipping container so that the entire candle will be covered with each dip, while means you'll have a potful of wax left over when you're through dipping.

For mass production, hanging a number of double-length wicks over a 1-inch dowel rod allows you to dip easily a dozen or so candles at one time. Multiple dowel setups keep you dipping while the other candles are hardening.

Safety First

Waxes and fats have low flash points and they will burst into flames if overheated. Use a candy thermometer to monitor temperatures, and never leave wax unattended while heating it. A fire extinguisher should be handy in case a small problem gets out of hand. (To make your own, see "Fire Extinguishers" in Index.) If flames do occur, you usually can contain them inside the pot. Pop a lid on the pot and turn off the heat. Do not move the pan. If flames persist, smother them with baking soda, *not water*, as water will make them spread.

Wicking

Wicking is readily available in different thicknesses for candles of different diameters. It is important to get the size just right. A wick too small will cause the flame to melt a channel down the center of the candle without melting the edges. On the other hand, a wick too large will cause the flame to melt too much wax, which in turn will drown the flame.

You can make your own wicking by braiding cotton string to the right diameter and soaking it in the borax solution below. To avoid some of the trial and error, use samples of commercial wicking from a craft shop to judge the size you need.

■ Wicking Solution

1½ cups hot water
¼ cup borax
1 tablespoon salt

Soak wicking overnight, then hang to dry straight. Do not use until the wicking is thoroughly dry.

Molding

Wash and thoroughly dry the mold. Secure the wick in place by tying a knot in one end, stringing it through the bottom of the mold, and drawing the top end taut around something like a wire from a coat hanger, then tying it securely. Block the wick hole in the bottom of the mold with a little beeswax. When the beeswax has set up, pour the wax down the side of the mold to avoid making bubbles.

Do not hurry the hardening process. A 3-inch candle will have to set a good 3 hours or more. The wax will shrink as it hardens, and the candle should slip right out of the mold. If not, give a tug on the wick with a pair of pliers. If that doesn't work, as a last resort, place the mold in a hot water bath and next time grease the mold.

Coloring and Scenting

Since paraffin, beeswax, and animal fats are all oil-based items, the colors and scents added to the wax have to be oil-based as well. Probably the easiest way to tint, and the way that offers the most even distribution and control, is the dye tab you can buy for candles at a craft shop. A dye tab is a waxy solid made of dye which is shaved into the hot wax, where it melts and diffuses to color the candle. You can also use artists' universal pigments in tubes, or try playing around with old crayons. Food coloring will not work.

[*Continued on next page*]

Wax in its liquid state always appears darker than it does when it is allowed to harden. To get a true picture of what your candle will look like, pour a quarter cup of hot, tinted wax into a small juice glass. The glass should be tapered, with the mouth larger than the base, so you can get the wax out easily. Let it harden. That's your color. Add more dye if you like, then test the color again. Be sure to pop the wax out of the glass and back into the pot. You won't want to waste any.

Pharmacies usually carry oils that can be used as scent. They'll be hiding among the liniments and include such oils as spearmint, camphor, and wintergreen. The more typical candle scents, such as pine, bayberry, and lemon, can be found in craft and candle shops. Oil scents added to wax in concentrations greater than 2 percent may cause the candle to smoke.

Standard Paraffin Candles

This standard formula for preparing candles from paraffin is a good one to use for starters. The materials can be purchased at a craft shop and you'll end up with a quality candle, one you'll be proud to give as a gift. Its only drawback is that paraffin is somewhat expensive. Using 2 pounds of candle material, you can make 1 candle, 3 by 8 inches, or 20 tapers, each 8 by ¾ inches.

Stearic acid, derived from tallow, serves as a hardener for candles to keep them from drooping in the heat. It also reduces the translucence of paraffin, to give candles a richer, more opaque appearance. Stearic acid is generally used sparingly because of its cost, but its concentration in the given formulas can be increased in order to further harden the wax.

■ Paraffin Candle

2 pounds paraffin
3 ounces stearic acid
1 teaspoon scent (optional)
dye (optional)

Melt paraffin in a double boiler (never over direct heat) to about 190°F. Add stearic acid. Add scent and dye, if desired. Dip or mold candles.

Yield: 2 pounds.

Beeswax Candles

Beeswax makes a special candle. It has a hue of colonial gold and a soft milky texture and smells a bit like honey as it burns. Use it sparingly if you have to buy it, since it easily can cost five to ten times as much as paraffin, if you can get it at all. If you have your own bees or can trade some homemade candles for some, you'll want to get as much as possible into your recipe.

Beeswax is not an ideal candle wax by itself. It will droop unless a hardener is added, and it's almost impossible to remove from an ungreased mold. But it is a superb additive to paraffin and tallow; it makes a slower-burning candle and imparts the benefits of its milky finish and pleasant fragrance when as little as 10 to 15 percent of the formula is beeswax. You can use up to 50 percent beeswax, but no more.

■ Beeswax Candle

1 pound paraffin
1 pound beeswax
1 ounce stearic acid
1 teaspoon scent (optional)
dye (optional)

or

1¾ pounds paraffin
¼ pound beeswax
1 ounce stearic acid
1 teaspoon scent (optional)
dye (optional)

For either formula, follow the procedure given for Paraffin Candle (above). If you are using a mold, lightly grease it with vegetable oil.

Yield: about 2 pounds

Candles from Animal Fat

Tallow, mutton and goat fat, and lard were used extensively to make candles during days past when they were necessary in quantity around the home. Tallow (beef fat) by itself produces a candle that droops in heat and has a smoky, smelly flame. Mutton and goat fat are harder than tallow and, therefore, are preferable for making candles, while lard (from pigs) is the softest fat of all and shouldn't be considered.

To render it pure, animal fat is teased away from veins and blood, cut into chunks, and melted over low heat. Impurities settle out as the liquid fat floats. Skimming fat off the top and straining it through fabric yields a clean product.

Animal fats are best used as fillers to stretch the more expensive paraffin and beeswax. But hardy souls who want the most light for the least cost and don't mind the dirty flame can have candles made from fat and stearic acid alone.

[*Continued on next page*]

The following table shows that paraffin and tallow can go together in many proportions. Mutton and goat fat can be used in the same proportions but the amount of stearic acid can be reduced by 25 to 50 percent, since they are harder fats. Follow procedure for Paraffin Candle (above).

Paraffin (parts)	**Tallow** (parts)	**Stearic acid** (ounces per pound)	**Scent** (ounces per pound)
2	1	2	2
1	1	2	2
1	2	2	2

■ Tallow and Beeswax Candles

2 parts tallow
1 part beeswax
2 ounces stearic acid per pound
½ ounce scent per pound (optional)
dye (optional)

Follow procedure for Paraffin Candle (above). If molding candles, grease molds lightly with vegetable oil.

Bayberry Candles

The original bayberry in bayberry candles came from the tiny fruit that grows on the bayberry bush, *Myrica pensylvanica.* It is a bushy shrub that grows along the eastern coastlands, around the Great Lakes, and in Pennsylvania and Ohio. The small, round berries have a thick coating of wax which, when boiled in water, floats to the surface where it can be skimmed off and strained.

It takes 10 pounds of berries to get a pound of wax. They do not grow in clusters but individually along the stem, making picking a slow process. Today, bayberry candles are produced synthetically.

Part II Natural Hygiene and Remedies

Jeanne Rose

Our bodies are our most valuable possessions—irreplaceable, and important to our personalities and perception of all things. It's important to care for our bodies, particularly by watching what comes in contact with them, both externally and internally.

Good hygiene protects us from bacterial disease, and improves our appearance and self-image. Natural hygiene and beauty care join both of these benefits, because herbal and other natural formulas perform just as well as commercial cosmetics, while they also soothe and help to heal our skin and bodies. A healthier skin, of course, makes natural beauty all the more easy to attain.

Sometimes physical hurts, aches, and ailments occur regardless of our efforts. Treating these problems with natural substances may help, and many people find that there is less likelihood that these substances will have some of the dangerous side effects more common with stronger pharmaceutical products. We hasten to add that the formulas offered in these pages are no substitute for consultation with a physician, and we caution you to confer with one in the event of an undetermined ache or hurt or serious ailment, or if you suspect that you suffer from any undetermined allergies.

Dogs and cats need their good health just as much as we do, so we've included formulas for them, too. For your pets' serious ailments, see your veterinarian.

The formulas presented in this section call for the use of dried herbs, measured by weight. If you'd like to substitute fresh herbs, triple the amount called for in the formulas.

As you read the next three chapters, you will notice that all the herbal ingredients are capitalized. This is according to the tradition of herbal practitioners. You may also see terms which are unfamiliar, so we have included a glossary of herbal definitions.

Herbal Definitions

Compress A compress is an external application of herbal waters to treat conditions such as acne, bruises, swellings, aches, and pains. Make an infusion or decoction of the desired herb and water. Strain the mixture, dip a linen or wool cloth into it, and apply it to the affected area. Cover with a piece of plastic, then a hot-water bottle, to keep the area warm. Alternate with cold compresses to stimulate circulation.

Decoction A decoction is a mixture of herbs and water that has been boiled, in a nonmetal pot if possible. Decoctions are used mainly to extract the essence from dried parts of the herbs, that is, the roots, bark, seeds, leaves, stalks, or stems. One ounce of herb and 1 quart of water are brought to a boil and simmered gently for up to 20 minutes. The heat is turned off and the herbs are allowed to steep. The material is strained and drunk or used in compresses, poultices, or plasters.

Essential Oil Essential oil is oil extracted from that part of the plant that possesses the fragrance, or essence, usually obtained by steam distillation. (Oil extracted from flowers by fats is generally called flower oil.)

Fomentation This is a hot, moist application of herbs or an herbal infusion directly to the skin to stimulate circulation or heal inflammation. When using an herbal infusion as a fomentation, dip a cloth into the hot liquid, and apply, repeatedly, to the affected area.

Friction Rub A friction rub is simply rubbing an area to provide friction. This is extremely stimulating and warming and is especially effective after a bath. Alcohol can be applied first to cool, or oil to warm the skin.

Herb When we use the word *herb* in plant medicine we mean any living plants. Herbs include all parts of the plant—the roots, seeds, bark, or flower of a tree, shrub, bush, or vine. In a formula, the word *herb* means the top part of a plant as opposed to its roots or seeds. Spices are always herbs but herbs are not always spices. It is more appropriate to use the terms *plant therapy* or *phytotherapy* than the term *herbal therapy*.

[*Continued on next page*]

Herb Water An herb water is made by simply simmering or soaking an herb in water, straining the water, and then using it. An herb water is more dilute than an infusion and usually more concentrated than a tea.

Infusion An infusion is a strong brew of herbs and water, used as a tea for internal treatment or as an external wash. Add 1 ounce of herb to 1 quart of water, bring to a boil, remove from the heat, cover, and let steep for at least 20 minutes. Strain the infusion if you use it as a beverage.

Poultice A poultice is a warm, moist mass of powdered or decocted herbs that is applied directly to the skin and covered by a warm cloth to retain heat. It is used for inflammation, bites, eruptions of any sort, or blood poisoning. A plaster is the same as a poultice, but is separated from the skin by a thin cloth.

Spice Spices are always herbs; they are the hard parts of aromatic plants and they are ordinarily indigenous to the tropics. Spices are usually pieces of bark (Cinnamon), roots (Ginger), flower buds (Cloves), or berries (Pepper).

Tea A tea is made with from 1 teaspoon to 1 tablespoon of herb to every cup of water. The best method is to bring the water to a boil, take it off the heat, add the herb, steep from 3 to 5 minutes, strain, and use. A tea is generally used as a beverage.

Tincture A tincture is an extract of herbal properties into alcohol. Place herbs in alcohol, cover, and steep. Shake daily for ten days. Isopropyl alcohol should only be used for external tinctures. For internal use, use only vodka or gin.

Tonic Herbs Herbs that are taken regularly to balance or nourish the system, or to counteract some sort of deficiency, are called tonic herbs. They help energize and are most useful when given for long-standing chronic conditions.

Chapter 8 Natural Beauty and Hygiene

We live in a complicated, difficult world full of unseen dangers in the air and water and in the food that we eat. Hazardous substances can build up in our bodies and cause sickness and irritations that seemingly come from nowhere. Many of these hazardous substances are found in cosmetic and beauty-aid products available in stores or supermarkets. Ingredients such as butylated hydroxy anisole (BHA) and butylated hydroxytoluene (BHT) are commonly used as preservatives to prevent oxidation of oils in cosmetics, instead of vitamin E, a natural ingredient that can do the same thing. Some people are allergic to the synthetics, BHA and BHT, but not to natural vitamins used in their place. Thickeners such as beeswax and Candelilla wax generally cause no ill effects when used externally, though this is not always true of synthetic waxes.

The lesson to learn from such knowledge is a simple one: If you make your own beauty aids *you* control the contents and the final products. Making your own products with simple ingredients and simple, tested formulations is much safer than using commercial products. Also, it is extremely easy to make one's own cosmetics. They might not have the shelf life of the commercial products, but they won't come in a 25-cent glass bottle with a $5 price tag, and they will be made of simple, natural substances. You can make clean, natural products with ingredients chosen especially for protection of the hair and skin, and you can apply these fresh products immediately, while the ingredients still have a useful life, unlike those in some stale, preserved goods.

Hair Products

Shampoos

Shampoo is easy to make. Baking soda is commonly used for washing hair by people who suffer from extreme allergies to regular shampoo. A good-quality castile shampoo is also easy to make and to use as well. The shampoo won't be gelatinously thick, but it certainly will clean properly. Most commercial shampoos contain sudsing agents as well as agents that quickly break down these suds when enough water is applied. Natural shampoos don't produce quite such copious amounts of lather, but they do combine with the dirt and allow for its easy removal through a good rinse.

■ Castile Shampoo

1 quart water
4 ounces castile soap flakes
4–8 drops essential oil (optional)
1 teaspoon isopropyl alcohol (optional)

Bring water to a boil, turn off heat, pour water over soap flakes in a bowl, and stir until soap dissolves. For scent, if desired, add essential oil of an herb you like, dissolved in a teaspoon of alcohol. If you wish to make this an herbal shampoo, start by making an herbal infusion. Instead of water, pour the hot herbal infusion over the soap flakes until the soap dissolves.

Yield: 1 quart

■ Dry Shampoo

Convenient, time-saving dry shampoos can be used during cold weather to strip the hair of grime, grease, and excess oils without the risk of wet hair that may contribute to chills and colds. They are also useful as conditioners for limp, greasy hair.

1 tablespoon finely ground Cornmeal
1 tablespoon finely ground Almonds
1 tablespoon powdered Orris root

Mix ingredients together. Thoroughly brush your hair, bending over at the waist to release tension from the neck and shoulder muscles, and brushing from the nape of the neck all the way down to the ends of the hair. Rub the mixture into the scalp. Brush the hair again. Some of the particles might be left in the hair, but this is all right. They can remain in your hair until the next time you intend to use a wet shampoo. Then you can simply brush the hair, shampoo, and treat as usual. Your hair will have an unusual luster and gloss unobtainable by any other means.

Rinses

You can make herbal rinses with herbs that you have chosen and premixed for your particular type of hair. These mixtures of herbs can be used as a base for the shampoo, as a rinse afterward that conditions the hair, or simply to help remove the soap.

■ Herbal Rinse for Normal Hair

1 ounce Camomile
1 ounce Marigold flowers
1 ounce Comfrey leaves
1 ounce Rosemary leaves

Mix the herbs together and store for later use in an airtight container. To rinse your hair, make an herbal infusion with ½ ounce of the mixed herbs and 1 quart water. Steep until cool enough to use, about 20 minutes. Strain carefully through a strainer or cheesecloth to remove all herb particles. Pour the strained liquid over freshly washed hair. Rinsing with water afterward is unnecessary.

■ Herbal Rinse for Problem Hair

This is a good mixture for restoring the natural balance in problem hair that is either too oily or too dry. However, it may prove to be too dark for very light hair. In this case you should use it only as an herbal infusion shampoo, followed by Herbal Rinse for Normal Hair (above).

1 ounce Burdock root
1 ounce Comfrey root or leaves
1 ounce Rosemary leaves
1 ounce Nettles

Mix the herbs together. To use, make an herbal infusion with ½ ounce of the herbs and 1 quart water, and use as a final rinse or with either castile soap flakes or your own shampoo.

You can use vinegar instead of water in either of the preceding herbal mixtures to make an after-shampoo vinegar rinse. Vinegar acts as a solvent of both natural and cosmetic oils as well as resins. It is about 5 percent acetic acid, which is found naturally in apples, grapes, and other foods. Apple cider vinegar is very effective for cutting any soap residue left after shampooing. It is also good for hair that is too oily or full of dandruff, or for very dark hair that needs to be conditioned. Since vinegar is naturally on the acid side and castile soap is naturally alkaline, they balance each other and work very well when used together. A vinegar rinse can be stored for some time, so you can make a quantity sufficient for a few months.

■ Vinegar Conditioning Hair Rinse

4 ounces dry ingredients for Herbal Rinse for Normal Hair *or* Herbal Rinse for Problem Hair (above)
1 quart apple cider vinegar
4–8 drops essential oil (optional)
1 tablespoon isopropyl alcohol (optional)

Add dry ingredients for the herbal rinse of your choice to vinegar. Put in a bottle and cap. Shake the bottle gently every day for 10 to 14 days to make sure that the herbal contents stay submerged in the vinegar. At the end of this time, separate the liquid from the herbs by straining through a double layer of cheesecloth. If you like, 4 to 8 drops of any desired herbal essential oil can be dissolved in 1 tablespoon of alcohol and added to the vinegar as a scent.

Put the rinse into a clean bottle, label, and store in a cool, dark place for later use. When needed, mix up to ½ cup of the herbal vinegar with 1 cup of water, and use as a final rinse after shampooing.

Oil Treatments

Oil treatments are occasionally necessary to condition a dry or scaly scalp, sun-tortured hair, dry ends, or any type of damaged hair. They are a little more difficult to apply than simple hair rinses, but the resultant shiny, healthy head of hair is well worth it.

■ Oil Treatment Formula

2 ounces Jojoba oil
2 ounces Olive oil
2 ounces Walnut oil (if available)
½ ounce Rosemary oil

Mix oils together. If Walnut oil isn't available, increase the Jojoba and Olive oils by 1 ounce each. Store mixture in closed container.

To use, first carefully brush the hair to remove all loose strands and grime. Wet the hair in hot water so that the oil is easier to remove later. You might also rinse your hair with an herbal rinse. Steaming the head facilitates the absorption of the oil and helps to remove any old sebaceous plugs from and increase the circulation to the scalp.

The oil treatment should be heated slightly and applied to the scalp section by section. Part the hair into sections with a rattail comb and apply, using cotton pads, a sponge, or even just your fingers. Note that the oil need only be applied to the scalp and not to the hair itself. Enough of the conditioning oil will drip down the hair shaft to penetrate it.

[*Continued on next page*]

After applying the oil, wind up portions of hair, and secure them in pincurls or with linen strips. Wrap your hair in a thin linen towel that has been wrung out in any hot herbal solution, then put a piece of plastic or a shower cap over this, and finally wrap a nice, thick towel around your head to hold in the heat. Leave this on for at least 30 minutes and up to 4 hours. Your head may get all itchy and feel sweaty, but this only means that the herbs and oil are working. Finally, remove all the wrappings and rinse the hair in hot water. Shampoo with Castile Shampoo (page 129). Shampoo a second time with the juice of a lemon added to the shampoo. Rinse again carefully and let the hair dry naturally. Your hair may still feel a bit oily, but this will lessen when you shampoo again in the next day or so. Use this treatment no more often than once every 2 weeks.

Yield: 6½ ounces

■ Daily Conditioning Oil

The finest combination of conditioning oils is a mixture of Jojoba, Rosemary, and Basil. Mix the oils together in equal proportions and use 1 or 2 drops at a time. Put the conditioning oil on your hand, rub your hand across your brush, and then brush your hair.

Setting Lotion

An easy-to-use, natural hair-setting lotion can be made with Irish moss.

■ Irish Moss Setting Lotion

¼ ounce Irish moss
1 quart water
8 drops essential oil (optional)
2 tablespoons isopropyl alcohol (optional)

Boil the Irish moss with the water for 20 minutes until it has thickened. Strain it through a coarse strainer into a squat, wide-mouth, glass jar. For scent, if desired, add essential oil dissolved in the alcohol. You can also use 2 tablespoons of Bay rum, which is alcohol-based, or start with any herbal infusion instead of plain water to further gain the benefits of the herbs. Rosemary water is especially good, as is Lemongrass water. To use the lotion, simply dip your comb in it, comb through your hair, and roll up your hair in the usual way.

Beverage Tea for Hair Health

It is a well-known fact that not by shampoos and herbal hair rinses alone will drab, lank hair turn into a mane of shining glory. Good nutrition and daily exercise are also important. Various nutrients may be needed for the hair to remain in good shape, such as biotin and vitamins A, B_6, and E. Various herbs may also supply needed hair nutrients, such as the absorbable iron that is contained in Nettles, silica in Horsetail, calcium in Oatstraw, and vitamin A in Strawberry leaves and Lemongrass. A vitamin- and nutrient-supplying mixture of herbs that can be drunk as a tea follows.

■ High-Nutrient Tea for Healthy Hair

2 ounces Nettles
2 ounces Lemongrass
2 ounces Violet flowers or Strawberry leaves
1 ounce Kelp or Dulse
1 ounce Beet tops
1 ounce Alfalfa
1 ounce Lemon peel
½ ounce Hibiscus flowers
½ ounce Camomile
½ ounce Oatstraw
½ ounce Horsetail
½ ounce Mint

Mix these herbs and bottle in a dry, light-proof container to keep for later use. Brew the tea, using from 1 teaspoon to 1 tablespoon of herbs to 1 cup of boiling water; steep, strain, and drink. Honey can be added, if desired. For best results, the tea should be taken regularly.

Body Care Products

Deodorants

Deodorants come in all forms, from a simple application of baking soda or white clay that absorbs moisture and odor to the chemical formulas that actually stop perspiration from forming. These latter can be harmful, as they actually stop the body from "breathing" through the skin. Homemade deodorants do two things: They minimize odor, and they absorb wetness. Some herbs that have a deodorant action (something that destroys or masks unpleasant odors) can stain garments, but deodorants made with white clay and baking soda will not. Normally, washing your underarms and feet several times a day and being scrupulous about the cleanliness of your underclothes and socks is all that is necessary to keep odors away. Naturally, a diet rich in vegetables and whole grains, and vitamin supplements such as zinc and vitamin C, may help to keep you sweet-smelling from the inside out.

■ Standard Deodorant Formula

1 part baking soda
1 part white clay

Mix baking soda and white clay together. Dust on with a puff whenever necessary.

■ Scented Deodorant

2 parts baking soda
2 parts white clay
1 part dried powdered Lemon peel *or* Orange peel

Mix baking soda and white clay together, and add Lemon peel powder or Orange peel powder as a scent. Dust on with a puff whenever necessary.

■ Deodorant Tea

Mix together Sage leaves, Melilot, Parsley, and Alfalfa in equal quantities. Store the mixture in a light-proof container. Drink ½ cup of tea, brewed with ½ to 2 teaspoons herb mixture, regularly.

Bath and Skin Conditioners

Mixtures of herbs that treat various skin conditions or that can be used for smoothing, soothing, and hydrating (adding moisture) the skin are easily obtained from herb or health food stores. However, they are also easy to make and are most economical. Bath herbs are the organic antidote to impure air conditions and harsh chlorinated water.

The herbs themselves can be placed directly in the bathtub (though they can plug the drain), or they can be wrapped in a washcloth, secured with a rubber band, and used as a scrub. You can also purchase or make small cheesecloth or muslin bags, insert the herbal mixtures, and throw the entire bag into the tub where it can release the essence of its herbal contents. My favorite method for taking an herb bath is to make a standard herbal infusion of mixed herbs, strain the entire contents directly into the warm bath water, and put the herbs themselves in a washcloth to use as a scrubber after I've soaked in the bath.

Skin conditioners can also be made from simple household ingredients such as Cornmeal, Oatmeal, Almond meal, and salt. These can be used separately or mixed together in any amounts. A small handful is scrubbed on the body to remove old dead skin, softening and smoothing the skin as well as conditioning it. Then a bath or shower is taken, and this constitutes an entire beauty ritual.

■ Dry Skin Conditioner

1 ounce Oatmeal
1 ounce Almond meal
1 ounce Comfrey leaves, ground

Mixed together, this is enough for 3 baths or showers. To use, make a decoction of 1 ounce of the mixed materials in 1 quart of water. Strain into bath water, and save the herbs to use as a scrubber. Step into the bathtub, and soak for at least 10 minutes. When you soak in the tub, you will begin to feel smooth and relaxed, and the herbal liquid in the bath water will complete the smoothing and hydrating process.

■ Oily or Scaly Skin Conditioner

1 ounce Lemongrass
1 ounce Cornmeal
1 ounce Witch Hazel
1 ounce Rose petals

Mix these ingredients together. Add 1 ounce of the mixture to 1 quart of boiling water. Turn off the heat, and let steep for 20 minutes. Use 2 times a week or more, following the instructions for Dry Skin Conditioner (above).

Sun Lotions

Lemon juice put on the skin hastens a tan; plain mayonnaise is a sun protectant; PABA, a member of the group of B vitamins, actually blocks the harmful rays; and vitamin E nourishes the skin and keeps it from burning. These can be mixed in various ways to protect the skin and also to encourage good color. My favorite substance for lubricating sun-soaked skin is simply pure Corn oil, which I slather on every few hours.

■ Suntan Lotion

2 ounces salt-free mayonnaise
2 ounces black tea
juice of 1 Lemon
5 400-IU vitamin E capsules

Mix the mayonnaise, tea, and Lemon juice together in a blender. (Ideally, the mayonnaise should be homemade from any recipe that uses Olive oil and Lemon juice, and the tea should be very dark.) Pour this into a storage container, and squeeze the contents of the vitamin E capsules into it. Keep in the refrigerator for no more than a week.

■ Sunburn Lotion

If you should get a nasty burn, the application of something cold will help to soothe the skin. This can be a cool bath, the juice of the Aloe plant, or simply a compress of Apple cider vinegar. If you have Aloe gel stored in a bottle, apply continually until the skin cools. Direct application of vitamin E oil is also extremely useful for cooling and healing burned skin. Liquid vitamin C mixed with Aloe plant juice and gel helps to heal a bad sunburn or, for that matter, any sort of a burn.

Massage and Other Body Oils

Massage and other body oils are mixtures of oils and, occasionally, herbal extracts. Through their application they are relaxing, healing, soothing, or stimulating. They also can act as a medium for the body to absorb essential oils or vitamin oils, as well as medicinal herbs. These oils can be scented, and they can be used as a creamy mixture to apply after a bath or a day in the sun.

Massage and body oils can be oily or watery, depending upon their ingredients. They work best in small amounts, either rubbed carefully into the skin of the face or body or added to baths for treatment of dry skin.

■ Massage Oil

1 quart oil
1 ounce herbs
4–8 drops essential oil (optional)

For the oil, you can use a combination containing all of the essential fatty acids, such as Corn, Safflower, Soy, Olive, and Peanut oil. Or the oil can be simply Olive oil, or a mixture of fruit or nut oils such as Apricot kernel, Almond, Avocado, and Walnut.

Listed below are a few herbs and the condition they'll alleviate or the sensation they'll enhance.

Alfalfa, Rose, and Camomile: dry skin
Lemongrass, Witch Hazel, and Marigold: oily skin
Peppermint, Rosemary, and Thyme: stimulation
Sage, Catnip, and Camomile: relaxation

Combine ingredients and make a decoction. Allow to cool, then strain oil through a double layer of cheesecloth, and add essential oil for scent, if desired. Store oil in a labeled, light-proof bottle.

■ Bath Oil with Soap

1 ounce liquid Ivory soap
1 ounce Wheat germ oil
3 ounces fruit or nut oils
¼ ounce essential oil

Mix the liquid soap with the oils to help the oil disperse somewhat in the bath water. Since bath oils are concentrated, use only 1 ounce per bath.

Sesame oil, Olive oil, and Almond oil make a good combination of fruit or nut oils for this formula.

For the essential oil, Mint oils are stimulating, Sage oil is useful for tired muscles, Rose and Jasmine oils are very relaxing, Lavender is cleansing and mildly stimulating, and Sandalwood is relaxing.

Baby or Body Powder

Powders can be made of mixtures of baking soda, Cornstarch, Rice powder, Oatmeal powder, herbs, and talcum. They can be used to soothe heat rash and chafing, or simply to absorb moisture and provide "slip" so that clothing can be put on and taken off easily. Most of these materials come in a powdered form, but for those that don't, it is a simple matter to run them through a seed grinder or coffee mill to create a soft powder. Oats and herbs possess many healing qualities and are good for diaper rash and any other sort of skin irritation.

■ Baby Powder

1 ounce powdered Camomile
1 ounce powdered Marigold flowers
1 ounce Oat or Oatmeal powder
½ ounce powdered eggshells
½ ounce Cornstarch (optional)

Purchase the herbs in the finest form possible, then put them, along with the eggshell, through a seed grinder or coffee mill until they have been ground still finer. Sift the mixture through a very fine sifter, then bottle. Discard the remainder that has not passed through the sifter. If heat rash is especially a problem, add about ½ ounce of Cornstarch.

■ Body Powder

1 ounce plain talcum
1 ounce powdered eggshells
½ ounce Sandalwood powder

Mix together, and grind as fine as possible. Sift mixture, discarding remaining particles. Dust on the body whenever desired.

■ Fragrant Body Powder

1 ounce plain talcum
1 ounce powdered eggshells
4 drops essential oil

Mix all these ingredients together except the essential oil. Drop the oil onto mixture, and stir with a fork. Set it aside for a few days, then sift and resift 5 or 6 times through a regular flour sifter. This will distribute the essential oil throughout the entire mixture nicely. Allow it to sit again for a few days or more until the oil can completely vaporize and mix. Dust on the body after bathing.

Perfume

Making your own perfume can be simple—just dissolve an essential oil that you like in pure alcohol and water, and use it as a cologne or toilet water. Or you can involve yourself in the complicated operation of picking your own flowers and extracting their scents through various, somewhat intricate processes.

Why should anyone even try to make his or her own fragrance? One shopping trip to any department store should give you the reason: cost! Commercial perfumes and colognes made from real flowers cost many, many dollars. Granted that they come in very attractive containers with designer labels, but after all, it is the contents that count.

Perfumes and toilet waters are not that difficult to make, and the contents can be controlled so that the fragrance you wear is something you really like that also works well with your own body chemistry.

■ Maceration Technique for Perfume

fresh flowers
Olive oil
tincture of Benzoin

To macerate means to extract and soften by soaking in a fluid. Pick fresh flowers and remove and discard all the green parts. Put the flowers into a container and add just enough Olive oil barely to cover them. As the flowers soak up the oil they will sink deeper into it. You need just the thinnest layer of oil over the flowers in order to extract the essence. After 24 hours, most flowers have given up their essential oil to the surrounding oil medium. Remove the flowers by carefully straining the oil. Smell the oil; if it has retained the fragrance of the flowers that you started with, you have a perfume oil. If not, then add fresh flowers to the oil and repeat the process. When your oil smells like flowers and not like Olive oil, you are through. This oil can be preserved by the addition of tincture of Benzoin, a natural preservative that occurs as a resin in certain trees. Add 4 drops of tincture of Benzoin for every ounce of perfume oil.

Treatment for Detergent Hands or Dry Feet

Sometimes when we have done dishes by hand for a number of years, or because of other types of work that we do, our hands become very dry, cracked, painful, and unsightly. The continuous application of a healing oil is helpful, but there are other emergency measures that can be very effective. A woman once called and told me that her hands had been cracked and bleeding for three years, and that she hadn't been able to do housework or dishes adequately in that time. My first suggestion was that she cut down on the amount of housework that she was doing, as well as wear rubber gloves. She had apparently become allergic to household cleansers and dishwashing liquids. Her doctor had suggested these same things, and in addition, had prescribed a medication that had not been helpful. My second suggestion was to use a three-hundred-year-old remedy that is called in the old "receipt" books, "To Whiten and Smooth the Hands." Within days, this formula totally cured and healed this woman's painful, cracked hands. Although slightly messy, it is very simple to make and use.

■ Soft Hands Formula

1 ounce ground Almonds
1 egg, beaten
¼ ounce ground Comfrey root
1 tablespoon honey

Combine Almonds, egg, and Comfrey root, add honey, and mix with your hands. At night, before you go to bed, carefully coat your hands from wrist to fingernails. Ask someone to help you put on a pair of old kid gloves. (You can use cotton gloves, but they'll leak during the night. Rubber gloves do not allow your skin to breathe, so don't use them.) In the morning, remove and rinse the gloves, and rinse your hands. Apply one of the lotions or creams below. Repeat this process every night for a week, then once a week for a month, and then once a month for as long as necessary. This is a very effective measure for sore feet as well as hands. For feet, sock moccasins work well to contain the solution.

Facial Products

Facial Masks

Masks can remove grime or old dead skin; improve circulation; treat and alleviate pimples; remove excess oil; hydrate dry skin; and generally nourish, texturize, and smooth the skin. Masks are so simple and easy to make, and so economical, that it seems foolish to spend $6 to $8 for a 4-ounce jar of a commercial product in a store.

The best ingredients for basic masks are egg white, clay, brewer's yeast, honey, any mashed fruit, and cooked Oatmeal. Any of these can be used singly or in combination, in any proportions you desire. Egg white refines, clay can remove pimples and grime, brewer's yeast is extremely powerful as a circulation stimulant, and honey is naturally acid-balanced and can balance either a too-oily or a too-dry complexion. Fruit tightens lax pores, and Oatmeal softens and cleanses the skin. Simply wash your face and pat it dry. Apply a mask, let it dry, and then rinse it off. If your skin is dry, apply a lotion. Use a mask regularly, but no more than three times a week.

Here are three formulas for specific skin conditions.

■ Refreshing Mint Souffle Facial Mask for Tired Skin

1 tablespoon ground or powdered Spearmint
1 tablespoon honey
1 tablespoon oil

Mix together in a blender until nice and fluffy, and apply to clean skin.

■ Mask for Oily Skin

1 tablespoon clay
1 tablespoon water or Lemon juice

Mix together in the palm of your hand and apply to clean skin. Potter's clay, or any other kind of sticky clay for absorbing toxins, will serve well here.

■ Mask for Troubled Skin

1 tablespoon Cucumber
1 tablespoon yogurt
1 tablespoon Parsley

Blend together in a blender until mixture is fluffy, then apply to clean skin.

Simple Lotions

Lotions contain more water than oils and are used for the entire body or complexion. They can soften lines that are beginning to form or remove excess oil from oily skin.

A very basic lotion is the one our grandmothers made from vegetable glycerin and Rose water. Rose water is made at home by gently simmering Rose petals in water for 10 minutes, then straining and preserving with alcohol (three parts water to one part alcohol), or simply refrigerating. Fine quality Rose water can be purchased in liquor stores or Middle Eastern grocery stores, and also in herb and health food stores. You can apply lotions anytime from morning until night, but only use them on clean skin. Remember that herbal lotions and creams should be used as soon as possible, as bacteria do build up in such mixtures that do not contain preservatives. Up to one week in the refrigerator should be the limit before throwing them out.

■ Rose and Rosemary Lotion

1 ounce Rose petal tea *or* Rose water
1 ounce Rosemary tea
1 tablespoon egg white

Mix this in a blender and keep the resulting liquid refrigerated.

■ Orange Lotion

½ ounce Cocoa butter, melted
1 ounce Olive oil, warmed
1 ounce Orange juice
2 drops essential oil (Orange flower if possible)

Mix all of these ingredients together in a blender until light and fluffy. This lotion need not be refrigerated, but should be used as soon as possible. It may separate, but it can be beaten together again.

Creams

Creams are more oily than lotions and are more suitable as nighttime applications and for dry skin. They are used to soften the skin, to moisturize, to provide essential vitamins, or simply to cleanse. The simplest, least expensive cream is any type of shortening that can be purchased in the supermarket, with herb waters or vitamins added. Shortening plus vitamin E oil is excellent as a nighttime moisturizer, and by itself is useful for removing makeup. Salt-free mayonnaise is an excellent cream as long as it is made with Olive oil and Lemon juice rather than with another oil and vinegar. The egg in the mayonnaise is extremely nourishing for dry skin.

■ Rejuvenating Cream

1 ounce beeswax *or* lanolin
3 ounces Almond oil
1 Elastin ampule *or* 4 400-IU vitamin E capsules
2 drops Rose oil

Combine ingredients, and heat over low heat until beeswax is melted. Remove from heat and whip with a whisk until cool.

■ Stimulating Cream

1 ounce beeswax *or* lanolin
3 ounces Wheat Germ oil
1 ounce Peppermint tea, brewed strong
1 drop Peppermint oil

Put all ingredients in a pan and place over low heat until beeswax is melted. Remove from heat and whip with a whisk until cool.

Protective Lip Gloss

Lip glosses are used to protect the lips and to give a little color. If you color this gloss, it can also be used on the cheeks or the chin for color. Lip glosses are especially useful for swimmers or skiers, as they protect the delicate lip tissue from overexposure to the sun and elements.

■ Lip Gloss

¼ cup Sesame oil
2 teaspoons beeswax, melted
1 ounce Camphor *or* Menthol
Alkanet root (optional)

Put the ingredients together in a very small pot and heat to the melting point. Remove from the heat and beat until mixture is cool. Put into a small container, and whip until mixture is cold or set. The Camphor is for chapped lips, and Menthol gives the gloss a minty taste. You can use both if you like, ½ ounce of each.

For colored gloss, soak Alkanet root in the Sesame oil for 2 weeks. This will color the oil a dark red. Strain the oil before combining it with the other ingredients.

After-Shave Lotion

Of course, men can use all the previous formulas, but in addition they need an astringent lotion or something to use after they shave to soothe the irritated flesh.

■ Standard Herbal After-Shave

1 part Witch Hazel
1 part Rose water

Witch Hazel is a simple, standard herbal remedy to use as an after-shave lotion. It is inexpensive and easy to find. Mixed with Rose water, it makes a more pleasantly scented soothing lotion.

■ Soothing Gel After-Shave

10 Quince seeds
1 cup water
herb water

This soothing lotion can be made by boiling Quince seeds in water until a gel forms. Then dilute the gel with an herb water such as Rose water or Orange water to whatever consistency you like, and it's ready to use. Make it in small amounts so that you can use it up before it spoils. Spoilage depends upon your area's climate, but you should be able to keep a batch on hand up to a week in your refrigerator.

■ Herbal Water After-Shave

1 part vegetable glycerin
1 part herb water

Simple after-shave is made by mixing equal parts of plain vegetable glycerin and any herb water. In place of the herb water, you can also use Bay rum, to close the pores, Mint tea, which is stimulating, and Rose or Jasmine flower, to soothe and add a nice scent.

■ Apple Cider Vinegar After-Shave

1 part Apple cider vinegar
1 part vegetable glycerin or Witch Hazel

Mix ingredients together. Vinegar Conditioning Hair Rinse (page 131) is a good base for this after-shave lotion.

Steam Treatment for Skin

Clear, beautiful skin is ultimately the result of good nutrition and regular exercise. Nutritional supplements help, as do pure, wholesome substances that are used on the skin. In extreme conditions, such as exposure to a lot of air pollution, or for special occasions when you want your skin really pore-deep clean, nothing beats a steam treatment. A steam bath is a steam treatment for the entire body, but steam can be used as a treatment for the face or scalp regularly, when you boil water or use a vaporizer in your bedroom.

Steaming naturally increases circulation and perspiration, which cleans the pores from the inside out. You'll find this practice to be very refreshing, and it adds moisture to moisture-starved skin. Steaming with the right herbs can also relieve tension and unclog stuffy sinuses.

■ Basic Skin-Steaming Formula

1 tablespoon Licorice
1 tablespoon Fennel seeds
1 tablespoon Mint leaves
1 tablespoon Parsley

Mix herbs together, and store in a tightly closed jar. To use, bring 1 quart water and about ½ ounce of the mixed herbs to a boil in a pot. Put the steaming pot on the table and put your face over the pot, no closer than 10 inches from the water. If you place your face any closer than this, you'll risk burns from the steam. Cover your head and the pot with a towel, and relax for at least 5 minutes. The boiling water releases the aromatic and healing essences of the herbs as well as the volatile oils that are then absorbed into the skin to do their magic work.

Facial Soap

Soap is normally alkaline, while the skin is slightly acidic. The alkaline suds dissolve the dirt and combine with it so that it can be washed off. The skin returns to its normal acid condition within minutes of being washed. For many people, alkaline soap is too strong and drying to use on the face. In these cases, one of the acid-balanced soaps or the gentle soap below can be used.

■ Gentle Soap

1 bar soap
1 dab honey
1 ounce herb water

You can "gentle" your own favorite commercial or homemade bar soap by simply chopping it up into a small pot and heating it with honey and herb water until it melts. Any type of herb can be used. Camomile or Lettuce for soothing the skin, Lavender for stimulating the skin and removing excess oil, or Rose water for toning. For information on making your own bar soap, read the special section "Homemade Soap" (see Index).

Tooth Powder

Beautiful teeth are an asset to anyone, and these, too, can be cared for with simple home remedies. Brush regularly with a soft brush and floss at least once a day.

■ Tooth Powders

Easy-to-make tooth powders include the combination of equal parts of baking soda and table salt, but you can substitute Kelp for the salt and add various powdered herbs for flavor. For scent, add 1 drop of essential oil to every ounce of soda and salt. Stir it and let it sit so that the soda and salt can absorb the scent. Press this through a strainer, bottle, and label. Cinnamon oil is good as a scent, Myrrh oil is especially recommended as an antiseptic aromatic, Wintergreen or Birch can be added for a minty taste, while Rosemary and/or Basil can be added to improve circulation.

Chapter 9 Homemade Remedies

Many people associate homemade remedies with herbal medicine, and for good reason, since the very earliest home cures were made from herbs. Human experience with herbal medicine goes back to prehistoric times when, most likely, people observed and copied sick animals that became well by eating certain plants. Trial and error expanded human knowledge of natural medicine until practitioners could provide relief for a number of illnesses. Priests or physicians assumed responsibility for this growing field of "magic," but families still fashioned simple cures at home for a variety of common ailments.

In recent times, researchers have gone further in working with natural substances by extracting such modern medicines as digitalis from Foxglove, morphine from Poppies, and penicillin from mold cultures. The priests and physicians of antiquity gave way to our present doctors, who receive intense training in medical schools to prescribe the relatively new, powerful drugs of today. And, for the most part, the general public allowed their stock in home remedies to lapse in favor of treatment available from medical doctors.

Doctors and prescriptions can be expensive, however, and some of the minor aches and hurts that we suffer may not warrant the use of concentrated pharmaceuticals. By renewing our knowledge of simple home remedies made from natural ingredients, we can take care of some common health problems safely while also saving time and money.

Herbal medicine is simply home medicine that is gentle and easy to use, with very few side effects. The formulas presented in this chapter are not meant to replace a physician's care. But herb teas and tinctures taken regularly can often alleviate even the most persistent ailment, and simple herbal remedies show the most dramatic results in the common, everyday problems that beset us—insect bites, blisters, bowel troubles, rashes, colds, and earaches. We will deal with these in this section, advocating common, safe herbs and other safe substances that are easy and economical to use.

Common Ailments and Their Remedies

Athlete's Foot

This fungus infection occurs when the chemical balance of the foot changes due to environmental conditions such as increased moisture or heat. Wash affected feet with soap and then rinse or soak in Apple cider vinegar or honey water twice a day. Wear white socks that can be sterilized by boiling. Before putting on your socks, sprinkle the area between the toes with a mixture of dry clay and Goldenseal powder. The clay absorbs the moisture, while the Goldenseal helps to destroy the fungus.

■ Goldenseal/Echinacea Capsules

1 ounce Goldenseal powder
1 ounce Echinacea powder

Mix these powders together and stuff into size 00 gelatin capsules.* You can purchase the herbs and the empty capsules from most health food stores. Many people have found that these capsules relieve problems like athlete's foot.

■ Healing Dusting Powder

1 part Goldenseal powder
1 part dry clay

Mix Goldenseal and clay together, bottle, label, and use when there is a problem with moisture or a rash. It can be used for athlete's foot, diaper rash, or crotch itch.

Beestings and Insect Bites

After a beesting or insect bite (with a beesting, first remove the stinger), rub the area vigorously with any handy green herb. This releases chlorophyll, which has a quick, soothing, and pain-killing action on the sting or bite. The best herbs to use are Savory, Plantain, or Comfrey, but even grass will do in a pinch. A moistened tea bag (preferably Papaya leaf tea or another black tea) is also useful as a poultice. Healing Dusting Powder (above) is very soothing and can be used after the initial sting goes away. If you have bottled chlorophyll, this can be dabbed on the irritation

*There is a new capsule filler available for home use, called the Cap • M • Quik, made by S. L. Sanderson & Company, 6911 Los Olivos Way, Carmichael, CA 95608. It's a very useful device with which to make your own herbal capsules for ingestion.

whenever necessary. The contents of a garlic oil perle applied to the sting or bite is another remedy.

Another useful remedy to use is a paste of Chlorella and water. Chlorella has a chlorophyll content of 7.5 percent, the highest in the plant world. You can also take Chlorella orally to detoxify the body in case there is a mild allergic reaction to the beesting or insect bite. It's also wise to take some pantothenic acid and vitamin C if you have a history of mild allergy. (If you have a violent allergic reaction to beestings, see your doctor at once.) Straight honey is also excellent as an application for any sting or bite.

Blisters

When you find a blister, make sure it is clean, cover it with moleskin or lamb's wool, and leave it alone.

I used a clay and Goldenseal poultice on my son when he picked up a hot plate and a huge blister formed on the palm of his hand. We put a thick, soft blob of white clay mixed with a bit of Goldenseal on the blister, covered it, and wrapped a towel around his hand. Several hours later the clay had dried and my son removed the towel. The blister was flat and reduced to the size of a quarter, and we covered it with a bandage. I have found that bandages by themselves are next to useless on blisters; I prefer moleskin or lamb's wool, and would certainly recommend that you always carry one of these in your first-aid kit, plus a bit of adhesive tape to attach it to the skin.

Bowel and Stomach Distress

The reasons for ailments of the bowel and stomach are diverse; they can result from eating too much or too little food or the wrong combinations of food. You can incur them from eating unripe or spoiled foods or strange, exotic foods. Or the problem simply may be a lack of enough digestive juices in the body, part of another illness that you are experiencing, or the result of stress or tension. (If the latter is the case, it is best to stay away from solid foods altogether until you and your body are calm and relaxed.) Bowel or stomach distress can result in constipation or diarrhea. These are the most common of problems, and yet people suffer from them needlessly when simple home remedies can almost immediately correct the situation.

Constipation may be the result of lifelong improper food habits, and this cannot be dealt with in this little paragraph. If temporary constipation is your problem, try drinking plenty of water or Prune juice to hydrate the bowel, or eat bran flakes to provide bulk. Lighten your food load with simple steamed vegetables until the bowels move. You may also need to take an Olive oil enema to break up the hard bulk so that it can pass.

■ Olive Oil/Orange Juice Drink for Constipation

½ cup Olive oil
½ cup Orange juice

Mix Olive oil into Orange juice and drink at night.

■ Senna Pod Tea for Constipation

6–12 Senna pods
1 cup cool water

Steep Senna pods in water, and drink. For children or older people, 3 to 6 pods steeped in cool water are sufficient. Senna pod tea is less griping (that is, easier on the system) than Senna leaf tea.

Have you ever put activated charcoal into a fish tank to absorb gases and odors and clean the water? You can use this same substance to treat stomach or intestinal distress. Activated charcoal is simple, cheap, and worthwhile to have on hand at home. It is processed from pure vegetable ingredients, has a very porous surface, and can absorb several times its weight in irritating gases and toxins. It also cleans up bad odor and reduces cramps. Activated charcoal works entirely in the digestive track and never enters the bloodstream. It is truly a *simple* (a single-ingredient remedy used to treat a particular condition). It has been in use for at least two thousand years as a treatment for gas and diarrhea.

Many people have found that charcoal tablets and a cup or two of Papaya leaf tea have relieved their stomachache or diarrhea. This is the best remedy, but if you have neither of these, then 1 to 2 teaspoons of liquid chlorophyll will also do the job

■ Vomiting and Flatulence Remedy

2 drops Peppermint oil
½ cup water

Of course, vomiting from a poison is a situation that should be handled by a physician, but if you just have traveler's diarrhea or queasiness accompanied by vomiting and/or flatulence, then you can use the same measures and remedies recommended for stomachache. Often the vomiting must be stopped before the other remedies can be used. The very simple Peppermint oil remedy is useful for halting vomiting. In addition, it will deodorize your excretions.

Bruises

Bruises are caused by a blow or compression that does not break the skin but does break small blood vessels beneath the surface, causing soreness and discoloration. They are treated best by the instant application of cold water or ice wrapped in a cloth. A gentle application of the herbal remedy called Calendula oil is excellent, and will encourage healing. Taking a sufficient quantity of vitamin C and bioflavonoids encourages the basic integrity of the tissues, and bruising will not be nearly as severe or painful as it otherwise might be.

Bruised fingers and toes are best treated by soaking the injured digit for as long as you possibly can in an infusion of Comfrey root. Comfrey is healing and helps to soothe pain. Calendula oil can also be applied externally.

Burns

Aloe vera gel, honey, or simple vitamin E are the easiest and most effective remedies for a burn. An Aloe vera plant grown in the kitchen is useful and handy if you get burned; just cut a bit of leaf and apply the cool gel from the leaf to the burn. Honey is most effective in cooling and healing burns, because it forms a protective cover that heals the tissue very quickly.

Coldness

To counteract the effects of extreme cold, warm the affected area of the body by immersing it in body-temperature water or by pressing the cold part next to a warm person. Cold feet or hands can be warmed by sprinkling Cayenne pepper into one's socks before putting them on, or on the palms of the hands which are then rubbed together. Be sure not to put your hands near your eyes, however. If you do, the eyes will burn and hurt, although no permanent damage will occur. (Cayenne pepper in the eyes can be treated by a direct application of yogurt.)

■ Oil for Friction Rub

Olive oil
Rosemary oil

Warm up the Olive oil and add a few drops of Rosemary oil to every ounce of Olive oil. Then rub this onto the cold area, first gently, then more vigorously until you are using friction. (This is called a friction rub.)

■ Cayenne Drink for Cold Weather

½ teaspoon Cayenne pepper
½ cup hot water

Drink the Cayenne in the water once every 2 hours. It'll warm you up from the inside out, and it also improves circulation.

■ Warming Soup

1 1-inch cube Ginger root
1 cup water
Cayenne pepper
1 bouillon cube (optional)

Simmer Ginger in water 10 minutes, adding a few grains of Cayenne for flavor, and then drink this healthful, warming soup. You also can add a bouillon cube for flavor if you like.

Colds and Fevers

At the first sign of a cold take plenty of vitamin C, reduce the complexity of the foods you are eating to just a few simple choices, wrap a nice, wooly scarf around your neck, and slow down your life a bit. If you have a fever, run a vaporizer in your house with a few drops of Peppermint oil in the well to cool you down. If chills are the problem, add Cinnamon oil, Rosemary oil, or Basil oil to the vaporizer to warm you up. For respiratory congestion, use Eucalyptus oil.

Keep a supply of Garlic oil perles in the house. These come in mighty handy to loosen congestion, induce perspiration, promote thirst, and fight the infection causing the cold.

Garlic oil perles are little gelatin capsules containing Garlic oil diluted with vegetable oil. These are sold in health food shops. Please read the label and purchase only this infused Garlic oil. Concentrated Garlic oil is too strong for first-aid use, and it can be harmful.

For a really serious cold or fever it is a good idea to strengthen the lymphatic system with a mixture of herbs noted for their cleansing and blood-purifying abilities. Echinacea helps the body build its own resistance, while it increases the leukocytes that counteract infection. Yellow dock is a noted blood purifier, and Goldenseal generates a powerful antibacterial action. Ginseng encourages and stimulates all of the organ systems.

■ Purifier for Colds and Infections

2 ounces Echinacea powder
1 ounce Yellow dock powder
1 ounce Goldenseal powder
½ ounce Ginseng powder

Mix ingredients together and stuff into size 00 gelatin capsules. These capsules are known to have provided relief for people suffering from colds. Take them for no more than 10 days.

Cuts and Scratches

All that is necessary for a small cut is that you wash it carefully with soap. Wash a large cut or deep scratch with a dilute tea of Goldenseal root or Echinacea, and close with a butterfly bandage if necessary.

■ Remedy for Infection

1 tablespoon Comfrey root
1 tablespoon Fennel seeds
1 cup water

If your cut or scratch becomes infected, you should boil this cleansing solution, allow it to cool somewhat, yet not too much, and soak your wound in it. Plain soap and water also works well, as does hot water and salt. When the wound opens and begins to drain, apply a poultice of clay. When the clay poultice dries out totally, remove it, rinse the area, and dust with Goldenseal powder. However, if you see no positive results in a day or two, be sure to see a doctor as soon as you can.

Diaper and Other Body Rashes

Rashes can be caused by a number of conditions, from too-acidic skin and secretions to too-alkaline ones. The affected area should be kept clean and dry by washing with a gentle, neutral soap and plain water, and by powdering with clay. Honey, yogurt, or lecithin is also an excellent application for a rash of any kind.

■ Rash Powder

4 teaspoons dry clay
1 teaspoon vitamin-C powder
1 teaspoon Goldenseal powder

Mix together and apply. When applying to a diaper rash, dab it on instead of shaking it on, to prevent your baby from inhaling any particles floating in the air.

Ear Problems

I cannot think of anything more painful than an earache. Earaches may be caused by a buildup of earwax, the yellow, waxy secretion of the external ear glands, that blocks the passageway from the external ear to the internal ear. Because of the shape of their ear canals, some people need to have a doctor remove the wax periodically. Never use a cotton swab on a stick to clean an ear; you may push it in too far and damage the eardrum. The cotton swab picks up only the wax that's on the verge of falling out of the ear anyway, while wax further in the ear can be compacted by the swab, thus possibly causing the very condition it's intended to prevent.

One substance that helps soften earwax without causing it to swell is glycerin. Often, nonprescriptive products for treating earwax buildup merely contain some kind of glycerin and peroxide. The antiseptic is important because traditional remedies, such as warm Olive oil or Garlic oil from perles mixed with vegetable oil, may lead to infection instead of relieving the earache. Also, a woman I once met used an extract concentrate of Garlic as an ear oil, and the substance ate totally through her eardrum, which had to be repaired surgically. So, be careful about what you put into your ears.

Some ear ailments seem to be related to diet. A high-nutrition, low-fat diet similar to that prescribed for heart patients may alleviate many inner ear symptoms, too. Restricting fats, sugars, and caffeine has helped some people with ear problems.

Eyes: Irritated, Sore, or Tired

Watching television, reading under poor lights, exhaustion, smoky rooms, and air pollution are a few of the reasons why your eyes might get sore and red. Avoiding smoke-filled rooms and making sure your home is properly ventilated will help to some extent to protect your eyes. And following a few simple rules when you read or watch television will also aid in preventing eyestrain and fatigue.

When reading, be sure that you provide good lighting—150- to 200-watt bulbs for overhead lights and 75- to 150-watt bulbs for floor or table lamps. Place your reading material against a light background to reduce contrast that can cause your eyes to work too hard. Sit up straight and keep the book at the same angle as the tilt of your head, about forearms' distance away, to prevent your eyes from becoming used to unusual angles. Also avoid reading in bed for this reason.

Take a break every 20 minutes or so by looking at a distant object to refocus your eyes. If your sight seems fuzzy, keep looking back and forth between far and near points until the blurriness is gone. Finally, get up and move around a bit to relax your entire body. Stretch your muscles, and breathe deeply for a minute or two.

Nutrition affects your eyesight, too. Zinc and vitamins A, C, D, E, and the B complex all have been shown to be necessary to good sight. So, be sure to eat foods or take supplements to provide these important nutrients for your eyes. Cod-liver oil is a good source of vitamin D, though if you find its taste unappealing, spending time outdoors in sunshine might be just as good.

■ Compresses for Eyes

Of course, sometimes eye fatigue is impossible to avoid. Here's how you can refresh weary eyes by using compresses that open and close facial blood vessels to reduce swelling from stagnant fluids. At the end of any day that you've used your eyes for a lengthy time, apply hot and cold compresses to your face, brows, closed eyelids, and cheeks. Use small towels or washcloths to soak up the hot or cold water. First apply the hot compress (but not so hot that it will burn your eyes), then follow with a cold compress. Alternate the compresses for a 2- to 3-minute period, finishing with a cold compress. Then, gently massage your forehead, closed eyelids, and upper cheeks with your fingertips.

Fatigue

The best remedy for fatigue is rest. Drink a cup of tea—any kind of noncaffeine herbal tea—and take a nap. However, if for some reason you absolutely must continue working or driving, there are a number of herbs that will stimulate you. (I certainly don't recommend regularly drinking beverages that contain substantial amounts of caffeine.) Guarana or Yerba mate, with their high content of caffeine, can be drunk as a tea or taken in capsule form.

■ Herbal Stimulant

1 part Guarana
1 part Yerba mate
1 part Echinacea root
1 part Ginseng root
1 part Rosemary

Mix these ingredients together, brew as tea, and drink. The above mixture can also be ground in a seed mill or coffee grinder and stuffed into size 00 gelatin capsules. Remember that this is a stimulant to be used when absolutely necessary, and it shouldn't be taken too frequently.

Headache

For relief from a headache, try one of these remedies: Rub your temples with a bit of Rosemary oil, put a cool compress of Apple cider vinegar on your forehead, or drink a cup of Rosemary or Valerian tea. If the headache is accompanied by a stomachache, drink a cup of Camomile tea. A cup of Cabbage soup is also an old folk remedy for headache, as is a compress of Cabbage leaves on the forehead.

Heatstroke or Sunstroke

Heatstroke occurs as a result of prolonged exposure to high temperature, when your body is simply unable to get rid of excessive heat and its internal temperature goes up. If the sun is the source of the high temperature, the condition is referred to as sunstroke. Your temperature may climb as high as 106° to 108°F. You may get weak and giddy, feel nauseous, and sweat profusely. If a person loses consciousness from heatstroke or sunstroke, contact a physician at once.

The best thing you can do for yourself is to submerge yourself in cool water with either a cold cloth or an Apple cider vinegar compress on your head. If a bathtub isn't available, you can press an Apple cider vinegar compress against any part of the body that feels excessively hot. A drop or two of Peppermint oil in a quart of water is very cooling when used as a compress. Also drink plenty of cool (not cold) fluids. Physicians recommend 0.1 percent saline solution as a drink to replace the electrolyte concentration of sweat. Keep cool, but not chilled, rest, and reduce activity during extremely hot spells.

Insomnia

If for some reason you are unable to sleep, get up. Do some work, exercise vigorously for 10 minutes, or even take out a difficult book and begin to read. These simple remedies could put anyone to sleep. The very act of brewing a pot of tea is time-consuming, very relaxing, and also sleep-inducing. If the pot contains Camomile, Valerian, Birch leaves, Lemon verbena, or Red Clover, your insomnia should be gone, as these are sleep-inducing herbs and most effective for relaxing you and easing you into the world of sleep. These herbs can be used individually or in combination, depending upon your taste and what you have on hand.

■ Camomile Sleep Tea

1 part Camomile
1 part Valerian
1 part Mint

Mix herbs together and store in a labeled bottle. To use, bring 1 cup of water to a boil, remove from heat, and add 1 tablespoon of the herbs. Let tea steep for 3 to 5 minutes, strain, and drink slowly.

■ Red Clover Sleep Tea

1 part Lemon verbena
1 part Birch leaves
1 part Red Clover

Mix herbs together and store in a labeled bottle. To use, follow preparation method for Camomile Sleep Tea (above), and drink slowly.

■ Valerian Sleep Tea

1 part Lemon verbena
1 part Lemon peel
1 part Valerian

Mix herbs together and store in a labeled bottle. To use, follow preparation method for Camomile Sleep Tea (above), and drink slowly.

■ Milk and Honey Sleep Remedy

1 glass warm milk
1 teaspoon honey
1 drop Vanilla

Mix ingredients together. Drink, while still warm, before going to bed.

Jet Lag

■ Remedy for Jet Lag

Put a few drops of Rosemary oil in ½ cup of water and drink. In a few hours or at your normal bedtime, drink a cup of Valerian Sleep Tea (above).

Nosebleed

If your nose starts to bleed, pinch the nostrils shut, and keep them shut as long as it takes to stop the bleeding—at least 15 minutes. A Rosemary tea compress on the forehead is also very helpful.

Poisoning

If poison is even a bit suspected as the cause of an illness, then by all means contact a doctor immediately and follow his directions. If you have Ipecac in the house, follow the directions on the package while you are calling the doctor. If the poisoning is in the form of a sick stomach or grumbling bowels, then take charcoal tablets. Every house should have a chart, easily accessible, that lists various poisons and how to treat them, but with our infinite array of chemicals, cleansers, and combination ingredients, it is often extremely difficult to know what a suspected poison contains. Take charcoal tablets and call the doctor. Many hospitals have poison control centers for dealing with such emergencies. Keep the phone number for one near you by your phone for quick access.

Poison Oak or Ivy

After being exposed to poison oak or ivy, wash the area immediately with a cleansing soap and cool water. Hot water will spread the oil, while cool water constrains it. Take plenty of vitamin C and possibly pantothenic acid to control the allergic reaction. Try not to scratch the blisters. Apply clay to the blisters to keep them from itching. Goldenseal powder is also helpful, although it stains clothing and makes your skin yellow. Chlorophyll liquid is also very good to apply to itchy poison oak, and certainly don't forget a dab of honey. The honey is sticky, but whenever you can use it, do so, as it is very effective. If the poison oak or ivy is on the legs, apply honey and/or lecithin and cover with a cotton sock.

Sore Muscles

Muscles become sore through a buildup of lactic acid that is incompletely metabolized in the muscular tissue. Saffron tea can help in this metabolism, but it's prohibitively expensive to drink as a tea (one cup would cost about $2). A simple remedy for sore muscles is to massage them and gently stretch them until they feel better. A massage with Rosemary oil is even more helpful. Here's a formula for massage oil that's particularly good for aching muscles.

Rosemary Massage Oil

¼ ounce Rosemary oil
8 ounces Olive oil

Mix together and use. Substitute Mint oil for the Rosemary oil if you want to stimulate your muscles.

Relaxing Tea

This tea is also helpful for easing the tension of sore muscles.

1 part Alfalfa
1 part Camomile
1 part Dandelion
1 part Horsetail
1 part Oatstraw

Mix together, and store in a labeled bottle. To use, steep 1 tablespoon in a cup of hot water for 3 to 5 minutes and strain. This drink is useful for rebuilding as well as relaxing worn tissues.

Sprains

A sprain is a tear or a very marked stretching of a muscle or ligament around a joint. Immediate application of cold is helpful to keep inflammation down; later, use heat to relax the sprained area. Alternate hot and cold soaks are also good to soothe the stretched or torn tissues. Hot and cold soaks are more helpful, of course, when they contain stimulating and relaxing herbs to help in the healing process. They should be done in sequences of 5 minutes hot and 2 minutes cold for at least 20 minutes. Drinking a relaxing tea will help, also. Rosemary Massage Oil (above) is very useful as a rub.

Hot Soak for Sprained or Aching Muscles or Joints

1 ounce Rosemary
1 ounce Comfrey root
1 gallon water

Bring the ingredients to a boil in a large, flat pan. Turn off the heat and let steep until cool enough to use, though the hot soak is most effective when it's as hot as possible. This liquid also can be used as a compress, and the herbs can be applied as a plaster. When you can, insert the sprained area into the hot water, and soak at least 5 minutes. Then immediately plunge it into a cold soak for 2 minutes.

■ Cold Soak for Sprained or Aching Muscles or Joints

¼ ounce Peppermint oil
1 gallon cold water
2 trays ice cubes

Put oil, water, and ice cubes into a large, flat pan. Keep mixture in the refrigerator, and use whenever necessary to soak aching muscles or joints.

Sunburn

With sunburn, the skin is actually cooked, and it will eventually peel off to expose the new skin underneath. It is, of course, best never to get sunburned; if your skin is very sensitive, alcohol-based PABA solutions are very helpful in blocking the harmful rays of the sun. If you do suffer a sunburn, the first thing you must do is cool the skin. Immersing in a cool water bath will soothe you, and adding baking soda to the water will make it even more effective. Vitamin E oil and Aloe vera gel are noted for their effectiveness in relieving a sunburn and should be applied immediately, either one or the other, or alternating. A cold Comfrey compress is excellent for cooling and soothing a sunburn. Keep reapplying any of these substances until the redness has turned brown and does not hurt any longer.

Toothache

Toothaches should be treated by a competent dentist, but if you cannot get to one quickly enough, put a drop of Clove oil on a tiny piece of cotton, and apply it to the aching tooth. It will quickly ease the pain. Taking bone meal or dolomite tablets is very relaxing and will also help by feeding the nerves. Purifier for Colds and Infections (page 152) can also help. Sometimes taking these capsules along with bone meal will cure whatever problem is causing the aching teeth. It should most certainly be tried. Taking Garlic oil perles may also help.

Chapter 10 Natural Dogs and Cats

Taking natural care of your dogs and cats is very much like taking care of your children. Their health is totally dependent upon your knowledge and how you put it into practice. This responsibility need not be as awesome as it sounds. Animals do not have to be smothered with attention; they will actually prosper with a certain amount of benign neglect. Give them an excellent diet based on sound nutrition, and you'll be freeing them from both internal and external parasites and keeping them in good health. Add a generous amount of exercise and a healthy dose of love, and you will have an animal without neuroses or physical problems.

Successful animal care has more to do with proper diet than anything else. If you feed your pet pure, wholesome food, based on its nutritional needs, chances are good that it will be healthy. If it does become ill, you can do much by treating it with herbs and diet. With a little knowledge and foresight, the intelligent owner can save many trips to the veterinarian.

Along with diet, exercise is one of the most important ingredients for successful animal care. It is only through vigorous exercise that your pet's lungs can fill with oxygen, a cleanser and revitalizer of the respiratory system. Indeed, all of the organs benefit from a regular exercise program. Pets that are kept indoors do not exercise enough. They should be taken outside to walk or run in the morning or evening, preferably both. Also, animals must exercise in all sorts of weather to maintain vital health. Cats can run loose in the smallest of backyards where they can climb trees, fight bushes, and joyously leap about. A dog, on the other hand, needs more space to be really free to jump and run.

Sometimes, though, even a healthy animal will get sick. Never ignore your animal when it pesters you repeatedly—it may be trying to tell you something is wrong. If you suspect your pet is ill, check for the following danger signals:

Breath: fetid or sour
External temperature: cold extremities
Eye clarity: dull, listless
Hair or fur: dry, rough, lifeless coat, excessive hair loss, dandruff
Internal temperature: resting rectal temperature for a cat or a dog below 101° or above 102.5°F
Nose: hot, dry
Odor: odor of body, mouth, ears, or hindquarters different from the normal body odor
Pain: flinching or crying out when you run your hands over any part of the body
Posture or stance: favoring a limp, wincing with movement, holding the head to one side or repeatedly shaking it
Skin: flabby, lips excessively pale

Taking an animal's rectal temperature is not as difficult as most people who have never done it assume. The procedure is basically the same for cats and dogs. Before insertion, shake the mercury column of a rectal thermometer down below 99°F, and lubricate the tip with any nontoxic, greasy substance, such as vegetable oil. With the exception of large animals, which can remain on the floor, stand your pet on a platform, at about your waist level. A standing position is preferable, but if the pet seems more inclined to sit or lie down, you can still take the temperature. Hold the pet's tail with one hand and insert the thermometer into the rectum with a firm, gentle push. If you encounter some resistance to the thermometer just after it passes through the anus, continue to push gently or rotate the thermometer. The muscles in this area will soon relax. For small- to average-size animals, insert the thermometer 1 to 1½ inches into the rectum. For large dogs, it takes half the length of the thermometer or more. If you feel the thermometer go into a fecal mass when you insert it, begin again. Ideally, for an accurate reading, the thermometer should remain in the anus for 2 to 3 minutes. If your animal is particularly jittery, you might remove it after 1 minute; some thermometers will register after this amount of time.

Diet

Diet can mean the difference between active, vibrant health and a weakened, unhealthy state. Wild animals that eat a natural diet suffer very little from nutritional diseases. If you feed your pet an approximation of the natural diet for its species, it is likely to thrive. A commercial pet food alone will almost inevitably result in unhealthiness. The same diet with the addition of vitamin, mineral, and herbal supplements, and a little unrefined oil, is certainly an improvement. The ideal, however, is homemade pet food from wholesome, nutritious ingredients. Animals that live on such a diet, while also receiving plenty of fresh, pure water to drink and adequate exercise, will have the resistance and stamina to fight off most ailments that may come along.

Making animal food from scratch is as easy as preparing a meat loaf or cooking oatmeal. It is also the best way to offer your pet low-cost, nutritious food. If your pet is finicky, introduce new foods gradually, perhaps mixed in with its commercial favorite. If at first it completely ignores the new offerings, stand firm and refuse to switch back to the old standby. When the food gets stale or moldy, replace it with a fresh batch of the same ingredients. Do not be insulted if at first your pet turns its nose up at your efforts. When your pet realizes that it isn't going to get anything else, it will adapt.

The amount to feed depends on the size of the animal and how much exercise it gets. The best way to determine how much to give your pet is to offer it all it will eat within a 30-minute span, twice a day. Remember to remove the leftovers after the allotted time. Always have plenty of fresh water available for your pets to drink day and night. The general proportions in each basic food group listed in Table 10.1 provide a healthy diet for cats and dogs.

Table 10.1 Recommended Animal Diet

Basic Foods	Percent Needed in Daily Diet (cats)	Percent Needed in Daily Diet (dogs)
Eggs: raw or slightly cooked, once a week, 1 to 5 depending upon animal's weight	-	-
Food supplements: nutritional yeast, wheat germ, milk powder; include a sprinkle of bran for roughage	5	5
Fruit: feed rarely, as a treat	-	-
Grains: Oats, Millet, Rice, Barley; cooked or sprouted	25	40
Muscle meats: any lean meat or fish, chopped raw or slightly sauteed; avoid pork and hamburger, as these meats are too fatty	10	10
Oil: unrefined vegetable oil (Safflower, Corn, Sesame) added to 1 meal, 5 days a week; 1 teaspoon per serving for a cat and up to 1 tablespoon for a large dog	-	-
Organ meats: heart, liver, kidney; chopped raw or slightly sauteed	50	30

Table 10.1—*Continued*

Basic Foods	Percent Needed in Daily Diet (cats)	Percent Needed in Daily Diet (dogs)
Vegetables: carrots, beets, and any dark green or dark yellow vegetables; raw or lightly steamed and chopped fine	10	15
Vitamin and mineral supplements: obtain from your health food store, or pet store	-	-

Sample Recipes

Vary any recipes according to the food you have left over or on hand in your refrigerator or garden. Balance the diet over the course of the week—more meat one day, more grain and vegetables another. Also, give vitamin, mineral, and herbal supplements with every meal. Oil is a must, too, if you wish your pet to have a shiny coat. (It also helps cats expel hair balls.) *Caution:* Mineral oil robs the body of oil-soluble vitamins and adds nothing to nutrition, therefore, do not use this oil. Avoid using butter and cheese because of their high fat content.

■ Burgers for Pets

Mix together 10 parts chopped organ meats; 2 parts chopped, slightly cooked carrots; 1 part minced raw greens (watercress, spinach, or kale); and 4 parts cooked grain (leftover rice or bulgur). Add 1 part nutritional yeast, 1 part oil, and 2 parts Herbal Supplement Blend (below). Form this mixture into thick patties, separate them with wax paper, and freeze what you don't immediately need.

■ Vegie-Grain Stew

Mix together 1 cup leftover Oatmeal, ¼ cup cooked or grated raw yellow squash, 1–4 tablespoons chopped Alfalfa sprouts, 1 raw egg, 2 teaspoons nutritional yeast, and 1 tablespoon Herbal Supplement Blend (below), and add oil. This will probably be enough for 1 or 2 meals, depending on the size of the animal. If you have already used egg earlier in the week, omit it from the recipe.

Herbal Supplements

In addition to having medicinal qualities, herbs are highly nutritive. They contain valuable minerals drawn up from the soil and vitamins synthesized by the plants through their own internal processes. The Herbal Supplement Blend (below) will provide some vitamins and many minerals. It also acts as preventive medicine by toning different organs and assisting in proper assimilation and elimination. Some of the herbs in the formula, such as Alfalfa and Nettles, have nutritional and blood-building qualities. Others, such as Red Clover and Burdock, are blood purifiers, while Garlic and Thyme are antiseptics. Camomile and Catnip are good for the nerves and the stomach. Other herbs in the formula serve a double function: Fennel seeds are good for the liver and the digestion and ease flatulence; Rosemary is antiseptic and serves as a tonic for the heart and nerves.

If you cannot obtain every herb called for in the formula, do not despair. By consulting any good herb book, you can learn the function of a given substance and substitute one that acts similarly. If you cannot find Mullein, for instance, you might use Coltsfoot, which is also good for the lungs. If you are temporarily out of Thyme, try Sage, another common antiseptic herb. Since Horsetail and Oatstraw are both rich in silica, you might use more of the latter if you cannot find Horsetail.

Buy the herbs mentioned at any good natural foods store or herb shop, or purchase them through the mail-order companies that sell herbs and herbal products. (See Appendix C, "Mail-Order Suppliers and Manufacturers.")

■ Herbal Supplement Blend

Use either cut and sifted or powdered herbs.

1 ounce each:	Alfalfa, Dandelion root, Marshmallow root, Mullein leaves, Nettles, Parsley
2 ounces each:	Burdock root or seed, Camomile, Horsetail, Oatstraw, Red Clover, Rose Hips, Rosemary, Slippery Elm bark, Thyme
¼ ounce each:	Catnip, Fennel seeds, Garlic powder
dash:	Cayenne pepper

If you are using cut and sifted herbs, put them into a blender or food processor and reduce to a coarse powder. Mix with the already powdered herbs and store in a dark jar in the refrigerator or some other cool place. For a cat, 1 to 3 teaspoons a day is adequate. Depending on the size of the dog, 1 tablespoon to 1 cup a day is adequate for a dog. Mix the herb powder with the food or sprinkle it on top.

This blend should be considered a mineral and preventive medicinal supplement, not a replacement for chopped, fresh, green, leafy vegetables and herbs in the diet.

■ Herbal Supplement for Pregnant or Nursing Pets

Use Herbal Supplement Blend (above) and include ½ ounce each: Chickweed, Milk Thistle, and Raspberry leaf.

Herbal Remedies

Every once in a while, despite all your care and attention to your pet's diet, your basically healthy pet will get ill. Here are some useful formulas that will help you treat simple symptoms and illnesses when they occur.

All-Purpose Remedies

These first two recipes are all-purpose remedies that can be used for a variety of conditions.

■ Cleansing Tonic

Use this remedy in cases of fever or any internal or external bodily infection. The antiseptic and blood-purifying herbs help the body to throw off infection and toxins. Finely powdered herbs should be used.

2 tablespoons Goldenseal powder
1 tablespoon Burdock root
1 tablespoon Garlic powder
1 tablespoon Chaparral
1 tablespoon Cayenne pepper

Mix herb powders together thoroughly, and stuff into size 0 gelatin capsules. The dosage is 1 capsule for every 10 pounds of body weight, every 3 hours. Give no more than 5 doses per day.

■ Antibacterial Powder

Use to prevent and treat general infections, parasitic infections (such as ringworm or mange), or hair loss.

1 part Goldenseal powder
1 part Garlic powder

Mix herb powders together and keep in your first-aid kit. Apply freely to any sore or abraded area where bacteria might become a problem.

Burns and Abrasions

Any simple scratch, burn, slight abrasion, irritated pad, or bitten ear can be treated simply. Wash the area carefully with soap and water and apply one of the following remedies.

■ Aloe Treatment for Burns and Abrasions

Split open the fleshy leaf of an Aloe plant. Apply the soothing, healing gel to the injury on a regular basis until you witness considerable improvement. You can buy these plants in most nurseries and even some supermarkets.

■ Vitamin E Treatment for Burns and Abrasions

With a needle, pierce a vitamin E perle (a soft capsule with an oil-based solution inside), and squeeze oil onto the injured area. Continue to apply on a regular basis until condition improves.

■ Comfrey Gel Treatment for Burns and Abrasions

Comfrey gel can be purchased at some health food stores. However, the plant is so prolific and easy to grow that any backyard gardener can have one. The plant also grows well in a tub on the back porch or fire escape.

Simmer 1 cup freshly chopped Comfrey root in 1 cup water about 20 minutes. Let the mixture cool, and strain it through a coarse sieve. You can use the resulting gel immediately or roll it into small balls and freeze them for future use. To treat your pet, rub the gel into the injured area on a regular basis. Continue treatment until condition improves.

Digestive Ailments

Sometimes your pet will "go off its feed" or show other signs of digestive disturbance, such as fetid urine or feces. Treat such conditions by simplifying the diet for a few days and adding more vitamin and mineral supplements to the daily feed. Also, use the Cleansing Tonic (page 165), and add digestive herbs such as Fennel, Catnip, and Camomile to the diet. The following cold infusion of Uva Ursi, an herb that cleanses the urinary tract and therefore assists in proper excretion of toxins, will help deodorize feces and urine.

■ Cold Infusion of Uva Ursi

1 tablespoon Uva Ursi
3 cups water

Tie Uva Ursi in a muslin bag, and place it in the water in the animal's dish. The herb also can be added loose, as it will sink to the bottom. Continue practice until you notice an improvement in your pet's condition.

Ears

Your pets will also develop painful earaches, which can be caused by bacteria fostered in dirty scratches or other types of wounds. If you notice that your dog or cat has an open wound inside of its ear, wash it with warm water, gently and carefully blot dry, and treat it with an antiseptic recommended by your veterinarian. This should prevent an infection from occurring. If you suspect that your pet is suffering from an ear infection already, consult your vet for proper treatment.

Cats are very susceptible to wounds around their ears from fighting with other cats, and sometimes these wounds turn into abscesses. For treatment, follow the instructions under Sores and Abscesses (page 169), or take your cat to a veterinarian.

Ear mites can cause your pets much discomfort, too. Dogs usually get them from cats. Cats with ear mites will scratch furiously when you rub their ears. You will see brownish black deposits in their ears. Dogs with ear mites will shake their heads vigorously and scratch their ears continuously. You'll need to have a veterinarian confirm an infestation, however, because ear mites are almost microscopic in size. Your vet most likely will prescribe an effective treatment, but frequent recurrences of ear mites could mean that your pet's vitality level is low. Improved nutrition will help to prevent incidences of ear mites, and can help in recovery. Increasing Garlic and brewer's yeast in your pet's diet may be helpful.

Eyes

Animals often get irritated eyes, especially in hot, dusty weather or in a polluted city environment. Sometimes a dog or cat will scratch its eye, and bacteria may cause an infection in the wound. Infections should be dealt with by your veterinarian. Also, see your vet if there is any blood in the eye or if some object such as a splinter is stuck in your pet's eye.

Minor scratches of your pet's eyes may not even be visible, though tearing, blinking, and your pet's general display of discomfort may indicate that a scratch has occurred. Doubling your pet's daily intake of vitamin E and adding cod liver oil to its diet may speed up the healing process.

Parasites, External

Particular vitamins, especially those of the B-complex, seem to work to increase vigor and help to build resistance to skin diseases and external parasites. A nutritional yeast supplement in your pet's food is a valuable source of these vitamins. In addition to being one of the richest sources of the B-vitamins, it supplies as much protein in a heaping tablespoon as does one egg. If you detect external parasites on your pet or when you know that a pest season is approaching, double the amount of yeast supplement in the diet. A further preventive measure to discourage parasites is the use of Flea Repellent Sleep Pillows that you make yourself, and an Herbal Flea Powder. Ingredients and instructions for both follow.

■ Flea Repellent Sleep Pillows

Herbs may be used cut or whole.

For cats
2 parts Pennyroyal
1 part Catnip
1 part Camomile

For dogs
2 parts Pennyroyal
1 part Thyme
1 part Wormwood

Mix together enough herbs to stuff a 2-foot-square pillow for a cat, or a 3-foot-square (or larger) pillow for a dog. Sew the pillowcase out of a tough, washable fabric such as denim.

■ Herbal Flea Powder

Use the herbs in powdered form only.

2 ounces Pennyroyal
1 ounce Wormwood
1 ounce Rosemary
1 teaspoon Cayenne pepper

Mix herbs together and store in a container. Use as often as you would any other flea powder and rub well into the skin. Be sure to keep the powder away from pets's eyes to avoid severely irritating them.

Parasites, Internal

Expel internal parasites, such as roundworms and pinworms, with one of two specific formulations that emphasize Garlic or Wormwood (any variety but *Artemisia absinthium*, which can be harmful).

Follow with a pure, wholesome diet with a preponderance of chopped, raw foods. At this point, add to the diet Pumpkin seeds, which have a vermifugal action, and Slippery Elm bark, which soothes irritated intestinal tissues. Avoid milk products and heavy meat meals for a week following worming.

■ Garlic Treatment for Internal Parasites of Pets

Fast the animal for 24 hours and bury all feces. Give an enema with a strong infusion of Catnip and Thyme in a child-size bulb syringe. Every hour, feed large quantities of fresh garlic, either chopped and hidden in a small amount of meat or eased down the animal's throat in small chunks or whole cloves. Give a dose of Castor oil at night.

■ Wormwood Treatment for Internal Parasites of Pets

Mix equal parts of powdered Wormwood, Thyme, and Garlic, and pack into size 0 gelatin capsules. Give 1 capsule for every 10 pounds of body weight at 4-hour intervals during the day. Give a mild laxative (Castor oil or milk of magnesia) morning and evening of the treatment day. Give a soothing Catnip enema after bowel movement.

Sores and Abscesses

Abrasions, sores, and abscesses are common in pets that are allowed to run free. Cats especially suffer from them. An abscess is a collection of pus under the skin, surrounded by red, inflamed tissue, usually caused by a scratch or bite that has become infected.

For infections, start with the Cleansing Tonic (page 165) to purify the bloodstream by helping the body throw off the poisons. Then use the following fomentation. The heat of the fomentation will help bring the infection to the surface, and if a scab is present, it will come loose easily and the wound will drain. After the wound has been opened and drained, sprinkle on Antibacterial Powder (page 165).

■ Antiseptic Fomentation

The herbs in this recipe can be fresh or dried, whole or cut.

1 part Camomile
1 part Comfrey root
1 part Red Clover
1 part Thyme

Mix herbs together. Make a strong infusion, dip a muslin or wool cloth into the hot liquid, and apply to the sore or inflamed area. Keep the fomentation hot and apply repeatedly.

Sprains and Rheumatism

Many pets suffer from the same type of rheumatic pain as humans do, and the treatment is similar. Add Alfalfa tablets, Rosemary, Devil's Claw, and Rooibos to the diet as internal treatment. Externally, use herbal rubs and tinctures.

■ Rosemary Rub

1 big handful fresh or dried Rosemary
3 cups water
essential oil of Rosemary (optional)

Simmer herbs in water in a tightly covered saucepan 20 minutes, then let them steep 2 hours. Dip a muslin cloth in the warm liquid, and apply it to the affected limbs. A few drops of essential oil of Rosemary may be added to the brew to give it strength and penetration, if desired.

Cleanliness

A clean animal will generally be a healthy animal. Brush cats and dogs daily to remove loose hair and flakes of dry skin. Sprinkle pets with Herbal Flea Powder (page 168) once a week, and give them a bath once a month with Rosemary Castile Soap (below).

To sanitize feces- or urine-spotted rugs or other fabrics, use Rosemary Spot Remover (below). Not only will it help remove the spots, but the smell will deter the animal from using the same area again.

■ Rosemary Castile Soap

1 bar castile soap, grated
3 ounces strong Rosemary infusion

Melt the soap in the top of a double boiler, add the Rosemary brew, and stir until incorporated. Pour the liquid soap into a wide-mouthed container and let it set. This soap will deter fleas, keep the skin clean, and give the coat a healthy shine.

■ Rosemary Spot Remover

1 bar castile soap, grated
1 ounce Rosemary oil
1 ounce alcohol

Melt the soap in the top of a double boiler, add the oil and alcohol, and stir until well blended. Pour into a wide-mouthed container and let it set. Use as you would any other soap.

Part III Natural Convenience Foods

Carol Meinhardt Hopkins

Shopping for food can be a harrowing experience these days. Beleaguered by extraordinary advertising claims, irresistible packaging, and children begging you to bring home the latest breakfast cereal to hit the shelves, you really have to keep your wits about you to make intelligent buying decisions. Even then, you may be apprehensive about the synthetic additives that are put into your food. And in these days of rising costs when food prices may jump as much as a whopping 15 percent in a single year, getting the best quality and the most quantity for the fewest dollars is always a challenge for the conscientious shopper.

Convenience foods make up about half of the food purchased for consumption at home. They also contain most of the chemical adulterants that pervade our food supply. Consider the convenience foods you can buy—frozen fruits, vegetables, and appetizers; canned foods; bakery-made desserts; snack foods; and dry mixes of every kind. These foods contain laboratory-produced preservatives, thickeners, thinners, bleaching agents, emulsifiers, artificial colors and flavors, and even boosters to replace the nutrients that are lost in food processing. Approximately 2,500 new substances appear yearly to add to an overall recorded total of 20,000. Chemical names on package labels have become so commonplace that some buyers do not even question the terms that they see with such regularity. They often assume that ingredients so widely used can't be all that bad.

So-called natural additives also play an important part in commercial convenience foods. A few are advantageous—iodine, for instance, prevents goiter—while others serve merely to make food more attractive to the consumers' tastes (that is, more marketable). Of this group of "naturals," sugar and salt head up the list.

Sugar is a highly processed carbohydrate that contributes nothing but calories. Nonetheless, it appears in virtually every kind of prepared food, from baby products to breakfast cereals. Some cereals contain more sugar per ounce than a candy bar. Salt, the other leading offender, sometimes acts as a preservative, but it is used in most processed foods primarily for taste. Instead of the ½ teaspoon of salt that provides the necessary amount of sodium for one day, the average person consumes about 3 teaspoons—not just from the salt shaker but from commercial food products of every conceivable kind. Unless you specifically seek out sodium-free foods, you will be consuming large quantities of sodium in potato chips, cottage cheese, hard cheeses, bouillon cubes, canned soups, even in puddings and breads.

Food companies depend upon a gullible buying public to keep them alive. In 1976, for example, the industry produced 6,300 "new" products, most of which were only modifications of existing ones. Along with the charge for someone else's labor to assemble these substances, you pick up the cost for mass advertising and some elaborate packaging. You also pay dearly for the development of ideas for pastries that pop up out of the toaster, prerolled cookie dough to slice and bake, and dinners to boil in plastic pouches.

Making convenience foods at home requires no special equipment or utensils apart from those you use in everyday food preparation. A food processor or blender will facilitate the chopping of certain substances, but neither is essential. For the soup mixes, we used a simple, commercial electric food dryer, but in lieu of this, you can dry foods in the sun or in an oven.*

Part of the convenience of these foods you make at home lies in the storage. Most common kitchen containers and ordinary wrappers that you probably have on hand will do. Plastic containers and glass jars with tight-fitting lids and sandwich and freezer bags will all be useful. In addition, keep on hand twist-ties or rubber bands, masking tape, and a permanent marking pen. The last two items will be especially important in helping you keep track of exactly what is inside those sealed packages in your freezer.

The ingredients in your mixes will help you determine where and for how long to store them. In general, keep foods made of all dry ingredients in a cool, dark place, in the refrigerator, or in the freezer. Store them for no longer than six to eight months. If you have cut shortening into the dry ingredients, you *must* keep them refrigerated or frozen. The same time period for storage applies. Piecrusts, breads, and most dishes you follow through to completion will store best in the freezer. Piecrusts and breads lose some of their taste and texture if frozen longer than three to four months.

*You can build your own solar food dryer, using the *Solar Food Dryer* book, part of the Rodale Plans series.

Chapter 11 Quick Classic Baking Mixes

"Homemade baked goods"—the phrase itself is enough to conjure up memories of homemade bread fresh out of the oven. But how many people have time to bake bread "from scratch" anymore? And what about the other baked goods (perhaps not as basic as bread but just as good when they are freshly made) like cakes, cookies, puddings, and pies? Fortunately, there are convenience mixes for all of these foods, so we can still enjoy baked goods even when we are pressed for time.

In the time that it would normally take to make one cake from start to finish, you can get together the dry ingredients for ten cakes. Then, whenever you get the urge, you can whip up a cake batter and have a dessert in the oven in less than 10 minutes. That's only the beginning. Almost any of the classic baked goods—cookies, muffins, piecrusts, yeast breads, and corn breads—many of which you may have dismissed as too time-consuming for your schedule, lend themselves easily to this make-a-mix cookery.

The Best Ingredients

If making your own baking mixes appeals to you, you may want to consult the following annotated list to make sure that your larder is well stocked. We recommend that you shop in natural foods stores, where whole-grain flours and unrefined sweeteners and oils are more commonly seen than in supermarkets.

Flavorings

Special tastes that distinguish one baked item from another are real vanilla extract, spices such as cloves and cinnamon, carob powder, fruits, cheese, and the flavors of particular vegetables (like onions and carrots).

Flours

Cornmeal Cornmeal is stone-ground from corn and is used in conjunction with wheat flour in breads and muffins for taste, texture, and nutritional value. Store in the refrigerator or freezer.

Soy Flour See Nutritional Supplements (below).

Whole Wheat Flour (bread flour) This flour is stone-ground from hard wheat containing a high proportion of the protein complex, gluten, which is so essential for causing bread doughs to rise and creating the texture of the finished product. Store in the refrigerator or freezer.

Whole Wheat Pastry Flour Finely stone-ground from soft wheat, whole wheat pastry flour is low in gluten. It is primarily used for cakes, cookies, and pastry doughs. Store in refrigerator or freezer.

Leavening Agents

Baking Powder Baking powder, a combination of sodium bicarbonate and cream of tartar, is used to increase the volume and tenderness of baked goods. Check the ingredients to be sure that it's an aluminum-free product.

Baking Soda Baking soda, or sodium bicarbonate, is used to increase the volume and tenderness of baked goods and to alkalize acid mediums, such as those containing sour cream, buttermilk, or yogurt.

Cream of Tartar This is a substance that is found in grape juice after fermentation. When used with baking soda it produces carbon dioxide to leaven batters. It is also sometimes used when beating egg whites to help hold their shape.

Eggs Beaten yolks and whipped whites incorporate large amounts of air into the batter and, therefore, act as leaveners.

Yeast Use dry yeast granules instead of the moist cakes; they are easier to dissolve and stay fresh longer. Store unrefrigerated for no longer than six months.

Liquids

Liquids such as milk, buttermilk, sour cream, water, and orange juice provide distinctive tastes and nutritional bonuses and aid in the development of gluten, which is not released until activated by a liquid.

Miscellaneous Ingredients

Such foods as dry rolled oats, a variety of unsalted and raw nuts, and unsweetened coconut supply texture and add bulk and flavor to many baked goods.

Natural Sweeteners

Blackstrap Molasses This is a highly nutritious, concentrated sweetener; 1 tablespoon supplies as much calcium as one glass of milk and as much iron as nine eggs. Blackstrap molasses also contains a generous amount of most B-vitamins.

Honey Honey is a natural, highly concentrated sweetener. Choose raw, unfiltered honey—refined honey often has water added to it.

Malt Malt is concentrated sugar from dry-roasted, sweet grain sprouts; read How to Make Malt (see Index) for information on how to make your own.

Nutritional Supplements

Blackstrap Molasses See Natural Sweeteners (above).

Brewer's Yeast This is an inexpensive, nonleavening nutritional yeast, rich in the B-vitamin complex, protein, and minerals. It is sold as "nutritional yeast," "primary yeast food," and more recently, as "good-tasting nutritional yeast," a more palatable form grown on molasses. Store any of the above yeasts in the refrigerator or freezer.

Powdered Milk Powdered milk is whole or nonfat milk removed from its liquids, and is a good source of supplemental protein and calcium. It comes in both instant and noninstant types. The noninstant has a slight edge in nutritional value but not enough to outweigh the convenience of the instant. If you choose to buy the noninstant, keep in mind that it does not dissolve as easily in liquid as the instant does. You may even have to use a blender to achieve a smooth liquid; the noninstant should be stored in the refrigerator or freezer, while the instant can be stored on the shelf.

Soy Flour Soy flour is a high-protein legume flour that supplies certain amino acids not found in wheat flour. Store in the refrigerator or freezer.

Wheat Germ This is an excellent source of protein, iron, vitamin E, and the B-complex. Store in the refrigerator or freezer.

Shortenings

Butter Butter is a highly saturated fat that produces a very flaky, tender pastry and rich batters. To use butter in recipes calling for oil, use one-sixth more butter than the amount of oil called for in the recipe.

Oil We recommend an unrefined vegetable oil, such as safflower, for most baking, because it has a subtle taste and is low in saturated fat. To use oil in a recipe calling for butter, use one-sixth less oil than the amount of butter called for in the recipe.

Bread Mix

If you are the baker in your household, you know what an investment of time and love goes into producing homemade bread. You are also aware of the return you get for your efforts. When those crusty loaves turn out just right, you are sure to receive your family's warmest accolades. After all, what smells and tastes better than freshly baked dough, and what gives more pleasure to others than the knowledge that you expended this energy just for them?

use a portion of the mix and add yeast, shortening, more flour, and the liquid ingredients. This dough adapts well to other purposes. As the variations in our recipe indicate, you can also shape it into dinner rolls or pizza dough.

Many never-ruffled cooks who appear to have time to bake while also preparing meals practice the following shortcut, based on the fact that unbaked bread dough freezes well. Follow this simple method, and you, too, can carry warm loaves to the table whenever you choose.

Wrap and freeze loaves in their pans before the last rising. About 2 hours before mealtime, remove dough from freezer and allow it to reach room temperature, then complete its last rising. Bake as recipe directions instruct.

The way we look at it, if you're going to give any part of yourself to this bread-baking project, the result should be the best-tasting, most nutritious product available. While you're assembling the ingredients, mixing and kneading the dough, and watching it grow, you may as well feel confident that it will sustain and nourish your family. For these reasons, we have put together a recipe fortified with calcium, B-vitamins, iron, and protein through the addition of such foods as soy flour, wheat germ, and powdered milk.

The different between this bread and most store-bought versions is that it includes natural supplements in addition to whole-grain flour. Most commercial breads contain refined white flour from which at least 12 substances essential to health have been largely removed in the milling. Only a portion is returned in "enrichment" and then only with synthetic boosters. Stone-ground whole-grain flour, on the other hand, is minimally milled and still contains all the properties of the original grain along with the rich, satisfying flavor of a real food. Baked in your own kitchen, your bread can be the absolute finest you'll find anywhere.

■ High-Protein Bread Mix

This bread mix improves upon the Cornell formula, which was developed to enrich white flour.

10 cups whole wheat flour
¼ cup wheat germ
½ cup soy flour
⅔ cup instant powdered milk

Combine above ingredients and store in refrigerator or freezer in tightly closed container. The mix can be kept for up to 1 year.

Yield: about 11½ cups

■ High-Protein Bread

Each portion of the dough will make 1 loaf of wholesome bread in a 8 × 4-inch pan, 12 crescent rolls, or 2 thin-and-crispy pizza crusts.

1¼ cups warm water
2 teaspoons yeast
1 teaspoon honey
1 tablespoon oil
1 tablespoon honey
3¼ cups High-Protein Bread Mix (above)

Combine water, yeast, and 1 teaspoon honey in large bowl. Allow to stand 10 minutes or until frothy. Add the oil, 1 tablespoon honey, and 2¾ cups of the bread mix, and mix 5 minutes, using a stationary electric mixer or a dough hook, if you have one.

Remove dough from bowl and place on a wooden board with the remaining ½ cup of bread mix. Knead bread mix into dough for 5 minutes. Shape dough into a ball and allow to rise in a greased, covered bowl in a warm place 15 minutes.

Remove dough from bowl and push into well-buttered 8 × 4-inch pan. The dough will almost fill the pan. Allow the bread to rise in a warm place until it is even with the top of the pan, 15 to 20 minutes.

Bake in preheated 375°F oven 45 to 50 minutes. To test for doneness, rap the bottom of the loaf with your fist—it should sound hollow.

To make crescent rolls, after allowing dough ball to rise, roll dough into a 12-inch circle and cut into 12 pie-shaped pieces. Roll up each piece from wide end to point. Place, point down, on a buttered baking sheet, and curve slightly into a crescent shape. Allow rolls to rise according to the directions above. Bake the rolls at 375°F 20 to 25 minutes.

After baking, remove bread or rolls from the pans, and allow to cool before storing them.

When making pizza crusts, divide dough in half and roll out each portion to fit a 13-inch, round pizza pan. Put desired toppings on, and bake at 400°F 15 to 20 minutes (the time will vary depending upon the amount of topping that is used). Remove pizzas from oven and serve immediately.

All-Purpose Baking Mixes

You'll be surprised at how many of these baked items will become a familiar sight on your table once you start using the master mixes below. For the greatest convenience, we suggest cutting the shortening right into the dry ingredients so that close to mealtime you will have nothing more to do than mix in the liquids and bake. To insure freshness, store the mixes in an airtight container in the refrigerator or freezer no longer than 8 months.

■ Multipurpose Baking Mix

9 cups whole wheat pastry flour
1½ cups instant powdered milk
3 tablespoons baking powder
2 teaspoons cream of tartar
1 teaspoon baking soda
1½ cups cold butter

Combine all ingredients, except butter, in a large bowl. Cut in butter until it is evenly distributed and the pieces are the size of small peas.

Yield: 12¼ cups

■ Biscuits

2 cups Multipurpose Baking Mix (above)
½ cup water

Preheat oven to 425°F. Put baking mix into a large bowl. Add water and stir until a stiff dough forms. Allow it to rest 5 minutes. On a floured surface, roll dough to a ½-inch thickness and cut out 2-inch circles. Bake them on an ungreased cookie sheet 10 to 12 minutes or until lightly browned.

Yield: 12 biscuits

Variations:

■ Buttermilk Biscuits
Substitute ½ cup buttermilk for water.

■ Cheese Biscuits
Add ¾ cup grated sharp cheddar cheese to baking mix before adding liquid.

■ Onion Biscuits
With liquid ingredients, add ½ cup coarsely chopped, sauteed onions.

■ Muffins

¾ cup cold water
1 egg
2 tablespoons honey
2½ cups Multipurpose Baking Mix (above)

Preheat oven to 400°F. In a large bowl, beat together water, egg, and honey. Add baking mix and stir until ingredients are just moistened. Fill greased muffin tins ⅔ full. Bake about 20 minutes or until muffins are nicely browned.

Yield: 12 muffins

[Continued on next page]

Variations:

- Blueberry Muffins
  Add 1 cup fresh blueberries with liquid ingredients.
- Date-Nut Muffins
  Add ¼ cup each finely chopped dates and nuts with liquid ingredients.
- Cranberry Muffins
  Add ⅔ cup chopped, fresh cranberries with liquid ingredients.

■ Pancakes

3 cups water
2 eggs
4 cups Multipurpose Baking Mix (above)

Begin warming pancake griddle over medium-low heat. In a large bowl, beat together water and eggs. Add baking mix and stir just until baking mix is moistened. Lightly oil griddle. Increase heat to medium. Ladle batter onto it to form 4-inch circles. Turn pancakes as soon as bubbles form on top side. Cook quickly on second side, and remove immediately to warm serving plates.

Yield: 20 4-inch pancakes

■ Coffee Cake

¾ cup sour cream
⅓ cup honey
2 eggs
2 cups Multipurpose Baking Mix (above)

Streusel topping
⅓ cup honey
½ cup chopped walnuts
1 tablespoon carob powder
1 teaspoon cinnamon

Preheat oven to 375°F. In a large bowl, beat together sour cream, honey, and eggs. Add baking mix and stir until all ingredients are well combined. In a smaller bowl, combine ingredients for streusel topping. Spread half the cake batter into a greased 8-inch-square pan. Spread the topping over the batter, then spread the remaining batter on top. Swirl a knife back and forth through the batter to distribute the topping and create a marble effect. Bake 35 to 40 minutes or until a fork comes out clean.

Yield: 1 8-inch-square cake

■ Shortcake

3 tablespoons honey
½ cup milk
1 egg, beaten
3¼ cups Multipurpose Baking Mix (above)
2 tablespoons butter, melted

Preheat oven to 425°F. In a large bowl combine honey, milk, and egg. Add baking mix and stir until everything is just moistened. Turn dough out onto a floured surface and knead about 30 seconds. Then, roll it to a ½-inch thickness and cut it into an equal number of 2½- and 3-inch rounds. Brush the larger ones with melted butter and place a smaller one on top of each. Put the cakes on an ungreased cookie sheet and prick the tops with a fork. Bake 12 to 15 minutes or until shortcakes are nicely browned.

Yield: 5 or 6 double shortcakes

■ Cornmeal Baking Mix

4 cups cornmeal
3 cups whole wheat pastry flour
1½ cups instant powdered milk
½ cup soy flour
½ cup wheat germ
¼ cup baking powder
1½ cups cold butter

In a large bowl, combine all ingredients except butter. Cut in butter until it is evenly distributed and the pieces are the size of small peas.

Yield: 11¼ cups

■ Corn Bread

4½ cups Cornmeal Baking Mix (above)
2 eggs, beaten
1⅓ cups water

Preheat oven to 425°F. Combine all ingredients and stir until the baking mix is just moistened. Pour batter into a greased 8-inch-square pan. Bake about 25 minutes or until a fork inserted into the center of the bread comes out clean. Cut into 8 pieces.

Yield: 8 pieces

■ Cornmeal Drop Biscuits

½ cup water
2 tablespoons honey (optional)
2 cups Cornmeal Baking Mix (above)

Preheat oven to 425°F. Combine water with honey, if desired. Add liquid to baking mix to form a soft dough. Drop by tablespoonfuls onto a greased baking sheet. Bake 10 to 12 minutes or until a fork inserted in the center comes out clean.

Yield: 12 biscuits

■ Cornmeal Muffins

2¼ cups Cornmeal Baking Mix (above)
1 egg, beaten
⅔ cup water

Preheat oven to 425°F. Combine all ingredients and stir just enough to moisten baking mix. Fill buttered or papered muffin tins ⅔ full. Bake about 18 minutes or until a fork inserted in the center comes out clean.

Yield: 12 muffins

Cake Mixes

For most people, just the suggestion of a homemade cake is enough to bring on a smile and a warm memory of some happy occasion. Once you get into the habit of making delicious desserts from your own convenience mixes, you won't need to wait for special events to light up faces around your house. In about the same amount of time it takes to pack lunches, you can whip together the batter for a first-rate birthday cake that's equally appropriate for other occasions—lunch-box snack, dinner dessert, or after-school treat. Since you will be using high-quality ingredients, you won't have to worry about your family's intake of sugary, empty foods. You can feel confident that the whole-grain flours, eggs, milk powder supplements, unrefined oils, and natural flavorings in these mixes and recipes are the basis of top-notch nourishment.

Most of these cakes are pleasing either all by themselves or with a few simple adornments. A dollop of homemade whipped cream, a smear of your own jelly, or a sprinkle of freshly grated coconut on each piece satisfies most people quite well. If you want more of a traditional icing, a good natural foods cookbook will give you some ideas. One easy combination that we find goes well on almost any of the cakes below is a mixture of equal parts of fresh butter and cream cheese flavored with a little honey, vanilla extract, and lemon rind, all to taste.

All of the following recipes call for oil as shortening. If you prefer a richer cake, substitute butter for the oil and increase the amount by one-sixth. If you are using glass pans, lower the oven temperature by 25°F. Store any of these mixes in a tightly capped container, preferably in the refrigerator or freezer, for up to eight months.

■ Basic Whole Wheat Cake Mix

16½ cups whole wheat pastry flour
½ cup plus 1 tablespoon baking powder
2 cups instant powdered milk

Sift together the flour and baking powder. Thoroughly mix in the milk powder.

Yield: about 20 cups

■ Homemade Vanilla Cake

3¼ cups Basic Whole Wheat Cake Mix (above)
¾ cup honey
⅔ cup water
½ cup oil
3 eggs
1 teaspoon vanilla extract

Preheat oven to 350°F. Place cake mix in a large bowl and add remaining ingredients. Beat with an electric mixer at slow-to-medium speed 2 minutes or by hand 3 minutes. Scrape the sides of the bowl frequently. Pour batter into greased and floured pans, either two 8-inch round pans, or a 13 × 9 × 2-inch pan. Bake 30 to 35 minutes or until a toothpick inserted in the center comes out clean. Cool cakes 10 minutes before turning out onto racks.

Yield: 2 8-inch cakes or 1 13 × 9 × 2-inch cake

Variations:

■ Carrot Cake

After batter is completed, stir in 2 cups raw, shredded carrots, 1 cup raisins, 1 cup coarsely chopped nuts, and 1 teaspoon cinnamon. Proceed as with regular recipe.

■ Raisin-Spice Cake

To the dry ingredients, add 1 teaspoon cinnamon, ½ teaspoon allspice, and ¼ teaspoon powdered cloves. Before baking, stir ½ cup raisins into the batter. Proceed as with regular recipe.

[*Continued on next page*]

■ Cranberry-Pineapple Upside-Down Cake

After batter is completed, stir in 1 tablespoon orange rind. In a separate bowl, combine 1½ cups chopped fresh cranberries, 1 cup drained, crushed pineapple, and 2 tablespoons honey. Spoon this mixture into the bottom of a 13 × 9 × 2-inch cake pan. Pour the batter over the topping, then proceed as with regular recipe.

■ Carob Cake Mix

14 cups whole wheat pastry flour
3 tablespoons baking soda
6 cups light carob powder, sifted
3 cups instant powdered milk

Sift together the flour and baking soda. Thoroughly mix in the carob and milk powders.

Yield: about 23 cups

■ Homemade Carob Cake

4 cups Carob Cake Mix (above)
1¼ cups water
¾ cup honey
¾ cup oil
2 eggs
1½ teaspoons vanilla extract

Repeat exactly the directions under Homemade Vanilla Cake (above).

Variations:

■ Coconut Carob Cake

After batter is completed, stir in ¾ cup desiccated coconut. Then, proceed as with regular recipe.

■ Citrus Carob Cake

Add 2 tablespoons grated orange or other citrus rind to the dry ingredients. Proceed as with regular recipe.

■ Nut-Raisin Carob Cake

After batter is completed, add ½ cup each coarsely chopped nuts and raisins. Proceed as with regular recipe.

Cookie Mixes

Cookies are very much a part of our culture. In many families, they are the common lunch-box dessert, after-school snack, and before-bed treat. Unfortunately, most commercial cookies (even adorable animal-shaped ones) have little, if anything, going for them nutritionally. Unless you've discovered some exceptional person who is baking and selling a high-quality product, if you want nutritional cookies, you'll have to make them yourself.

Starting out with a homemade convenience mix with the butter already cut in makes producing a batch of warm, fragrant cookies child's play. You can make up a quantity of the mix when you have a free 15 minutes. When you're ready to bake, you can add the liquids and put your dough on cookie sheets in no time. Store these mixes in the refrigerator or freezer for no longer than eight months.

■ Basic Oatmeal Cookie Mix

6 cups whole wheat pastry flour
¼ cup baking powder
2 cups instant powdered milk
5 cups rolled oats, broken slightly in a blender or food processor
2 cups room-temperature butter

In a large bowl, sift together the flour and baking powder. Add the powdered milk and oats and mix well. Cut the butter into these dry ingredients until it is very evenly distributed. Store in refrigerator or freezer.

Yield: about 15 cups

■ Oatmeal Drop Cookies

3½ cups Basic Oatmeal Cookie Mix (above)
1 teaspoon cinnamon
1 egg
⅓ cup honey
¼ cup water
1½ teaspoons vanilla extract

Preheat oven to 350°F. In a large bowl, toss oatmeal mix and cinnamon. In a separate bowl, stir together egg, honey, water, and vanilla. Add to oatmeal mixture and combine thoroughly. Drop batter by teaspoonfuls onto buttered cookie sheets. Bake about 12 minutes or until a toothpick inserted in the cookies comes out clean.

Yield: about 2½ dozen cookies

Variations:

■ Raisin Oatmeal Cookies

To dry ingredients, add ¼ cup coarsely chopped sunflower seeds and ½ cup finely chopped raisins. Proceed as with regular recipe.

[*Continued on next page*]

■ Applesauce-Oatmeal Cookies

To dry ingredients, add ¼ teaspoon each powdered cloves, grated nutmeg, and baking soda and mix in thoroughly. Substitute ½ cup applesauce for the water in the liquid ingredients. Proceed as with regular recipe.

■ Basic Cookie Mix

9 cups whole wheat pastry flour
¼ cup baking powder
1 tablespoon cinnamon
2 cups cold butter

In a large bowl, sift together the flour, baking powder, and cinnamon. Cut the butter into the dry ingredients until it is very evenly distributed. Store in refrigerator or freezer.

Yield: about 11 cups

■ Drop Cookies

½ cup honey
1 egg
1 teaspoon vanilla extract
¼ cup water
2½ cups Basic Cookie Mix (above)

Preheat oven to 350°F. In a large bowl, mix honey, egg, vanilla, and water. Thoroughly combine this mixture with the cookie mix. Drop batter by teaspoonfuls onto buttered cookie sheets. Bake about 12 minutes or until a toothpick inserted in the center of cookies comes out clean.

Yield: about 2½ dozen cookies

Variations:

■ Carob-Spice Cookies

To cookie mix, add 3 tablespoons sifted carob powder, ¼ teaspoon grated nutmeg, and ¼ teaspoon powdered cloves. Then proceed with regular recipe.

■ Peanut Butter Cookies

Substitute 1 cup unsalted peanut butter (creamy- or chunky-style) for water in liquid ingredients. Thoroughly combine it with the mixture. Then proceed as with regular recipe. Before baking, flatten cookies and make the traditional crisscross pattern on top of each with the tines of a fork.

Delectable Pies and Puddings

The combination of an appropriate crust and any one of a number of sweet fillings is the essence of a dessert pie. The choice of those fillings is, of course, up to the discretion of the cook. The most typical ones are fruit centers, custards, and creams.

Cream pies are a favorite among busy homemakers for a number of good reasons. First, each starts with a simple, foolproof pudding to which other ingredients and flavorings are added. And the crust almost never becomes soggy, since the filling goes into a completely baked shell. After the filling has been added the pie requires no more than a moderate amount of chilling. An additional bonus to preparing cream pies is that decorating them is always a fun job. They go nicely with a whole array of fancy, yet rather effortless toppings—a layer of homemade whipped cream or fresh fruit slices or dollops of sour cream.

Cream pies are easy to make, but we have some suggestions for making them even easier. The first one involves preparing piecrust-dough mixes and piecrust-dough balls in advance, and freezing them until you want to use them. The other entails making up dry pie filling mixes that you reconstitute after baking the crust. With these tricks of the trade in hand, you'll be surprised at how simple it is to prepare delicious, homemade pies.

Piecrust Mixes—Some Basics

The crust often makes the difference between the success or failure of a pie. In general, a rolled crust made from basic ingredients—flour, water, and shortening—should be light, crisp, and flaky. It should be tender enough to break easily but not so delicate as to crumble when cut. Pressed crusts made from such foods as oats and nuts will have a much different texture, of course, but like any other filling casing, they should never be soggy.

Proper ingredients also play an important part in superior piecrusts—both in taste and food value. In some of these mixes, we use whole wheat pastry flour made from finely ground, soft, whole wheat. It produces a tender pastry, somewhat coarser and darker than one made with white flour. You benefit because the bran and the germ of the wheat are still intact. For shortening, we use either butter or oil. Some other ingredients that provide texture, taste, and nutrition are soy flour, wheat germ, coconut, and nuts. In order to ensure freshness, store these doughs or mixes in the refrigerator or freezer.

Certain preparation techniques also help to ensure perfect crusts. Pressed ones are fairly easy to deal with, and for this reason, beginners often start with this type. After pressing them to the bottom and sides of the pan, a little tamping with a cup or glass is usually all of the fussing you need do.

Thinner, flakier rolled crusts require a little more expertise. There is one major rule to remember when working with them: Never overhandle the dough. Quickly combine oil or butter with the flour, and work rapidly so that the oil or butter remains suspended in small particles in the flour. In the same vein, use only ice water, and add it gradually to the flour and oil or butter mixture. Stop as soon as a doughlike consistency forms. Too little water results in a dough that crumbles and falls apart; too much makes a sticky substance that is hard to roll and causes the finished crust to be tough.

Make sure that the dough is well chilled when you get ready to roll it, and avoid incorporating any additional flour into the substance. To overcome sticking, roll the dough between two sheets of wax paper or two linen tea towels. You can store the towels, unwashed, in a plastic bag in the freezer and use them again the next time you bake.

If your tale of woe is that your prebaked crusts shrink to small disks in the oven, there are steps you can take to prevent the problem. Roll the dough larger than your pie plate to prevent stretching it just to fit the pan. Gently drape the circle over the surface of the pan, press it into the corners, and make a heavy, fluted edge all around the rim. Prick holes in the crust every inch or so over the bottom with a fork to prevent buckling. You can lay commercial pie beads, pellets, dry beans, or a sheet of aluminum foil over the area to achieve the same result. Bake shells in a preheated 400°F oven anywhere from 10 to 15 minutes, until they are golden brown.

Rolled pie doughs work well with any type of filling. If you plan to use cooked ingredients inside, prebake the shell as directed above before adding the filling.

When making fruit pies that have a top and bottom unbaked crust, bake the filled pie in a preheated 400°F oven 45 minutes to 1 hour.

■ Basic Rolled Piecrust Dough

4 cups whole wheat pastry flour
1½ cups cold butter
1 tablespoon apple cider vinegar
1 egg
¼ cup water

Using a pastry blender or knife, combine flour and butter. Beat vinegar, egg, and water together and combine with flour and butter mixture.

Form the dough into 5 balls (about 7 ounces each). Wrap individually in freezer bags and store in freezer.

When ready to use, defrost about 30 minutes or until dough is easy to roll but still chilled.

Yield: 5 dough balls, each making 1 9-inch piecrust

Variations:

■ Coconut Piecrust Dough

Add ¼ cup desiccated coconut with the flour, and proceed with directions above.

■ Sunflower Seed-Wheat Piecrust Dough

Add ¼ cup finely ground sunflower seeds to the flour, and proceed with directions above.

Pressed Piecrust Dough

Without any special handling techniques, you can make an excellent piecrust with one of these pressed doughs. In lieu of a rolled top crust, you might want to scatter a handful of chopped nuts over the filling or some of the crumbled dough itself mixed with a little nutmeg, cinnamon, and small pieces of cold butter.

■ High-Protein Piecrust Dough

This is a general all-purpose crust, nice for cooked or uncooked fillings. If you plan to use cooked ingredients inside, prebake the shell first, then add contents. With uncooked ingredients, treat as you would any other unbaked dough.

4½ cups whole wheat pastry flour
¾ cup soy flour
¾ cup wheat germ
⅓ cup instant powdered milk
1¼ cups soy oil

Combine both flours, wheat germ, and powdered milk in a large bowl. Pour in 1 cup of the soy oil and toss with a fork until all ingredients are well coated. If the mixture looks dry, use the remaining ¼ cup soy oil. Divide the contents into 6 equal parts and freeze each in a freezer bag.

To use, place 1 ball in a bowl and cut 2 tablespoons of water into it. Transfer mixture to a pie plate and press it with your fingers along the bottom and sides. Fill crust with preferred contents.

Yield: 6 dough balls, each making 1 9-inch piecrust

■ Nutty Piecrust Dough

Although you can use this dough for a baked tart, it seems to stay together best when it is filled with cooked ingredients, then chilled until serving time. See "Puddings and Pie Fillings" (below).

3 cups raw almonds, finely ground
3 cups walnuts, finely chopped
1½ cups pecans, finely chopped
1½ cups sunflower seeds, finely ground
¾ cup honey

Combine all ingredients in a large bowl and mix thoroughly. Divide the mixture into 6 equal parts (about 1½ cups each). Wrap each in a freezer bag and store in refrigerator or freezer.

Yield: 6 packets, each making 1 9-inch piecrust

Puddings and Pie Fillings

Puddings—the dessert kind, or entrees including meat and vegetables—stem from the days when ovens were unreliable appliances. Instead of serving baked dishes, homemakers turned eggs, milk, and flour into a vast array of stove-top puddings for almost every occasion, from daily meals to holiday fare.

In general, modern menus do not emphasize many egg-and-milk-based main dishes or desserts, and for this reason many cooks don't know just how easy it is to prepare a pudding from scratch.

One glance at the ingredients in the pudding and pie filling base below will tell you that it is time to get back to basics. Making your own pudding from a homemade mix is extremely simple, quick, convenient, and soundly nutritious. In moments, you can get together a bulk base of instant powdered milk with a portion of cornstarch. When you are ready to make your pudding, you can add other healthful ingredients, such as whole eggs, unrefined honey, blackstrap molasses, and a few favorite tastes and textures, like nuts, coconut, and raisins. Starting from your own mix, you should be able to cook up a smooth, luscious pudding in 20 minutes.

Once pudding desserts catch on at your house, you will discover that they have a variety of purposes. They provide an effortless way to encourage the children to eat some high-protein food. Pack up individual servings in thermal lunch-box containers for school. Leave dishes of them in the refrigerator for after-school snacks. They are also the bases for some special desserts. Spread them between layers of homemade sponge cake and top with some fresh fruit for an easy but elegant after-dinner treat. Mound them in pie shells and crown the contents with some freshly whipped cream and a dash of nutmeg. As you find other ways to use puddings, you'll also discover how well they fit the term *convenience food* in their versatility and easy preparation.

■ Pudding-Pie Filling Base

6 cups instant powdered milk
1 cup plus 2 tablespoons cornstarch

Thoroughly blend ingredients and store in a tightly capped container. Since this mix is made with instant powdered milk, it can be stored in your kitchen cabinet. You may also keep it in the refrigerator or freezer if you wish.

Yield: about 7 cups

■ Vanilla Pudding

2 cups water
1 cup plus 3 tablespoons Pudding-Pie Filling Base (above)
¼ cup honey
2 egg yolks, beaten
1 teaspoon vanilla extract
1 tablespoon butter

Put water in a heavy-bottom saucepan or the top of a double boiler, and slowly add pudding base. Add honey. Stirring constantly to prevent scorching, bring mixture just to a boil, then reduce heat to simmer. Cook until pudding is thickened and coats a spoon, 10 to 15 minutes.

Blend a small amount of the hot pudding mixture into the beaten egg yolks, then stir this liquid back into the pan. Simmer 1 minute longer. Remove from heat. Mix in vanilla and butter until butter melts. Pour pudding into dessert dishes or a piecrust, and allow to cool before garnishing. Cover with pieces of waxed paper to prevent a film from forming on the top of the pudding.

(You may want to give the two leftover egg whites from this recipe to your friendly feline—they are a great source of albumin.)

Yield: 4 dessert servings or filling for 1 9-inch piecrust.

Variations:

■ Vanilla-Raisin Pudding

Add ⅓ cup coarsely chopped raisins with vanilla and butter.

■ Molasses-Walnut Pudding

Substitute ¼ cup molasses for the honey, and stir in ⅓ cup coarsely chopped walnuts with vanilla and butter.

■ Carob Pudding

Mix 3 tablespoons carob powder with Pudding-Pie Filling Base. Proceed with directions.

■ Banana-Coconut Cream Pie

Here's an old standard with a few modern touches. Starting with a homemade pudding mix and a premade piecrust dough, you can whip up a scrumptious dessert offering in moments.

2–3 ripe bananas
1 tablespoon lemon juice
1 9-inch piecrust made from Basic Rolled Piecrust Dough (page 188), prebaked
¼ teaspoon almond extract
½ cup desiccated coconut
1 recipe Vanilla Pudding (above), chilled
½ pint heavy cream, whipped

Peel and slice bananas. (Use a stainless steel knife to avoid discoloration.) Place banana slices in bowl and toss with lemon juice. Then place them in baked piecrust. The bottom should be covered completely.

Mix almond extract and coconut into pudding, and cover bananas with mixture. Chill several hours before serving. Garnish with whipped cream.

Yield: 1 9-inch pie

Chapter 12 Herbal Blends and Sprouts

Certain foods almost cry out for particular herbs and spices. Most tomato and cheese combinations, for instance, depend upon sweet basil for their special taste. Spaghetti sauce rarely arrives at the table without the distinctive flavor of oregano. Dill and fennel go part and parcel with a number of fish dishes, and rosemary and mint are practically first cousins to roast lamb.

In this country, most people have come to appreciate the tastes and smells of a vast array of dishes enhanced by particular seasoning blends. Unfortunately, many busy cooks do not have the time to devote to intricate forms of herb cookery and restrict themselves to scattering parsley over the boiled potatoes or throwing a few basic herbs into the vegetable soup pot. Understandably, except for holidays and special occasions, the evening meal often is just plain fare.

One way to put a little more "spice" into everyday meals is to keep on hand a supply of your own prepared seasoning blends and coating mixes. With a variety of them at your fingertips, you need not hesitate to undertake homemade spaghetti sauce one night and baked chicken the next. In addition to the main dishes, you could serve a fresh salad with homemade dressing or turnips in an exotic curry sauce.

Herbs and spices complement many foods and make meals more exciting. Another way to add variety to your meals rather effortlessly is actually to add a new food to your basic dishes. We're talking about sprouts. Raw or lightly cooked, sprouts lend themselves to all sorts of culinary creations—soups, salads, entrees, and side dishes. Their unique tastes and textures aid in determining their place on the menu. Wheat and rice sprouts, for example, are sweet and nutlike. Alfalfa and clover, light and unobtrusive in flavor, easily replace part of the greens in a salad. The distinctive quality of sprouted rye in soups can suggest the chewiness of wild rice. Cress, radish, and mustard sprouts are the peppery ones; they add zing to a bowl of lettuce or a sandwich. Finally, there are the ubiquitous mung and soybean sprouts. Their crisp, substantial nature makes then an attractive part of many oriental meat, fish, or vegetable main dishes.

Sprouts can also satisfy your sweet tooth. When they are dried and ground into a powder, their simple sugars are turned into malt, a sweetener used in both egg creams and beer. You can make your own malt with a formula in this chapter (page 207).

On the following pages, you'll find a number of easy-to-prepare herbal mixes, along with instructions for growing your own sprouts and some good ways to use them in meals. No doubt, in a short time you'll be putting together your own delicious herbal blends and sprouting combinations.

Herbal Blends

Before you start mixing the herbal formula themselves, you should take note of their storage requirements. The general points outlined below will help you make the most of whatever herbs and spices you use.

Once you have mixed up a variety of herb and spice blends, do not be tempted to show off these pleasing groupings of colors and textures (or any of the separate fixings) in clear glass jars over the stove or at the kitchen window. Like other perishable foods, these substances are delicate products of nature that require special treatment. Since time, light, and heat are the agents that rob them of their essential oils—the root of their flavor—you must store them carefully. Keep your blends in tightly capped, opaque or clear, dark containers away from heat and sunlight. (Even under these conditions, most of the volatile essential oils will be lost after about 3 months.) Another idea is to pack up the mixtures, either in bulk or in individual portions, and freeze them. Try to use them within 6 months.

When you are ready to cook with any of the seasoning blends, transfer the amount you need to a mortar and grind the ingredients with a pestle. This will release the oils and meld the flavors that otherwise might not mingle quite so well in your particular dish.

Seasoning Blends for Soups

The dominant taste of the soup before herbs are added will dictate which ones will season best. In general, cream soups take well to delicately flavored herbs, poultry-based soups can make use of ones a little stronger, and beef and lamb foundations can sustain a still stronger accent of herbs. Most vegetable, grain, and bean soups made with a vegetable rather than a meat stock also can support herbs in this latter category.

Each formula below makes about 1 to 1½ cups dry mixture. Premix ingredients, and store them in an airtight container. Fifteen minutes before completion of any soup, grind 1 to 2 teaspoons of any of the following blends for each cup of liquid in the recipe, and add the herbs to the soup. Further adjust seasonings to taste. For specific information on drying vegetables, such as the celery listed below, read "Dehydrated Soup Mixes" (see Index).

■ Cream Soup Seasoning Blend

Use dried ingredients for this blend.

¼ cup marjoram
¼ cup parsley
¼ cup celery flakes
¼ cup basil
4 teaspoons chives
4 teaspoons thyme

■ Poultry Soup Seasoning Blend

Use dried ingredients for this blend.

¼ cup savory
¼ cup chives
¼ basil
¼ marjoram
¼ cup tarragon
4 teaspoons sage

■ Beef and Lamb Soup Seasoning Blend

Use dried ingredients for this blend.

¼ cup savory
¼ cup celery flakes
¼ cup parsley
¼ cup basil
¼ cup marjoram
¼ cup thyme
¼ cup chives

Seasoning Blends for Ethnic Dishes

These blends are specially designed mixtures of herbs and other seasonings that allow the cook to produce quickly a number of popular ethnic dishes. Beyond its specific purpose, each unique formula adapts well for other uses. Try mixing, for example, a desired amount of one of these combinations in a portion of yogurt or sour cream for an interesting dip or baked potato topping. Season your meat loaf, bread dough, or plain tomato sauce with the Italian Salad Dressing Mix (page 200). For a snappy after-school snack, treat the children to pieces of warm, buttered pita bread sprinkled with Curry Powder (below).

Remember to grind any of these mixes briefly with a mortar and pestle before adding them to your recipe to release the oils and give you more flavor. For drying vegetables such as those in the Spaghetti Sauce Mix (below), read "Dehydrated Soup Mixes" (see Index).

■ Pilaf Herb Mix

¾ cup dried basil
5 tablespoons dried oregano
3 tablespoons dried thyme
3 tablespoons garlic powder
1 tablespoon black pepper
2 teaspoons allspice
2 teaspoons coriander

Combine ingredients and store in an airtight container. Use 2 tablespoons for each cup of rice, barley, bulgur, or other grain.

Yield: 1½ cups

■ Bulgur Pilaf

1 cup bulgur
2 tablespoons oil
1 teaspoon minced fresh ginger root
2 tablespoons Pilaf Herb Mix (above)
3 garlic cloves, minced
½ large onion, coarsely chopped
1 cup mushrooms, quartered
¾ cup thinly sliced celery
2 tablespoons tamari soy sauce
2 cups vegetable stock *or* water
2 teaspoons powder *or* 1 cube vegetable bouillon
¼–½ cup raisins (optional)

In a large skillet, toast bulgur in oil, stirring constantly, over low heat until it just begins to brown. Add ginger root, herb mix, garlic, onion, mushrooms, and celery, and cook 3 minutes. Add soy sauce, stock or water combined with vegetable powder or cube, and raisins, if desired. Bring mixture to a boil, then cover, lower heat, and simmer about 25 minutes or until liquid is absorbed. Remove skillet from stove and let sit 15 minutes before serving.

Yield: 6 servings

■ Curry Powder

½ cup ground coriander
¼ cup chili powder
¼ cup dry mustard
¼ cup ground cardamom
¼ cup ground cumin
1 tablespoon ground cloves
1 tablespoon turmeric
1 tablespoon ground fennel seeds
4 teaspoons cinnamon

Combine all ingredients and store in an airtight container.

Yield: about 1¾ cups

■ Curried Parsnips

1½ pounds parsnips
3 tablespoons butter
⅓ cup water
1 tablespoon Curry Powder (above) *or* to taste

Wash and scrape parsnips and cut them into ¼-inch-thick slices. In a heavy skillet, melt butter and add parsnips and water. Cover and steam 5 minutes. Remove top; add curry powder and a little more water if necessary. Cover and steam about 3 more minutes or until tender.

Yield: about 6 side-dish servings

■ Spaghetti Sauce Mix

6 tablespoons dried carrot pieces
6 tablespoons instant minced onion
6 tablespoons dried parsley flakes
6 tablespoons cornstarch
3 tablespoons dried green pepper pieces
3 tablespoons dried celery flakes
1 tablespoon dried oregano
1 tablespoon dried basil
2 teaspoons dried thyme
2 teaspoons garlic powder
1 teaspoon Malt (page 207)

Combine ingredients and store in an airtight container. Whether making spaghetti sauce or some improvised dish, as rule of thumb, use 2½ tablespoons of dry mix to each pound of ground meat or to every 3 cups of cooked grain in meatless recipes.

Yield: about 2 cups

■ Spaghetti Meat Sauce

1 pound ground beef
1 large onion, coarsely chopped
1 large green pepper, finely chopped
3 garlic cloves, minced
2½ tablespoons Spaghetti Sauce Mix (above)
1 6-ounce can tomato paste
2½ cups water

In a large skillet, brown meat and drain off any excess fat. Add onion, pepper, and garlic and cook 10 minutes. Blend in sauce mix, tomato paste, and water. Simmer, uncovered, 20 minutes, stirring occasionally.

Yield: enough sauce for 6 servings

■ Taco Mix

½ cup instant minced onion
5 tablespoons chili powder
3 tablespoons dried oregano
3 tablespoons cornstarch
2 tablespoons dried basil
2 tablespoons crushed red pepper flakes
2 tablespoons garlic powder

Combine ingredients and store in an airtight container. Use 1½ tablespoons of this mix for each pound of meat in any recipe in which you would find these flavors pleasing. For meatless grain and bean dishes, start with 1½ tablespoons for every 2 cups bulk, and adjust seasoning to taste.

Yield: 1½ cups

■ Taco Meat Sauce

1 pound ground beef
1 large onion, coarsely chopped
3 garlic cloves, minced
1½ tablespoons Taco Mix (above)
½ cup water

Brown meat in a large skillet. Drain off excess fat except for about 1 tablespoon. Mix in onion and garlic and cook 5 minutes longer. Add taco mix and water and simmer, uncovered, about 10 minutes or until liquid just about evaporates. Spoon mixture into taco shells and top with shredded lettuce, chopped tomatoes, onions, and grated Monterey Jack cheese.

Yield: 6 servings

■ Italian Salad Dressing Mix

¾ cup dried oregano
6 tablespoons dried basil
3 tablespoons onion powder
1 tablespoon dry mustard
4 teaspoons garlic powder
4 teaspoons paprika
2 teaspoons black pepper

Combine ingredients. Store in an airtight container. One tablespoon of this mixture for each cup of liquid ingredients seasons sauces and dressings.

Yield: about 1½ cups

■ Italian Salad Dressing Supreme

1½ cups unrefined oil, preferably part olive
¼ cup apple cider or wine vinegar
¼ cup lemon juice
2 tablespoons Italian Salad Dressing Mix (above)

Combine ingredients in a 1-quart jar. Cover and shake well to blend. To allow flavors to further meld, place dressing in refrigerator for at least 4 hours, then remove to room temperature directly before serving.

Yield: enough dressing for about 6 servings

Coating Mixes

Coating mixes have become increasingly popular lately for a number of good reasons. They give fish, meat, poultry, and bean- and grain-based patties added flavor. They also provide an appealing crisp outer surface without deep-fat frying. Some cooks also have discovered that they can pan-fry these foods using a small amount of good-quality oil, and they do not have to worry about excess fat.

The easiest way to apply a coating mix is to put the dry seasoning and the food to be coated in a paper or plastic bag and shake to cover the ingredients. This method will not work, of course, with patties made of such foods as cooked mashed beans or grain. An alternative method involves a little more work, but it also produces a crisper finished product. Using this method, you first dip the food into a beaten egg-milk combination and then into the coating mix.

Making any of these mixes is a simple undertaking. Blend the ingredients for any one of them, and store the mixture in an airtight container. Each yields about 2⅓ cups. One-third cup is enough to cover a 1-pound fish fillet or 3 pounds of chops, chicken pieces, or patties of any type. When they're dipped in a batter first, all may require slightly more coating.

Table 12.1 Cooking Times for Coated Foods (in minutes)

Coated Food	Baking Time	Frying Time	Broiling Time
Chicken	350°F 60	25–30 (about 12–15 per side)	20 (10 per side)
Fish fillets	375°F 15–20	10 (5 per side)	5–10, unturned (brush with melted butter after coating)
Hamburger (medium-rare)	350°F 30	10 (5 per side)	10–15 (about 5–7 per side)
Pork chops	350°F 60 (30 per side)	30 (15 per side)	15 (about 7 per side)
Bean- and grain-based patties (made from precooked ingredients)	Not recommended	8 (4 per side)	8 (4 per side)

A guide to baking, frying, and broiling times is given in Table 12.1. You might want to vary these suggestions according to the thickness of the food and how well done you like your meat or fish.

Almost any of the master mixes work interchangeably with fish, meat, poultry, and bean- and grain-based patties. We also have made a notation of any foods that they complement particularly well.

■ Basic Coating Mix

You can't go wrong with this blend. The flavors subtly enhance almost any food.

2 cups whole wheat pastry flour
1 tablespoon paprika
1 tablespoon dry mustard
1 teaspoon ground celery seed
1 teaspoon black pepper
1 teaspoon dried basil
1 teaspoon dried marjoram
1 teaspoon dried thyme

■ Curry Coating Mix

The taste of chicken takes on a nice twist with this simple but uniquely flavored mix.

2 cups whole wheat pastry flour
3 tablespoons curry powder
1½ teaspoons black pepper

■ Seafood Coating Mix

Although originally designed to complement fish, this seasoning mixture works equally well for most nonmeat bean- and grain-based patties.

5⅓ cups whole wheat pastry flour
5 tablespoons dried parsley flakes
2 tablespoons ground celery seed
2 tablespoons dried thyme
2 tablespoons dried marjoram
1 tablespoon onion powder
1 teaspoon black pepper
2 bay leaves, crushed

■ Tarragon Coating Mix

Guests seem to appreciate the taste of tarragon in this mix, especially when it's used on hamburgers or fish.

2 cups whole wheat pastry flour
2 tablespoons dried tarragon
1½ teaspoons black pepper

■ Savory Coating Mix

This combination acts as a pleasing complement to chicken and pork chops.

1 cup whole wheat pastry flour
1 cup yellow cornmeal
2 tablespoons dried summer savory leaves
1 tablespoon onion powder
1 tablespoon garlic powder
1½ teaspoons black pepper

Sprouts

You remember Jack and his wondrous beanstalk. Little did he know as he tossed those five magical gems out the window that they would eventually lead to the goose that laid the golden eggs. Now, completely unaided by any storybook magic, you can produce miracles from beans in your kitchen every day.

Beans, grains, nuts, and seeds possess tremendous potential as sources of food. When they are exposed to the proper amount of moisture, the correct temperature, and adequate air circulation, these capsules evolve, or sprout, into tiny embryos that temporarily live on their own food supply. Despite their small size, sprouts contribute a large variety of nutritive value to a meal. They are a good source of vitamin C. And the fresher they are, the better: Scientists at the University of Pennsylvania have proven that soybean sprouts increase their own ascorbic acid (vitamin C) during the first 72 hours of life.

Don't allow supermarket packages of week-old sprouts or canned specimens to deter you from kitchen gardening. Absolutely no store-bought product compares in taste, quality, or cost with fresh-grown sprouts. On the following pages, you'll find that sprouting is easier than rinsing the breakfast dishes and soon becomes second nature to you. You'll also find instructions for making various mixtures so that you can conveniently combine the tastes and textures of a number of different sprouts at one meal.

Getting Started with Sprouting

First, buy yourself mung beans and alfalfa seeds, making sure they are chemically untreated and certified edible. Then, start with either 2 tablespoons mung beans or 1 tablespoon alfalfa seeds. (You'll need fewer alfalfa seeds because they expand more.) You'll need water to cover, too.

Begin by soaking seeds in water overnight (8 to 12 hours). Use an ordinary, wide-mouth, 1-quart glass jar. Cover the top with a nylon stocking, several thicknesses of cheesecloth, or pliable fiberglass screening (sold for windows at hardware stores). Use a rubber band to secure the cover. Place the jar in a dark place such as under the kitchen sink or in a cabinet.

After soaking, drain the water through the screening. (Save the liquid for stocks or treat your plants to a rejuvenating drink.) Twice a day, pour fresh water in the jar, swish it around, and drain it off immediately.

Throughout the process, keep the crop in a dark place until the last day of sprouting. At that time, place the container in a sunny window for about 4 hours. The green chlorophyll, a miraculous body cleanser and builder, will begin to develop in the first set of leaves, at which time the sprouts will be ready to serve.

Sprouts are usually ready to use anywhere from 3 to 8 days after germination. Their flavor, texture, and nutritional value depend upon the size they reach. After you've experimented enough times, you'll know instinctively when to eat the sprouts, but in the meantime, you may want to refer to the "Handy Sprouting Guide" to determine an average time for specific beans, grains, and seeds.

Sprouting Mixes and Recipes

Mixing compatible dry seeds will allow you to enjoy different sprout tastes together while sprouting in only one container. Experiment with your own combinations or use the proportions given below. When you are ready to use the seeds, follow the directions under "Getting Started with Sprouting" above. Wrap each batch in a plastic bag and twist closed. Each mix yields about 1 quart of fresh, delicious vegetables.

■ Breakfast Bounty

Add finished sprouts to omelets and pancake batters. One cup mixed into a cup of oatmeal makes an interesting cereal.

⅓ cup wheat berries
⅓ cup rye grain
3 tablespoons flax seed

Handy Sprouting Guide

Bean, Grain, or Seed	Desired Sprout Length	Average Sprouting Time (in days)
Adzuki	½–1 inch	4–5
Alfalfa	seed length to 1 inch	3–5
Almond	¼ inch	3–5
Barley	seed length	3–5
Cabbage	½–1 inch	3–5
Chick-pea*	¾–1 inch	5–8
Legumes	½–1½ inches	3–5
Millet	seed length	3–5
Mung bean	½–3 inches	3–8
Pumpkin	just opening	3–5
Radish	½–1 inch	2–4
Rice	seed length	3–4
Rye	seed length	3–4
Sesame	just opening	2–3
Soybean*	¾–1 inch	4–6
Sunflower	just opening	5–8
Triticale	seed length	2–3
Wheat	seed length	2–4

*Chick-peas and soybeans require more than one or two rinsings per day, or they will spoil before they have fully sprouted. Swish them with water at least four times within 24 hours, and make sure they are well drained.

■ Breakfast Salad

2 cups Breakfast Bounty (above)
½ cup chopped walnuts
½ cup sunflower seeds
2 large apples, grated
3 bananas, thinly sliced
½ cup raisins
½ cup plain yogurt
¼ teaspoon cinnamon
honey (optional)

Mix all ingredients together thoroughly. Sweeten with honey to taste, if desired.

Yield: about 6 servings

Bonanza Batch

This mixture of sprouts is excellent in salads, added to sandwiches, or sprinkled on soup just before serving.

2 tablespoons lentils
2 tablespoons mung beans
1½ teaspoons radish seeds
1 teaspoon alfalfa seeds

Solid Gold

This sprout combination can stand on its own or goes well as a part of salads, soups, and stir-fries. It has a variety of tastes and textures that may well make it one of your favorites.

½ cup lentils
¼ cup mung beans
1 teaspoon alfalfa seeds

Vegetarian Sukiyaki

2 tablespoons unrefined vegetable oil
1 cup thinly sliced onion
3 garlic cloves, minced
½ teaspoon minced ginger root
3 cups Solid Gold (above)
¾ cup diagonally sliced celery
¾ cup thinly sliced mushrooms
½ cup thinly sliced water chestnuts
½ cup bamboo shoots
1 large red pepper, cut into 1-inch lengths
1½ cups rich vegetable stock
2 tablespoons tamari soy sauce
1 tablespoon unsulfured molasses
1 tablespoon cornstarch
black pepper to taste
1 cup finely shredded celery cabbage

Heat oil in a wok or large frying pan. Stir-fry onion, garlic, and ginger root in oil until onion is just transparent. Add sprouts and all other vegetables. Stir-fry 5 minutes.

In a small bowl, combine stock, tamari, molasses, cornstarch, and pepper. Add to vegetable mixture, and stir and cook until sauce thickens enough to coat a spoon. Scatter celery cabbage over top of vegetables. Cover pan and allow mixture to steam 1 minute. Serve immediately.

Yield: 6 servings

■ Sweet and Tart

The sprouts from this mix are best eaten raw. Try them in salads of any kind.

2 tablespoons radish seeds
1 tablespoon alfalfa seeds

Malt

Malt can replace other sweeteners, completely or in part. When making yeast breads, it serves as the sugar on which the yeast spores can feed. Until you are accustomed to the concentrated sweetness of this product, however, turn to other recipes in this section to give you an idea of proper proportions.

■ How to Make Malt

Sprout 1½ cups dry wheat berries according to sprouting directions. (See "Getting Started with Sprouting," page 204.) Your yield should be about 1 quart. Spread sprouts on cookie sheets. Bake them for several hours at a very low temperature, about 150°F, until they become crisp and dark brown but not burned. Cool the sprouts, then grind them in a grain mill, blender, or food processor. Store in the refrigerator in a tightly capped container.

Yield: about 2 cups

Chapter 13 Quick Cereals, Soups, Beverages, and Snacks

Of course, any time is the right time for cooking to be more convenient, but there are certain times when easily prepared foods are truly a blessing. For instance, early morning hours tend to be rather hectic, with everyone rushing off to school and work. At the same time, breakfast is the most important meal of the day and should not be slighted.

Camping trips pose other special problems in meal preparation. No one arranging a vacation in the great outdoors wants to haul along a slew of pots, pans, and kitchen fixin's. Yet hiking, swimming, and just being in the fresh air usually lead to tremendous appetites.

Finally, snacking has become something of a national pastime. The best snack foods are quick, nutritious foods that require no cooking and a minimum of preparation.

Convenience Cereals from Scratch

Many recent cereal developments, touted as high-fiber, multivitamin, and iron supplement foods that meet 100 percent of the United States Recommended Daily Allowances for essential vitamins and minerals, are, in fact, strange facsimiles of real food. Sugar makes up a major portion of just about every one of them. (One of the big companies' recent "health" cereals lists sugar as its third main ingredient.) In addition, preservatives such as butylated hydroxy anisole (BHA) and butylated hydroxytoluene (BHT) are included, along with salt and a long line of synthetic boosters that are there primarily because the original vitamins and nutrients were taken out of the grain in the first place.

In spite of the preponderance of worthless cereals on the market today, some of the products in the stores are acceptable food items. Shredded wheat, for example, is still a simply produced, whole-grain substance. But if you really want to be sure of what you are getting, making up your own bulk quantities of cereals at home is a sensible, economical, and nutritious alternative.

Once you have established a regular pattern for selecting, buying, and storing the basic ingredients, your home cereal processing system is just about ready to go. Next, you'll need a few suggestions to get you started. In looking through recipes in cookbooks and magazines, don't become overwhelmed by the vast number of different recipes. Each is just one idea of what a natural cereal ought to taste like. Make up a small amount of different recipes to see how you like each one. Then take an inventory and decide from all the ingredients which ones appeal to you the most and best fit your needs. If, for example, you are allergic to wheat, substitute rye flakes in a recipe. If a molasses taste is too strong for you in another, reduce the amount in the master recipe. Pretty soon, you'll have a collection of wholesome, appealing cereal favorites that include nature's most distinctive tastes and textures—grains, dried fruits, nuts, and spices. Finally, make up a big batch of one or two of them and store each in a convenient container. Easy, delicious, and worth the time you have invested in putting them together, they'll be on hand each morning.

■ Grain Mix for Hot Cereal

2 cups rye grain
2 cups wheat berries
2 cups brown rice
2 cups bran

In an electric blender or grain mill, crack the rye, wheat, and brown rice into small particles. In a dry, heavy skillet, toast grains and bran until the mixture is lightly browned. Stir occasionally to prevent scorching. Remove from heat and cool. Store toasted cereal in a tightly capped container in a cool, dark place, preferably refrigerated.

Yield: 8 cups

■ Hot Grain Cereal with Raisins

This recipe makes a delicious morning dish that you can easily turn into a scrumptious dessert course with the addition of extra garnishes. Desiccated coconut, chopped dates or other dried fruits, nuts, and some sweet spices (such as cinnamon, nutmeg, and coriander) are all possible choices.

5 cups milk
1⅓ cup Grain Mix for Hot Cereal (above)
½ cup raisins

Pour milk into a heavy, 3-quart saucepan. Warm it thoroughly over medium heat until small bubbles cover the surface. At this point, stir in the cereal mixture and blend well. Lower heat immediately and simmer, uncovered, about 15 minutes or until thickened sufficiently. Serve in individual dishes, topped with raisins.

Yield: 6 servings

■ Granola Crunch

3 cups uncooked rolled oats
½ cup wheat germ
2 cups desiccated coconut
½ cup bran
½ cup sunflower seeds
¼ cup mild-tasting oil
½ cup honey
½ cup unsweetened apple juice
2 teaspoons cinnamon
½ teaspoon nutmeg
½ cup coarsely chopped cashews
½ cup coarsely chopped walnuts
½ cup coarsely chopped almonds
1 cup raisins

In a large bowl, mix together oats, wheat germ, coconut, bran, and sunflower seeds. In another bowl, whisk oil into honey. Mix in apple juice, cinnamon, and nutmeg. Pour this liquid over the oat mixture and toss thoroughly.

Lightly grease 2 baking sheets with oil. Transfer and distribute the oat mixture evenly over the surfaces. Place the pans in a 250°F oven and bake 20 minutes. Check and stir every 5 minutes to prevent burning.

Combine all the nuts and distribute them evenly between the pans. Bake another 10 minutes. Stir occasionally. Leave the cereal in the oven a little longer if it has not browned sufficiently.

Remove granola from the oven and add raisins to mixture. Cool before storing.

Keep granola in a jar with a tight cover in a cool spot. Serve with warmed or cold milk or yogurt. Store in the refrigerator whatever cannot be used within a week.

Yield: about 9½ cups

■ Maple Granola (uncooked)

2 cups uncooked rolled oats
1 cup wheat germ
½ cup wheat flakes
1 cup bran
1 cup sunflower seeds
½ cup coarsely chopped cashews
½ cup coarsely chopped almonds
½ cup coarsely chopped walnuts
¼ cup coarsely chopped pecans
1 cup raisins
1 cup coarsely chopped mixed dried fruit (any combination)
2¾ cups instant powdered milk
1 cup maple syrup *or* to taste

In a blender or food processor, quickly break up oats so that they have a part-powder, part-oat consistency. Pour them into a large bowl. Add all remaining ingredients except maple syrup and toss well. Slowly pour in the syrup and mix thoroughly. Refrigerate mixture in an airtight container (mixture will keep for 3 to 4 weeks). Serve with warmed or cold milk or yogurt.

Yield: about 12 cups

Easy-to-Make Soups, Beverages, and Snacks

Today's fast-moving world often makes demands upon us that cut into our time for preparing and eating full-course meals. For those frequent instances of hurried preparation and eating of school lunches, after-school snacks, and meals eaten on the run, premade convenience foods can be a real boon. However, many natural foods cooks, accustomed to taking time to make meals from scratch, draw blanks when they try gathering together a good variety of convenient foods. Some of the ideas presented here might simplify the preparation of these foods.

The key to making any food easy to use is to have it ready in your larder in advance. The most suitable types of food to store for quick use are dried soup mixes, beverage mixes, and simple snacks. Bad-weather days are good times to make a large quantity of mixes. You'll find that the recipes that follow do not require a great number of cooking utensils to ready these convenience foods for eating. A couple of pots and a good knife should do to put together some great, simple meals, such as nutritious soup accompanied by a loaf of homemade bread, and perhaps some cheese. Without much trouble, you can set out a meal like this that both adults and children will appreciate. And since the preparation of these soups, drinks and snacks doesn't require elaborate equipment, they're perfect for outings such as camping trips or picnics.

Dehydrated Soup Mixes

In this section, two master mixes form the base for nine delicious, quick soups. As part of these foundations, we have used a variety of dried vegetables. Although a good number of them are becoming more readily available in natural foods stores and some supermarkets, you can dry your own with an electric or solar food dryer. In general, the thickness of the sliced vegetable pieces will determine the length of time they remain in such a dryer. In addition, certain vegetables, such as spinach and carrots, taste better if they are blanched before they are dried. Blanching tomatoes briefly makes skinning them easier.

Most well-stocked food stores carry a selection of the herbs and spices in these mixes. Certain herb powders, however, may be difficult to find or they may be completely unavailable. In order to make them at home, grind the leaves or flakes of the indicated herb in a coffee grinder, electric blender, or mortar until they become powdery.

■ Cream of Celery Soup Mix

2⅔ cups instant powdered milk
½ cup celery powder (from stalks and leaves, not seeds)
3 tablespoons arrowroot powder *or* cornstarch
3 tablespoons onion flakes
1 tablespoon dried, crushed parsley flakes
½ teaspoon paprika
1 teaspoon white pepper

Stir the ingredients together. Divide the mixture into individual packets, each containing 7 tablespoons. A small piece of plastic wrap or aluminum foil, a small plastic bag, or even a paper envelope will work well. Close securely and mark.

Yield: about 7 packets, each making 1 serving

■ Cream of Celery Soup

1 cup water
1 packet Cream of Celery Soup Mix (above)

In a small saucepan, whisk together water and soup mix. Stirring frequently, simmer over medium-high heat, uncovered, 15 minutes.

Yield: 1 serving

■ Cream of Potato Soup

1 cup water
1 packet Cream of Celery Soup Mix (above)
¼ cup shredded raw potatoes

In a small saucepan, mix water, soup mix, and potatoes. Stirring constantly, simmer soup, uncovered, over medium-high heat about 15 minutes or until thick and bubbly.

Yield: 1 serving

■ Cream of Carrot Soup

1 cup water
1 packet Cream of Celery Soup Mix (above)
2 tablespoons dried carrots *or* ¼ cup raw, sliced carrots

In a small saucepan, mix water, soup mix, and carrots. Stirring frequently, simmer, uncovered, at a medium-high temperature about 20 minutes or until thick and creamy.

Yield: 1 serving

■ Cream of Mushroom Soup

1 cup water
1 packet Cream of Celery Soup Mix (above)
3 tablespoons dried mushrooms
½ teaspoon arrowroot powder *or* cornstarch

In a small saucepan, mix all ingredients together. Stirring occasionally, simmer, uncovered, at a medium-high temperature about 20 minutes or until thick and creamy.

Yield: 1 serving

■ Cream of Chicken Soup

1 cup water
1 packet Cream of Celery Soup Mix (above)
1 tablespoon dried mushrooms
¼ cup diced, cooked chicken (turkey may be substituted)

In a small saucepan, mix all ingredients. Stirring occasionally, simmer, uncovered, at a medium-high temperature about 20 minutes or until thick and creamy.

Yield: 1 serving

■ Vegetable Soup Mix

Use dried ingredients for this mix.

¼ cup carrots
¼ cup celery
1 tablespoon crushed parsley flakes
2 teaspoons onion flakes
1 teaspoon crushed thyme
1 teaspoon crushed basil
½ teaspoon white pepper

Stir together all ingredients. Divide mixture into individual packets, each containing 4 teaspoons. A small piece of plastic wrap or aluminum foil, a small plastic bag, or even a paper envelope will serve as containers. Close securely and mark.

Yield: about 8 packets, each making 1 serving

■ Tomato Vegetable Soup

1 cup water
1 packet Vegetable Soup Mix (above)
½ cup tomato juice *or* vegetable cocktail juice
1 teaspoon butter

In a small saucepan, stir together all ingredients. Bring to a boil and reduce heat to simmer. Cook, covered, 20 minutes.

Yield: 1 serving

■ Tomato Vegetable Barley Soup

1 cup water
1 packet Vegetable Soup Mix (above)
½ cup tomato juice *or* vegetable cocktail juice
¼ cup barley
1 teaspoon butter

In a small saucepan, combine all ingredients and bring to a boil. Reduce heat to simmer and cook, covered, 45 minutes to 1 hour.

Yield: 1 serving

■ Hearty Vegetable Soup

1 cup water
1 packet Vegetable Soup Mix (above)
½ cup tomato juice *or* vegetable cocktail juice
¼ cup diced, cooked chicken *or* beef
1 teaspoon butter

In a small saucepan, mix all ingredients together and bring to a boil. Reduce heat to simmer and cook, covered, 20 minutes.

Yield: 1 serving

■ Vegetable Macaroni Soup

1 cup water
1 packet Vegetable Soup Mix (above)
2 tablespoons whole wheat elbow macaroni
1 teaspoon butter

In a small saucepan, mix all ingredients together and bring to a boil. Reduce heat to simmer and cook, uncovered, until macaroni is tender. Stir occasionally.

Yield: 1 serving

Beverage Mixes

Creating your own drink mixes from delicious, nourishing foods will help you relish occasions for relaxation and refreshment without any negative side effects. In the beginning, you may want to present the finished products as "substitutes" for more popular flavors. Carob, for example, the predominant taste in a few of the following recipes, appeals to some people because of its chocolatelike taste. Roasted grain is an ingredient in others. It produces a beverage with a strong, hearty flavor and dark color reminiscent of coffee. In time you, your family, and friends most likely will welcome these flavors as unique tastes in themselves.

Almost all of the ingredients in these drinks are readily available in most natural foods stores and some groceries. Specialty herb and spice merchants will most certainly carry any of the herb tea ingredients we suggest. In addition, you can make up a few of these yourself. Consider foraging for some tea herbs and drying your own lemon and orange peels.

■ Carob Drink Mix

1½ cups carob powder
1 quart instant powdered milk

Combine the ingredients and store mixture in a tightly capped container.

Yield: 5½ cups

■ Hot Carob Drink

1 cup Carob Drink Mix (above)
½ cup hot water
1 quart milk
2 tablespoons honey
1 teaspoon vanilla extract

In a saucepan, dissolve drink mix in hot water. Gradually add milk and honey. Heat thoroughly, remove from the stove, add vanilla, and serve.

Yield: 4 servings

■ Carob Smoothie

2 tablespoons Carob Drink Mix (above)
2 tablespoons hot water
1 cup cold milk
1 tablespoon molasses
½ teaspoon vanilla extract
3 ice cubes, crushed
1 banana (optional)

In a blender jar, dissolve drink mix in hot water. Add remaining ingredients and blend quickly. Serve immediately or chill first for about 30 minutes.

Yield: 2 servings

■ Grain Coffee-Substitute Mix

To make your own malt, read How to Make Malt (see Index).

1 cup Malt
⅓ cup ground dandelion root
¾ teaspoon cinnamon

In a 200°F oven, on a cookie sheet, roast the malt and the dandelion root until the mixture turns a light toast color. Remove mixture from oven, add cinnamon, allow to cool, and store in a tightly capped jar.

Yield: 1⅓ cups

■ Malted Cream

2 heaping teaspoons Grain Coffee-Substitute Mix (above)
1 cup boiling water *or* warmed milk
milk, cream, or whipped cream (optional)

Stir together mix and liquid until powder is well dissolved. Strain liquid through a wire sieve into a serving cup; discard grain sediment. For a special treat, add a little milk, cream, or whipped cream to the finished beverage, especially if you have used water in the original preparation.

Yield: 1 serving

Due to popular demand, the commercial market is full of interesting herb tea blends that contain no caffeine. Nonetheless, some people will always take a better-than-store-bought approach to life, and for them, these next examples will be a good jumping-off point.

To assemble any of these blends, combine the ingredients and store them in a tightly capped container away from heat and light. The yield will be about 2 cups dried herbs. When you are ready to use a mixture, 1 tablespoon will be sufficient for each cup of boiling water. Allow the brew to steep for several minutes before serving. For a cold beverage, make the tea double strength, add honey when still lukewarm (if desired), and refrigerate until chilled.

■ Lemon Licorice Tea

Use dried ingredients for this blend.

1 cup licorice root
½ cup coarsely chopped lemon peel
½ cup dandelion root

■ Lemon Wintergreen Tea

Use dried ingredients for this blend.

1¾ cups wintergreen leaves
¼ cup coarsely chopped lemon peel

■ Spiced Spearmint Tea

2 cups dried spearmint leaves
1 heaping tablespoon whole cloves
1 tablespoon cinnamon

■ Anise Spearmint Tea

1½ cups dried spearmint leaves
¼ cup coarsely chopped, dried lemon peel
¼ cup anise seed

Pick-Up Snacks

Some snackers prefer to munch on plain nuts, seeds, and dried fruits. Others appreciate these treats even more when they are mixed together in different combinations. Either way, they are top-quality foods to toss into lunch bags, backpacks, or the snack jar at home.

If you are one of those people who like creating something unique from just basic ingredients, the idea of a snack mixture may appeal to you, and there are several advantages to preparing it at home. Apart from the satisfaction that you will get out of making it yourself, your snack mix will be free of the salt and sugar that are often found in commercial mixes. Instead, you can use your favorite spices to flavor your snacks.

And you'll save money at the gift shop. Spooned into an attractive jar and tied up with a pretty ribbon, these snack combinations make wonderful holiday or hostess gifts. If you don't mind imitation being the most sincere form of flattery, you might want to make a label listing the ingredients in the mixture, so that your recipient can keep on refilling the jar.

■ Fruit and Nut Snack

½ cup sunflower seeds
½ cup cashew halves
½ cup hazelnuts
½ cup raisins
½ cup small dried apricot halves
½ cup banana chips
½ cup pitted dates

In a 200°F oven, lightly toast the sunflower seeds and the nuts about 20 minutes or until they are slightly browned. Stir occasionally. Remove from the oven and allow them to cool. Combine the seeds, nuts, and the remaining ingredients in a large bowl and toss well. Store mixture in a tightly capped jar.

For a gift idea, prepare an attractive layered mixture. Using a 1-quart canning jar, layer each ingredient in the order it is listed above. Enough space should be left at the top of the jar to mix the ingredients at serving time.

Yield: about 3½ cups

■ Deviled Raisins

1 pound raisins
½ cup oil
2 teaspoons chili powder

In a saucepan or wok, combine the raisins and oil. Cook at medium-high heat about 10 minutes or until raisins are plump. Stir frequently. Drain raisins through a strainer or sieve. Place them in a bowl and toss with chili powder. Transfer to absorbent toweling to remove any excess oil. Store in the refrigerator in a covered container. The mixture should keep for up to 3 months.

Yield: 2 cups

■ Curried Nuts

1 cup almonds, walnuts, cashews, *or* pecans
1 cup raisins
1 teaspoon oil
1 teaspoon Curry Powder (see Index)

Combine nuts and raisins in a skillet or wok. Add oil and curry powder and mix over medium-high heat about 10 minutes or until raisins are plump and almonds toasted. Stir frequently. Store in the refrigerator in a covered container.

Yield: 2 cups

■ Home-Roasted Nuts

The brewer's yeast that flavors these nuts is a special variety grown on molasses. Ask for "good-tasting, nutritional yeast" in your store.

2 cups nuts (any variety), shelled
2 teaspoons oil
2 teaspoons brewer's yeast

Preheat oven to 300°F. Spread shelled nuts, with or without skins, in a single layer on a rimmed cookie sheet. Drizzle on oil and brewer's yeast. Then bake—allow 10 to 20 minutes for almonds, peanuts, pecans, pine nuts, and walnuts; allow 20 minutes for filberts and cashews. Stir occasionally.

Spread the roasted nuts on paper toweling to crisp and cool. Store in the refrigerator in an airtight container.

Yield: 2 cups

Part IV Outdoor Formulas

Shrewd homeowners today strive to make the most of their resources, including those outside and around the house. Garages, workshops, gardens, and yards can be transformed into well-organized centers for activities that usually aren't conducted indoors, and we've developed several useful formulas for these activities. The formulas will help you to economize, too—you'll be able to save by using less expensive, homemade products. You can extend the lives of costly items like tools, cars, sporting goods, and gardening equipment with these formulas to help with their proper maintenance. And if you're a gardener, the homemade soil improvements, insect controls, and other garden aids will assure a large, nutritious harvest for a smaller dollar investment.

Years of involvement with organic gardening methods have taught us that the overall nourishing and rebuilding of the soil accompanied by an effort to maintain natural ecological balances are the only ways to sustain a bountiful yard. In practical terms, we maintain the all-important microbial life in the soil through composting, the practice of creating friable soil humus by allowing organic matter to decompose. We further add to the buildup of soil nutrients with organic fertilizers, such as natural mineral substances and soil-amending mulches. We keep within reasonable bounds insect pest populations, weeds, and harmful fungi with controls that have little or no residual effects on any living plant or animal.

Throughout the following pages, we present some of this information as lists, tables, formulas, and general advice for each category. We garnered this information from our own experiences and also those of other organic gardeners. Our suggestions are guides for you, not strict calculations to which you need conform. Perhaps more important is an experimental attitude toward our formulas and gardening—one that most likely will lead you to discover some original developments of your own.

Sound cultural practices are the essential techniques that enable us to keep the land and environment in a healthy condition in order to produce nourishing food. In addition to composting and mulching on a regular basis, an organic gardener fertilizes with an eye toward what nutrients his soil actually requires, and controls pests by natural means. Most of these techniques seem to defy a formula approach but are nonetheless essential.

General tidiness—composting weeds and pruning scraggly and diseased growth to help keep garden pests from overwintering—is a primary cultural practice. The annual tilling of garden soil before covering with a mulch is important, too; it gets rid of weeds (or keeps them in check) and creates a loose, aerated, porous earth conductive to moisture retention and the breakdown of essential minerals from rock particles. Crop rotation is another elemental procedure. It is based on the principle that different crops make unique demands on the nutrient value of soil. Growing them in a different spot each year helps to balance out the nutrients taken from the soil. Crop rotation also helps to reduce soilborne diseases that occur when the same crops grow in the same place year after year. (For example, tomatoes, when they are not rotated annually, sometimes develop a fungal disease called anthracnose.)

Interplanting (growing two plants together that have complementary physical and chemical demands) and companion planting (choosing neighboring plants that repel each other's insect enemies) are two other traditional approaches. Both work by making use of inherent compounds within the plants that affect nearby ones positively or negatively.

Another cultural method, succession planting, calls for the continual planting of one crop after another in the same space during the growing season. This practice ensures the gardener good overall yields, but it also has the added advantage of preventing weeds from taking hold in barren spaces. A further expansion of this plan is green manuring, planting a winter crop of rye or another soil-building plant. Over the dormant season, the growth serves as a protective blanket that collects the sun's energy for use by the spring crops that come along later. Most general organic gardening books or encyclopedias elaborate on all of these practices. (See Appendix D, "Books for Further Reading.")

Chapter 14 Compost, Fertilizers, and Soil Mixtures

Carol Meinhardt Hopkins

To grow the best plants, trees, and vegetables naturally, you must first of all practice sound cultivation. Guaranteed success, however, calls for a bit more effort in upgrading your soil. If you are fortunate enough to live on land with soil that's fully aerated and rich in plant nutrients, you still have to maintain it at that level. If you live where topsoil is minimal and subsoil is compacted clay, you'll gain even more from the soil mixtures offered here.

Good organic soil depends upon two classes of material: compost or humus and organic fertilizers, which are also called soil amendments. Both compost and fertilizers introduce the same essential elements into your soil—nitrogen, phosphorus, and potassium (NPK). The distinction between compost and soil amendments is mostly a matter of function; compost, which is fully decomposed organic materials, acts as a nutrient reservoir and aids in moisture retention while still keeping soils from compacting. It also provides vital soil microorganisms with a healthy environment, and, along with the NPK, fertilizers introduce specific trace elements needed by plant life. Some gardeners use soil amendments that also work through decomposition, such as green manures and seaweeds.

Our aim is to help you determine the best use of compost and fertilizers in your garden. These formula guidelines will benefit your backyard crops, and you'll do even better by using some of the following good soil mixtures for starting seeds and growing plants indoors. Efficient gardening is a year-round matter, and these formulas and the suggestions for using them can give you a good head start at any time of the year.

Compost

Without our intervention, nature carries on the breakdown of organic matter—leaves, animal carcasses, dead plants and trees—into compost, technically known as humus. We can get involved in this process by composting garden by-products and other organic matter and returning to the soil those nutrients that we have taken from it in our planting practices. Common sense tells us that we cannot raise a patch of corn, harvest it, pull the stalks, and bag them for the trash collector, and hope to find that land in good fertile condition the following spring.

By applying compost to our gardens and fields, we are returning many of those elements that were previously lost to crop removal, wind and water erosion, and excessive temperatures. Because compost contains so many vital elements in their proper proportions and releases them to plants slowly, it offers an insurance against poor growth or reduced vigor caused by soil deficiencies. In addition, it tends to neutralize soil that has become too alkaline or too acidic. Extremes in either direction tend to tie up various nutrients and can cause imbalances in the soil that ultimately affect plants.

Composting is done most often without any structure at all. Tucked in the corner of a postage-stamp backyard or rising out of a field close to a barnyard, exposed compost piles work quite well. Some gardeners, however, choose to use holding structures—some simple, some quite complicated. We have found that many of the most modest are often the most practical. For example, an unmortared 5-foot-square wall of concrete blocks on three sides with an open fourth side helps contain organic materials, shields the family garbage and waste from wary neighbors, and provides a measure of protection from high winds. A removable board or other barrier on the open side keeps out scavenging pets and wildlife. Your own imagination and further reading may suggest to you a design geared for your particular needs.

The prerequisites for a successful compost heap are that the proper basic materials are placed in a specific balance, that correct temperatures are achieved and maintained, and that the heap has adequate moisture and is aerated to allow oxygen to get deep inside. It is also important to layer the composting materials to a minimum height of 4 to 5 feet. All of these factors must exist in order to house and feed adequately the billions of soil microorganisms—bacteria and fungi—that eat away at the pile and cause it to ferment and decompose.

Achieving the Proper Balance

All organic matter contains both carbon and nitrogen. Soil scientists refer to this combination as the carbon/nitrogen ratio, and it is important in composting because the microbes in the heap require a specific balance of the two in order to function. They use carbon to grow and nitrogen to synthesize protein. They demand a proportion of roughly 30 parts of carbon to every 1 part of nitrogen.

This carbon/nitrogen combination activates the microorganisms that heat up the composting materials. If too little nitrogen is present, the decomposition process may take as long as a year instead of an average of three months. If, on the other hand, too much is present, ammonium gas forms and the nitrogen seeps out into the atmosphere. The microbes do not function in a characteristic fashion, and the pile may take on an extremely undesirable odor.

Substances high in carbon come mostly from harder forms of matter, such as dried leaves and straw. Softer substances, such as kitchen wastes and green material like grass clippings, usually contain high amounts of nitrogen. As you experiment with these combinations, you may want to work with some of the figures in Table 14.1.

Table 14.1 Carbon/Nitrogen Ratios in Various Organic Materials

Organic Material	Carbon Parts to 1 Part Nitrogen
Activated sludge	6
Alfalfa	13
Alfalfa hay	12
Cornstalks	60
Digested sludge	16
Food wastes (table scraps)	15
Fruit wastes	35
Grass clippings	19
Naturally occurring humus	10
Leaves	40–80
Legume-grass hay	25
Oat straw	80
Paper	170
Rotted manure	20
Sawdust	500
Straw	80
Sugar cane residues	50
Sweet clover (green)	16
Sweet clover (mature)	23
Wood	700

SOURCE: Gene Logsdon, *The Gardener's Guide to Better Soil,* Emmaus, Pa.: Rodale Press, 1975.

An ideal compost heap should also contain two other essential elements, potassium and phosphorus. Along with nitrogen, they are considered the major nutrients of plant life; without them in the soil no growth takes place. Potassium (more commonly referred to as potash when talking about fertilizers) plays a part in all functions of plants; it helps them to resist disease and aids in protein synthesis. It also protects them from cold and dry weather by preventing excessive moisture loss and takes part in the formation of plant sugars. In ways that even scientists still do not completely understand, phosphorus accelerates growth and disease resistance and produces a vigorous root system.

We include potassium and phosphorus in our compost heaps, because the intense bacterial activity there produces heat that breaks them down into soil nutrients that are more readily available to plants. If merely applied directly to the soil, these relatively insoluble minerals take a long time to disintegrate and are useful only in small amounts over a long period of time. Major sources of potassium and phosphorus are ground forms of specific natural rocks and seaweed.

If you are just starting to compost, you may want to begin with the two approaches below. Once you have mastered each, alternatives to them will be easier to execute.

The Indore Method (layering)

Sir Albert Howard originated the first organized plan for composting, the Indore method, in 1931. The name derives from the state of India where he conducted his experiments. Today, through the use of more recently developed cutting, grinding, and masticating equipment, Sir Albert's method has been popularly supplanted by faster-working approaches that employ shredded material. Nonetheless, his basic formulation is still easy to follow and relatively effortless. In several months, it produces the precious stuff from which all gardens and farmlands can benefit.

Indore Composting

1. In the base of composting structure or on the open land, place a layer of brush.
2. Next, layer 6 inches of green matter (for example, weeds, crop wastes, leaves).
3. Follow the green matter with a 2-inch layer of manure or other nitrogenous material.
4. Sprinkle on limestone, topsoil, and phosphate rock.
5. Repeat layers until the pile reaches a 5-foot height.
6. For good aeration, as the pile begins to grow, force pipes or thick stakes (about 3 inches apart) through the organic matter to the bottom. Once you have finished layering, pull out the stakes.
7. Form a shallow basin on the top of the pile to catch rainwater.
8. Lightly press the entire outside surface of the pile to prevent blowing. Then cover the surface with a thin layer of rich earth.
9. To get more oxygen into the pile, turn it once or twice during the decomposition process. You might turn it at the sixth week and again at the twelfth. The pile should be completely decomposed in three months.

The 14-Day Method (shredding)

This quicker approach is actually a variation of the Indore method. As its name indicates, the 14-day method produces a finished product six times faster than the classic technique, but it requires more initial labor and more attention throughout the process.

All materials that go into a "quick" heap must be well shredded. Your object should be to increase the surface area so that microbial action can begin immediately. You also must supply generous amounts of nitrogen so that the pile actually starts cooking right away. (Within 24 hours, bacterial activity will be so great that the heap temperature will increase to anywhere from 140° to 160°F.) Watering and careful attention to the times when the pile is turned are also all-important if composting is to take place quickly. Last, depending upon weather conditions, the materials included, and the exact procedures, finished compost can take anywhere from ten days to as long as four weeks. There's no absolute guarantee of a fortnight's humus, so plan to leave yourself a couple of weeks of leeway in your garden schedule for compost applications.

Keep in mind that the materials proportions and basic principles remain the same for both the 14-day and the Indore methods.

14-Day Composting

1. Grind or shred all materials that go into the pile. You need not fuss over creating layers; if the materials are mixed together, all the better for encouraging microbes to begin their work.
2. The microorganisms require a humid environment in which to live and work. Too much moisture, however, will drive out the air that's also necessary to their survival. Therefore, keep your pile only as moist as a well-wrung sponge. This means dampening the initial materials and further watering, especially during the first three days when most of the heating is taking place. Form the same sort of depression in the top of your pile as that for the Indore heap. Water directly into it.
3. For better aeration, run stakes or poles (as in the Indore method) at intervals down to the base. Remove them once you've built the mound to a 4- or 5-foot height.
4. Starting on the third day, turn the pile at three-day intervals. Air will then arrive at all parts of the pile and the slower-decaying surface materials will have a chance to meet with the hot core.

Composting Variations

Aside from the Indore and the 14-day methods there are numerous other composting techniques. If well built and maintained, each produces a beneficial product.

Natural Composters If you raise chickens, a method is available to you that requires almost no work. Bed the flock with straw or old hay, and let the material build up for about a year. Chicks, by scratching for grain and other food bits, will compost their "linens" with nitrogenous manure, and turn them into a top-quality fertilizer.

Earthworms are also natural composters, especially if you just give them some food to squirm in. Build shallow composting pits no more than 2 feet high, but as long and as wide as you want. Fill the pits with mixed, shredded composting materials in the usual proportions. Loosely cover the pits with boards (earthworms prefer darkness) and let these industrious workers begin mixing and breaking down the organic matter into rich humus. The whole job should take no more than two months. Water the pile by removing the boards to expose the contents to periodic rains.

Sheet Composting Sheet composting is the most efficient way to compost large areas. Employed in conjunction with other sound organic growing practices, such as proper tilling and covering the ground between crops, this method involves placing a mulch of manure and other organic raw matter directly on the soil where it can decompose. Additional nutritive elements, such as limestone, phosphate rock, granite dust, or other natural mineral fertilizers, will also add to the overall value of the compost. Although the decaying process may take longer, and the results may be less controllable than those in a heap, the importance of this approach for large-scale growers is invaluable.

Airless Composting For years, some insightful city municipalities have been composting citizens' organic discards and offering them back to them in the form of humus. The system usually involves community cooperation. In most cases, residents who choose to participate deliver their raked grass clippings, weedings, and prunings to a central depository. Sometimes the municipality provides trucks to make pickups. At the main location, employees erect piles of the material in specially designed, air-free enclosures or on and under heavy plastic sheeting. The method, an anerobic one, makes use of microbes that work to break down materials in an airless environment.

Anerobic composting has certain advantages over the more popular aerobic method. A covered heap will naturally decrease the chances of animals getting into the piles. Oxidation, which inevitably destroys part of the carbon and nitrogen in aerobic piles, occurs only to a limited extent. In addition, many of the valuable liquids cannot leach directly into the soil beneath.

The results of home anerobic methods are not quite as predictable as those for the Indore and the 14-day procedures. Nonetheless, a number of home gardeners have reported successes with the practice. Some build their heaps on 3-mil-thick plastic sheeting and closely cover them with the same type of sheeting. Others fill large plastic bags with shredded composting materials, seal them, and place the containers in as much sunlight as possible.

Checking and Using the Final Product

Appraising Your Compost

Finished compost should be crumbly, not matted or lumpy.

Resultant color should be black brown. A pure black compost is often soggy and smelly, conditions that indicate too much moisture and too little air.

Good compost smells like good earth. A bad odor indicates that the bacterial process is not completed or that the proper conditions did not exist and, therefore, molds have developed.

The pH range of a good pile should fall between 6.0 and 7.4, 7.0 being neutral. Too much acidity is often the result of a lack of air and too much moisture.

Applications

Feeding flower gardens: Put compost through a ½-inch sieve, then shread it with a hoe, or roll it with a rolling pin to make it very fine. Use it alone as a 1-inch-thick mulch, or mix it with soil and top-dress with it.

Feeding lawns: Every spring, make holes over your lawn with a spike-tooth aerator. Then spread a mixture of fine humus combined with some bone meal. Rake this combination into the holes and lightly over the rest of the lawn. Dig up bare spots to about a 2-inch depth. Work in generous amounts of finished compost, tamp down the area, and rake to smooth the spot. Sow new seed after soaking patches well. For new lawns, work copious amounts of compost into bare ground to a depth of at least 6 inches in the fall.

Feeding shrubs: Yearly, fall or spring, work a half-bushel of compost into the soil surface. Also see Yearly Feeding for Established Trees and Shrubs (page 239).

Feeding trees: see "Fertilizing Trees" (page 238).

General application to the soil: One cubic yard of your finished pile will equal approximately 1,000 pounds of compost. As a rule of thumb, use 2 pounds every 4½ square feet of ground (10 tons per acre). Apply a depth of ½ inch to the top 4 inches of soil each year.

Mulch for growing crops: Mix compost with topsoil and apply as a "top dressing" around the base of already established plants. In this way their roots will not be disturbed, while the layer will also hold down weeds.

Planting trees and shrubs: Always make sure the planting hole is twice the size of the root ball. Mix equal parts of compost, topsoil, and leaf mold. Carefully shovel this medium around the plant and tamp it down as you work. Soak the ground well, then spread 1 to 2 inches of pure compost on top. Finish with a mulch of leaves or hay to keep soil moist and to control weeds.

Sowing seeds indoors or in a cold frame: Prepare compost as for feeding flower gardens. Mix it with equal amounts of sand and soil.

Natural Fertilizers

Dollar for dollar, mass-produced chemical fertilizers are cheaper to buy than organic ones. These synthetics are less expensive, however, only if quick plant growth and high yields are your only concerns. In the long run, you may be paying much more than you realize for many of the side effects they carry along with them.

Chemical fertilizers are made from by-products of petrochemicals and a combination of some earth product and a strong acid. In their many guises, they are quick-acting, short-term "boosters," created primarily to stimulate rapid plant growth. Natural (or organic) fertilizers are indeed much slower acting. Since they are made up of pure earth and animal materials untreated with acid or other substances to increase their solubility, for the most part they are not immediately available to plants. Instead, over a much longer period of time, they gradually give to the soil a wide variety of unadulterated nutrients. Phosphate rock, for instance, provides only about 1.5 percent of its phosphorus content the first year, even though an accumulated amount of 28 to 30 percent will accrue over a three- or four-year period. Chemical superphosphate, on the other hand, treated with an equal amount of sulfuric acid to make it more soluble, bears a phosphorus rating of 19 to 21 percent. The essential phosphorus is highly available, but only for a short period of time, after which it leaches out of the soil and leaves behind salt deposits that retard beneficial bacteria.

Unlike organic substances that continually decompose and add valuable humus to the soil, chemical fertilizers do not break down over a long period of time. Instead, their inorganic salts accumulate and destroy the resistance of certain plants to disease. In dry areas, particularly in the West and Southwest, these salts tend to amass on the ground where they form a compact, somewhat impervious layer that ultimately brings about erosion. Another disturbing aspect of chemical fertilizers is that they can lower the nutritional content of fruits and vegetables. Tests have proven, for example, that laboratory-made nitrogen will lower the vitamin content of oranges and the capacity of hybrid corn to produce seeds with a high protein content.

Composting, mulching, green manuring, and the addition of natural soil enrichers are organic gardeners' alternatives to chemical fertilizers. These methods and materials return to the soil the major elements and trace minerals that plants have removed during their development. They also inhibit the effects of wind and water erosion and other weather extremes. Most of the materials that go into the compost heap are the same ones organic gardeners rely on to correct deficiencies or to maintain productive soils. The first step toward a balanced growing environment, though, is to find out just what types of organic fertilizers your garden needs.

Professional Soil Tests

The staff at the Rodale Research Center highly recommends that every serious gardener and farmer start a fertilization program with a reputable soil test. Although many home kits on the market can provide a fair idea of what's happening to the garden floor, a much better indicator is a professional evaluation from a chemical laboratory. Under controlled conditions, experienced chemists judge your soil and return to you a form indicating the levels of important plant nutrients and the acid-alkaline (pH) balances in it. It will take a good deal of the guesswork out of your gardening endeavors.

The least expensive professional soil test is available from the soil-testing laboratories of state universities. The cost at this writing is $2 to $3 in most states. For this amount you'll get an envelope which is attached to a small cloth bag. Inside is a plastic insert for your soil sample. In addition, you'll receive a questionnaire on which to indicate the use of your growing area (for example, lawn, golf course, garden). If cropping is your purpose, specify what plants you have grown previous to this year and what your plans are for the next season. The test packet is available through your county agent who usually can be found in the cooperative extension service office of the county court house. This official works in conjunction with the soil-testing laboratory of one of your state universities, where the sample will be analyzed.

The best time to take the sample is in the fall, on a day when the soil is fairly dry. If you wait until spring, the laboratories may be excessively busy, and you may get your results too late to make use of them.

If you garden or farm in an area with topographical differences (for example, hilly terrain and flatland), you will need to perform more than one test. However, for an average garden of fairly even features, one should be sufficient. In order to get a composite sample of the entire garden area, you may want to combine soil from several spots in the garden.

Use a trowel or spade that is free of rust to take a sampling. (Any foreign element that gets in the soil will influence the results.) Pull aside any hay or leaves so that no decaying mulch is included in the sample. Dig in about 6 inches to retrieve dirt from the surface down to that depth. (Another way to gauge the depth is to dig about as far as pepper, tomato, and eggplant roots extend—in other words, to the farthest level from which most plants derive sustenance.) A trowelful of dirt should be plenty to fill the plastic enclosure. Break up clods and remove any stones from the sample. If the soil is still moist, air-dry it, preferably indoors, in a shallow dish near a sunny window.

If you are taking a composite sample, scoop up the same amount of soil from every 30 to 35 feet of your field or garden. Mix the dirt together well in a clean bucket, and take out a small amount for the test.

Place the soil sample in the plastic bag and seal it tightly. Then, pack it into the outer cloth container, being sure not to detach the cloth bag from the end of the accompanying envelope. Fill out the forms and envelope. If you find no space to request specific information, write a note and ask for details. (Sometimes your request will be honored; if not, read on for our recommendations.)

The results of your soil test should come back to you within a few weeks. They will probably arrive via the county agent who will hold a copy and send one to you. If you have questions on the information, call your agent, not the state university.

Table 14.2 Percentage of Nutrients in Common Organic Materials

Material	Nitrogen	Phosphorus	Potash
Activated sludge	5.00	3.25	0.60
Alfalfa hay	2.45	0.50	2.10
Animal tankage	8.00	20.00	0
Apple leaves	1.00	0.15	0.35
Basic slag	0	0.8	0
Blood (dried)	12.00–15.00	3.00	0
Blood meal	15.00	1.30	0.70
Bone meal	4.00	21.00	0.20
Brewers' grains (wet)	0.90	0.50	0.05
Castor bean pomace	5.50	2.25	1.13
Cattle manure (fresh)	0.29	0.17	0.10
Cocoa shell dust	1.04	1.49	2.71
Coffee grounds (dried)	1.99	0.36	0.67
Colloidal phosphate	0	18.00–24.00	0
Cornstalks	0.8	0.40	0.90
Cottonseed	3.15	1.25	1.15
Cottonseed hull ash	0	8.70	23.93
Cottonseed meal	7.00	2.50	1.50
Fish scrap (red snapper)	7.76	13.00	0.38
Granite dust	0	0	5.00
Greensand	0	1.50	5.00
Guano	12.00	8.00	3.00
Hoof meal and horn dust	12.50	1.75	0
Horse manure (fresh)	0.44	0.17	0.35
Incinerator ash	0.24	5.15	2.33
Oak leaves	0.80	0.35	0.15
Peach leaves	0.90	0.15	0.60
Phosphate rock	0	30.00–32.00	0
Poultry manure (fresh)	2.00	1.9	1.9
Rabbit manure (fresh)	2.40	0.6	0.1
Red clover	0.55	0.13	0.50
Seaweed	1.68	0.75	4.93
Sheep manure (fresh)	0.55	0.31	0.15
Swine manure (fresh)	0.60	0.41	0.13
Tankage	6.00	5.00	0
Tobacco stems	2.50	0.90	7.00
Wood ashes	0	1.50	7.00

SOURCE: Anne M. Halpin, *The Organic Gardener's Complete Guide to Vegetables and Fruits*, Emmaus, Pa.: Rodale Press, 1982.

Depending on what laboratory performs them, soil tests generally indicate the pH of the soil and the availability of phosphorus (P) and potash (K). Many also include calcium and magnesium rates. Unless you specifically request a reading, however, most do not indicate the nitrogen (N) content. Since this latter, important nutrient is a very unstable, soluble element, a test for it will indicate only the condition of the soil at the time you took the sample.

Test results for levels of nutrients range from low through medium and high to excessive. No emphasis is placed on trace elements such as iron, copper, and boron. The assumption is that once you bring your soil to a slightly acid-to-neutral pH (between 6.5 and 7.0), most likely you've established sufficient amounts of these micronutrients as well. Finally, somewhere on your report you will find a recommendation for a suitable fertilizer for your particular conditions. Numerical labels such as 10-10-10, 0-5-0, and 5-10-5 indicate respectively the percentage of nitrogen, phosphorus, and potassium in a synthetic fertilizer. Thus, a 100-pound bag of fertilizer would contain 5 pounds of nitrogen, 10 pounds of phosphorus, and 5 pounds of potash.

If the results of your test suggest that your soil contains adequate levels of the major elements and a midpoint pH, your job will be to maintain that precious loam. In addition to sound cultivation practices, application of organic substances together with inorganic natural mineral powders yearly or every several years will help to maintain high fertility levels. Some commonly used organic materials and their percentages of N, P, and K appear in Table 14.2.

If your soil test comes back and at the bottom it reads something like this: "Use 20 pounds of limestone and 4.5 pounds of 5-10-10 fertilizer per 100 square feet," you'll have some decoding to do to translate the report into organic language and to correct a few deficiencies.

The following example suggests the steps involved in moving from a recommendation for a synthetic chemical formula to an organic mixture.

1. The recommendation calls for 20 pounds of limestone per 100 square feet and 4.5 pounds of 5–10–10 fertilizer for the same area. For liming, apply crushed limestone as directed.
2. In order to substitute organic ingredients for commercial fertilizer, you must first calculate how many pounds of each nutrient the fertilizer provides. A 5–10–10 mixture contains 5 percent nitrogen, 10 percent phosphorus, and 10 percent potash. When you use 4.5 pounds of such a fertilizer, you are getting the following amounts of each nutrient:

   $0.05 \times 4.5 = 0.225$, or 0.23 pound of nitrogen when rounded off;
   $0.1 \times 4.5 = 0.45$ pound of phosphorus;
   $0.1 \times 4.5 = 0.45$ pound of potash.

3. To create your own custom organic fertilizer that supplies comparable amounts of these essential elements, look at Table 14.2. Check first for materials readily available in your area. Among those, look for one that contains a high percentage of one nutrient. For example, animal tankage contains 8 percent nitrogen, 20 percent phosphorus, and 0 percent potash. Since the 20 percent phosphorus content of animal tankage is twice as much as the 10 percent recommended by the test results, you'll need to use only half as many pounds of animal tankage to meet your phosphorus requirements. Thus, 2.3 pounds of animal tankage will supply you with approximately the correct amount of phosphorus ($2.3 \times 0.2 = 0.46$).
4. Animal tankage also contains 8 percent nitrogen, so 2.3 pounds of animal tankage will provide 0.18 pound of nitrogen ($2.3 \times 0.08 = 0.18$). Therefore, you still need 0.05 pound of nitrogen ($0.23 - 0.18 = 0.05$) and the full quantity of potash to meet the soil requirements. Returning to Table 14.2, you'll discover that tobacco stems contain 2.5 percent nitrogen, 0.9 percent phosphorus, and 7 percent potash. To meet the rest of the test's nitrogen recommendation, it's necessary to compute the quantity of tobacco stems that will supply 0.05 pound of nitrogen. Divide

Table 14.3 Example of Organic Materials Necessary to Approximate the Nutrient Weight in 4.5 Pounds of 5–10–10 Commercial Fertilizer

Organic Material and Amount	Nutrient Percentages and Pounds		
	Nitrogen	Phosphorus	Potash
Animal tankage 2.3 pounds	8% = 0.18 pound	20% = 0.46 pound	0% = 0 pound
Tobacco stems 2 pounds	2.5% = 0.05 pound	0.9% = 0.02 pound	7% = 0.14 pound
Granite dust 6.2 pounds	0% = 0 pound	0% = 0 pound	5% = 0.31 pound
Total 10.5 pounds	0.23 pound	0.48 pound	0.45 pound
Compared to 4.5 pounds of 5–10–10 commercial fertilizer	5% = 0.23 pound	10% = 0.45 pound	10% = 0.45 pound

0.05 by 0.025 and you'll find that 2 pounds of tobacco stems will supply the necessary nitrogen. This will also give you extra phosphorus ($2 \times 0.009 = 0.02$), an amount that's too small to affect your phosphorus level significantly.

5. Two pounds of tobacco stems will also supply you with 0.14 pound of potash ($2 \times 0.07 = 0.14$), which leaves you with 0.31 pound of potash to find ($0.45 - 0.14 = 0.31$). Table 14.2 shows that granite dust contains 5 percent potash and no nitrogen or phosphorus to disturb the balance you've attained with these nutrients. Divide 0.31 by 0.05, and you'll find that 6.2 pounds of granite dust will supply you with the recommended amount of potash per 100 square feet of garden. Table 14.3 lists the total quantities of natural materials necessary to equal the test results in this example.

General Organic Fertilizer Formulas

The fertilizers listed in Table 14.4 present some typical organic blends based on the soil-test recommendations for nutrient balances most commonly required. Because of the shortcomings involved in setting down absolute NPK formulas for natural substances, however, these mixtures suggest primarily that there are an infinite number of ways to combine soil enrichments for specific purposes. The numbers above each formula represent the percentage of N, P, and K found respectively in the total blend. If, for example, your soil test should call for a 10-10-10 fertilizer, you can substitute any organic material with the same ratio of nutrients (in this case, equal percentages of N, P, and K). Keep in mind that you must vary the amount of materials used per 100 square feet to supply the same amount of nutrients called for by weight in the synthetic. If the test calls for 5 pounds of 10-10-10 per 100 square feet, you could use 25 pounds (5 times the weight) of a 2-2-2, which has only one-fifth the concentration of a 10-10-10, for the same area. Or, you could use 12.5 pounds (2½ times the weight) of a 4-4-4 and obtain the same results.

In mixing organic fertilizers, attempt to combine quick- and slow-release ingredients. A general rule to follow is that most of the rock powders are slower to decompose than the organic matter and, therefore, the two substances work best in combination. This approach keeps plants growing well throughout the season while assuring balanced soil for the next season.

If a fertilizer formula contains raw organic matter, try to turn it under at least several weeks before planting. In addition, grind up organic matter such as leaves, hay, or straw, so that it will decay more quickly.

Table 14.4 Formulas for Organic Fertilizers

- 2–4–4 Mix
  2 parts animal tankage
  2 parts tobacco stems
  5 parts granite dust
  or
  1 part blood (dried)
  1 part phosphate rock
  6 parts granite dust

- 2–4–2 Mix
  4 parts coffee grounds (dried)
  1 part bone meal
  1 part wood ashes

- 3–6–3 Mix
  1 part blood meal
  2 parts bone meal
  4 parts granite dust

- 1–1–1 Mix
  2 parts wood ashes
  1 part blood (dried)
  10 parts basic slag

- 2–2–2 Mix
  1 part poultry manure (fresh)

- 4–4–4 Mix
  4 parts blood (dried)
  1 part phosphate rock
  8 parts wood ashes

- 0–1–0 Mix
  1 part basic slag

- 0–5–0 Mix
  4 parts basic slag
  1 part colloidal phosphate

- 0–10–0 Mix
  1 part basic slag
  1 part colloidal phosphate

- 0–20–0 Mix
  1 part colloidal phosphate

Fertilizing Trees

Perhaps the grandeur and long life of a number of native trees builds for all species an image of indestructibility. As a result, many of us often employ our green thumbs in the garden while we forget the needs of the massive oak or the spiraling arborvitae growing nearby. The fact is, however, that trees growing outside of woodlands, forests, and jungles do not receive nature's uninterrupted ministrations. Lush carpets of rich leaves and centuries-old accumulations of humus do not fall undisturbed at our tree's roots. Growing out of concrete sidewalks and planted in cultivated settings, they are our charges, and it is up to us to nourish them.

Today, professional arborists are discovering the need for periodic feeding to make up for shortages exhibited by trees, but not all of them agree on the best formula for particular trees. Virtually all concur, however, that a complete mixture containing the three major soil elements, nitrogen, phosphorus, and potash, should be used.

Gardeners must look to themselves to determine when to use fertilizers and how much to use. Some arborists recommend spring applications—about the time the ground is free from frost but well before buds appear. Others staunchly support the idea that late fall is the best time. Late-season applications cause some nutrients to enter roots immediately and others in very early spring. The remainder will be available over an extended period of time. One rule, however, must be observed: Do not fertilize woody perennials in the fall with a soluble, high-nitrogen fertilizer. If the trees are encouraged to produce succulent growth too late in the season, they will not harden off properly in preparation for winter.

Amounts applied depend a great deal on what the individual gardener wants to achieve. If a tree is young and you want it to grow as rapidly as possible, then extra food is called for. On the other hand, use less fertilizer to maintain an older tree while restricting further growth.

Mere application of fertilizer in the soil around a tree is no guarantee that the tree will benefit from it. All professionals know that, regardless of the method of application, fertilizers must be placed at the location of the feeder roots.

Feeder roots usually occupy the outer band of a circular area, the circumference of which lies just beyond the spread of the outermost branches (the drip line). The width of this band is equal to about two-thirds of the radius of the circle. The extent of this band cannot always be determined by the spread of the branches. The roots can extend at least 1½ to 3 times beyond that line. To determine the region where most of these roots occur, follow this rule of thumb: The number of inches of the tree's diameter 1 foot above the soil is equal to the number of feet of the spread of the root radius. As an example, a tree with a diameter of 1 foot will have most of its roots within a 12-foot radius and its feeder roots in the outer 8-foot-wide band.

■ Starter Formula for Transplanted Trees

This solution is an immediately available plant food. It stimulates leaf and root growth and gives the tree a quick pick-up after transplanting.

Fill a barrel or other container one-fourth full of compost. Fill the rest of the container with water and stir several times in the next 24 to 48 hours. To use, dilute liquid to a light amber color with water. Pour 1 pint around each planted sapling. This solution can be used at 10-day to 2-week intervals, especially when soils are not high in fertility.

This starter formula also works well for established trees. Apply approximately 1 gallon to each tree at the feeder roots.

■ Yearly Feeding for Established Trees and Shrubs

The only material you will need for this excellent fertilizer is compost—approximately half a bushel per tree. Start about 2 to 3 feet from the trunk, and cultivate the soil shallowly to a foot beyond the drip line at the end of the branches. Rake 1 to 2 inches (3 to 4 inches for fruit trees) of compost into the top 2 inches of soil. Spread any remaining portion over the surface. Cover compost with a mulch of leaves or hay to help keep the soil moist and free of weeds.

To pep up old fruit trees, auger holes 1 foot apart all around the feeder root area of the tree, and pack each with compost. A time-release action will take place.

■ All-Purpose Tree-Fertilizing Formula

This formula provides substantial amounts of all the major soil elements plus generous proportions of calcium, magnesium, and other trace minerals. It helps to maintain healthy trees and revitalizes less-youthful specimens. Some gardeners who use it regularly even report fruit trees that produced worm-free apples.

3 parts cottonseed meal, soy meal, *or* blood meal
2 parts finely ground raw phosphate rock *or* steamed bone meal
3 parts wood ashes, granite rock, *or* greensand
1 part dolomitic limestone

Mix all materials together. Under small trees, broadcast the mixture evenly from a 6-inch circle left free around the trunk to a point slightly beyond the end of the drip line. For larger trees, determine where the feeder roots occur, and concentrate applications in that band around the tree. Apply 1 pound of fertilizer for each foot of the drip line diameter of the tree. For example, if the tree measures 12 feet from the tip of the branches on one side to those on the other, use 12 pounds. For deeper penetration of fertilizer, make holes with a crowbar. Space them 1 foot apart all around the feeder-root area and place mixture in each.

To build up humus content in the soil, each spring add and work about a 3-inch covering of compost into the immediate area surrounding the tree.

■ Fish Fertilizer for Fruit Trees

Fish fertilizer is an excellent means for building up minor nutrients and adding nitrogen to soil in which fruit trees grow. This method provides a simple way to feed an orchard.

For the first year, at planting, add 1 teaspoon of concentrated liquid fish fertilizer to each 5 gallons of water and mix. Increase amount of fish liquid by 1 teaspoon each year. By the time the tree is full size, you will most likely be using about 10 times the original amount to every 5 gallons of water.

Apply the diluted fertilizer in stages—one-third in the early spring when the trees are dormant, one-third after the blossoms fall, and one-third in the early summer to boost fruiting. Completely soak the feeder-root area at each watering.

Soil Mixtures

All homemade mediums must meet a number of important requirements, no matter what the final use of the product is going to be. All should be free from insects, disease, and weeds. (This doesn't necessarily mean soil sterilization is required, however.) The mixtures must drain well but still hold ample moisture, and they should be loose enough to allow oxygen and water to reach the roots of young seedlings or cuttings. Also, they should be made of inexpensive, easily attainable, and easy-to-work-with materials. For the most part, these mixes need little nutritive value, since the plants contained in them are young and have smaller nutrient requirements than mature plants. Most mixes that have either topsoil or compost in their makeup probably need no additional fertilizers.

We mentioned earlier that soil sterilization may not be needed to free the medium of soilborne insects, disease, and weeds. We've found little or no damping-off (a fungus that affects seedlings) with our mixes, even though we use some topsoil and compost. What appears to be happening is that the medium we use is teeming with life from many types of microorganisms, none of which tend to dominate the entire environment. Theoretically, they should keep each other in check so that the harmful fungi that cause damping-off will not become a problem. Weeds and insects can also be kept to a minimum right from the start, too.

If the desired mix you intend to use includes compost or topsoil, make sure the compost comes from piles that were thoroughly composted and that also were not located in areas where weeds may have been deposited accidentally. Good compost should not have insects' eggs in it, because the heat generated by compost should have destroyed them. Any topsoil you use should be obtained from an area that has no weed or insect problems. Even so, weeds still will appear occasionally in your mediums made with topsoil. However, their numbers will be few and a minimal amount of hand weeding will be necessary.

Usually, the mix used for houseplants needn't be sterilized unless there are definite insect or special disease problems associated with it. Also, never use straight topsoil as a medium, since it tends to crust and compact and becomes rather impervious to thorough watering.

If you feel you must sterilize your mixes that include topsoil and compost, or if you have a perennial problem with soilborne pests in your homemade mixes, then you should pasteurize it. Fortunately, most harmful insects, diseases (including most viruses), and weeds can be controlled with heat treatments of 150° to 175°F, while many of the beneficial soil microbes will not be totally killed if temperatures don't go higher than this and are not maintained for an extended period.

Table 14.5 Soil Sterilization Temperatures for Different Pests

Pest or Group of Pests	40-50 Minutes at Temperature
Nematodes	120°F
Damping-off and soft rot fungi	130°F
Most pathogenic bacteria and fungi	150°F
Soil insects and most plant viruses	160°F
Most weed seeds	175°F
Resistant weed seeds and resistant viruses	212°F

SOURCE: George and Katy Abraham, *Organic Gardening Under Glass,* Emmaus, Pa.: Rodale Press, 1975.

Sterilizing Soil

When sterilizing or pasteurizing, make sure the medium is somewhat moist but not soggy. Put it in trays that fit into your oven, if you don't have regular equipment for this purpose. Use a meat thermometer to determine the soil temperature you desire, and hold the temperature at that point for 40 to 50 minutes.

■ Solar Energy Sterilization

This method is worthwhile to try, since it is clean, inexpensive, and easy. Also, if you can get temperatures high enough it will be effective without creating a bad odor in the house, as does sterilizing in your oven.

Place soil in shallow pans (4 inches deep or so), and moisten the soil somewhat. Place a meat thermometer in the center. Put an airtight plastic covering over the container and place in full sun for the required time if temperatures can be maintained at 150° to 175°F. Try to keep the covering about 1 to 2 inches above the soil surface.

Whether or not you are using heat-treated soil, the greatest possible care should be taken not to contaminate or recontaminate your mix. The following are things that can be done to avoid this problem.

1. Never reuse soil mixes without heat-treating them. They run too high a risk of carrying soilborne diseases.
2. Keep clean all tools used for seeding, grafting, or making cuttings. Dip equipment in a mixture of 1 part liquid chlorine bleach to 10 parts water.
3. Old seed flats and trays should be thoroughly cleaned, again using a bleach solution.
4. Store your mix in clean containers that admit very little outside air. Large plastic garbage bags hold enough mix for the needs of most gardeners over a substantial period of time.
5. Use good, sanitary techniques when raising seedlings or cuttings. Never overwater. Also, try not to water late in the day when temperatures are apt to be cooler. Damping-off thrives in cool, moist conditions. Also make sure that plants have ample light, ventilation, and moisture for optimum growth.

Formulas for Soil Mixtures

■ Seed-Starting Mix

This mix is good and airy, and holds enough moisture to cause excellent germination. This is the most common mix for starting seeds at the Rodale Research Center. Also, if damping-off is still a problem, the addition of slight amounts of milled sphagnum moss applied over the surface of the soil mix will help to deter this fungal disease naturally in most cases.

1 part finely sifted topsoil
1 part finely sifted compost *or* high-quality leaf mold
1½–2 parts inert substances—preferably vermiculite, perlite *or* coarse builder's sand

■ Transplant Mix

This mix is slightly "heavier" than the mix used to germinate seeds. Since the plants are actively growing now, there is less chance of damping-off and, therefore, less aeration is needed from the inert substances. Also, since plants are using larger quantities of water and nutrients, they need a higher percentage of topsoil and compost in the total mix. The extra fertilizer can give a great boost to the plants at this stage as well. This sort of a mix appears to be very acceptable for all vegetable varieties we have tried.

2 quarts finely sifted topsoil
2 quarts finely sifted compost *or* high-quality leaf mold
1 quart inert substances—coarse builder's sand, perlite, *or* vermiculite
1 teaspoon weak organic fertilizer (3–2–2) *or* dehydrated poultry manure *or* 2 teaspoons dehydrated cow manure

■ Cuttings Mix

Any of the following can be used either alone or in mixtures with one another: coarse builder's sand, perlite, vermiculite, or milled spaghnum moss. The reason for using these materials is that they are inert; inexpensive; and, for the most part, sterile; and thus have excellent air and moisture drainage. They need to be kept moist to get good rooting of cuttings, but they never should be oversaturated. It is important that the rooting zone receives plenty of oxygen, so make sure the container has adequate drainage. This mix has no nutritive capacity, because cuttings get all their nourishment for rooting from the plant material itself. Once roots are actively growing, the plant depends upon the medium to supply nutrients. Therefore, the rooted cutting should be promptly transferred to a new container and planted in Transplant Mix (above).

■ Houseplant Mix

This mix calls for about 50 percent compost or leaf mold, because these materials provide good drainage, yet keep phenomenal amounts of moisture available to the houseplants. This helps reduce the chance of overwatering or underwatering. The rest of the ingredients provide an adequate store of nutrients and good soil aeration.

1 quart finely sifted topsoil
2 quarts finely sifted compost *or* high-quality leaf mold
1 quart coarse builder's sand, perlite or vermiculite, *or* premoistened peat or sphagnum moss
½ cup dehydrated cow manure *or* ¼ cup dehydrated poultry manure

Put 1 inch of loose gravel at the bottom of the container for better drainage. Apply Manure Tea (below), according to the needs of the particular plant.

■ Manure Tea

Poultry manure is the best to use for this because of its high concentration of nutrients.

40–50 pounds manure
water

Suspend manure in a burlap bag in a 55-gallon metal drum ¾ filled with water, for 3 to 4 days. Keep the drum covered to control odors. Remove the burlap bag, and use the solid manure as you normally would for your garden. About half of its nutrients still remain. To use the tea, dilute it to half strength with water and spray on plants, or apply directly on soil.

Chapter 15 Managing Garden Pests

Carol Meinhardt Hopkins

There is more than one way to approach garden problems and so-called pests. Insects, soil diseases (like fungi), prolific weed growth, and trespassing wildlife can be viewed as enemies that need to be obliterated as soon as they are discovered—or they can be considered natural occurrences that call for careful management.

Wildlife and insects that we most often think of as pests may actually be helpful in some situations. Take skunks, for example. Few animals have as bad a reputation as they do; we avoid them like the plague. Yet how many people know that they are mild, harmless creatures that help to control a much nastier pest—the wasp. Rabbits are food for owls and hawks. Garter snakes eat slugs that suck life out of plant leaves, and redwing blackbirds search out cutworms and other troublesome bugs. Before we so much as give a plant a forceful spray of water to remove aphids, we should consider first the extent of the damage. These pernicious little insects are also food for lacewings and ladybugs, voracious little life forms whose presence as overall insect sweepers may be more valuable than the few leaves they destroy.

Integrated Pest Management

Through trial and error, organic growers and researchers have evolved a practical, ecological system that has been appropriately labeled integrated pest management. In empirical terms, integrated pest management means structuring a garden or farm in such a way that a mixture of different plant and animal species can coexist and complement one another. The result, as test after test has shown, is a stable growing environment where no species get out of control. The grower is no longer involved in a perpetual battle to destroy the enemy; rather, he works to create balance in what first appears as conflicting conditions and elements in the garden environment.

One of the first steps to integrated pest management is establishing good soil health. Compost, mulches, crop covers, natural rock fertilizers, and lots of animal manure create substantial, beneficial microbial and bacterial activity that wards off the start of most soil diseases. In addition, plants raised in such rich ground are generally able to withstand soilborne diseases if or when these diseases arise. It's the old truism that a healthy body has a much better chance of resisting disease, while a weak one succumbs more easily to the malady.

Good cultural practices are also a vital part of integrated pest management. These essential techniques alter the habitat in many diverse ways to make it inhospitable for pest reproduction and survival. Most are logical procedures that virtually all organic growers instinctively follow. Soil cultivation (chisel-plowing on the farm and tilling in the garden) prevents many insects and diseases from making headway in the soil. Destruction of crop residues (through turning under or composting) prevents insects from overwintering on the grounds. Careful watering during the growing season is another step that is more important than many people imagine. An even, regular amount of moisture helps maintain the proper microbial activity in the soil and discourages certain fungi from starting where there are overly damp conditions.

In addition to following these universal cultural practices, the staff at the Rodale Research Center has experimented with plant varieties to find those that have been bred to resist disease or those that are naturally resistant to it in the first place. Over the years, they have discovered that blueberries are rather pest-free, acorn squash shows more tolerance to squash bug than do most other cucurbits, and corn that forms a tightly wrapped husk on the cob is physically protected against corn earworm. (See Appendix C, "Mail-Order Suppliers and Manufacturers" for mail-order sources for some resistant varieties.)

Another good pest control measure is either to grow specific crops when particular enemies are inactive or to put out seeds or seedlings so that the crops are most vulnerable when the pest is least prolific. For example, many Easterners plant squash at the very earliest date possible to avoid borers that lay eggs in July. By that date, the vines are less vulnerable than younger, more delicate ones would be, and also strong enough to withstand damage if it occurs. All in all, organic growers attest to the fact that when many of these cultural practices are combined, the soil fertility remains high, plant production is at a maximum, and insects and soil diseases are generally kept below bothersome levels.

Yet, in spite of dutiful adherence to organic principles, pest imbalances will occur on occasion. The following formulas and sources should help you to deal with just such an eventuality.

Out of approximately one million named plant-feeding insects and mice, only about 1 percent can actually be considered pests. And to control this paltry 1 percent we use inordinate quantities of chemicals each year. As a matter of fact, the greatest amount of synthetic poisons produced in this country are used against insects and mice, and over 50 percent of these are used on agricultural pests. We are all too aware of the health problems and environmental damage these poisons create. While most of us cannot do anything about pesticides used on farms, we can control those used in our gardens. On the following pages you'll find good, safe pest control alternatives that have been used and proven successful by scores of organic gardeners.

Homemade Organic Sprays

If your plants are plagued with an infestation of mealybugs or spider mites, give them a good spraying of cold water directly from the hose. (Try the same method on your bug-ridden houseplants.) Be persistent and continue to spray every day for about a week. If the insects seem to have subsided considerably, you have in your hands an easy method to control some species of bugs.

When water does not quite do the trick for a pest upsurge, many organic gardeners turn to spray formulations that they concoct themselves from common substances—water, soap, plants, and sometimes even the pests that are doing all the damage. Depending on the materials in the brew, these sprays eliminate insects in a number of different ways. Some compounds smother, others infect, and still others just downright repulse any bug who dares approach.

Used in proper proportions, soap solutions work by smothering unwanted insects, particularly soft-bodied ones, without harming the plants themselves. The most effective ones control pest populations just as well as the conventional synthetic insecticides for several days after treatment. Without the residual effect of chemical products, however, they must be applied weekly to provide lasting protection. Be sure that you don't use too concentrated a solution, since soap can burn leaves. Dry soap leaves unslightly spots, especially on plants with dense, pubescent leaves.

There is good indication that certain plants have insect-repelling qualities. Gardeners and researchers have noted that some plants are seldom disturbed by pests. Particular compounds in them act as natural barriers. Tobacco may be habit-forming for humans, but most bugs stay away. Elderberry leaves, poplar leaves, and horseradish are all relatively free of insect damage.

Focusing on the repellent quality of some plants, researchers in California successfully used sprays of neem seed and tung nut extracts as repellents to 12 species of native insects, including yellow scale, citrus mealybug, wooly whitefly, and boll weevil. Gardeners report success with all-purpose sprays made of citrus and banana peels. Others have encouraging results with an alfalfa, clover, and garlic solution for controlling some pest species on field legumes. Greenhouse plant growers now recognize poplar leaf sprays as a reputable remedy for mites.

Actual insect pests are the basic material of insect juice sprays. Preparing them involves capturing a handful of whatever insect is causing the damage, grinding the bugs in a blender with water, straining the mixture, and spraying it on the infected crop. Although formal experiments have not yet been able to substantiate its effectiveness, two theories have been offered to explain its mode of action.

Careful observations indicate that the insect juice sprays have repellent qualities.

Some bugs, it seems, pick up the odor of the decomposed remains and find it so intolerable that they stay away from the protected plant. The other popular assumption is that the sprays contaminate the pests to which they are applied. (All tests so far indicate that humans and animals are unaffected.) When a gardener takes up a handful of the unwanted bugs, the probability is that a certain percentage harbor some insect disease, and it may be the disease-causing substance in the solution that kills a number of the living members of the group. A number of scientists are experimenting with the use of disease sprays for small- and large-scale pest management programs. One of the most notable results to date is the discovery of the bacterial disease, *Bacillus thuringiensis*, used in the control of destructive moth larvae such as the gypsy moth.

Following are a number of simple formulas that have worked under specific conditions for other organic gardeners. Before you begin to mix up any brew, however, you'll want to review the spraying tips listed below. Once you get ready to spray, you won't want to experience the frustration of a clogged machine.

Essential Spraying Information

1. Prepare solutions according to directions. Concentrations that are too strong may clog the nozzle.
2. Strain mixture through several thicknesses of cheesecloth before pouring it into the sprayer.
3. During the spraying operation, stop and clean the nozzle occasionally to get rid of any accumulation.
4. When you are finished spraying, empty the sprayer of its contents and wash the body and the nozzle well. If you have been using insect juices, be certain to sterilize the parts with boiling water. Allow the machine to dry well before you put it away.

Soap sprays work best on soft-bodied insects, particularly psyllids, spider mites, exposed thrips (a species that feeds on fully expanded leaves), mealybugs, whiteflies, chinch bugs, and aphids.

Choose a liquid or dry soap detergent or any bar soap. Liquid dish detergents, such as Ivory and Palmolive, are the easiest to use and have killed greater than 85 percent of certain insects in tests. Powders such as Fels Naphtha, on the other hand, are sometimes difficult to dissolve, and some (for example Tide) burn leaves of many plant species. Shaving soaps, like William's, form too many suds, which clog the sprayer. Shaklee's Basic H, a liquid, nontoxic, biodegradable soap, does not achieve high scores as an insecticide.

Apply sprays at high pressure with a houseplant mister, a hand-pump compressed-air sprayer, a hose-end sprayer, or other suitable equipment. Test the spray on only a few leaves at first, to be sure the solution doesn't burn the plant. Apply weekly and after each rain until infestation is no longer excessive.

Adhere to suggested proportions. More concentrated solutions work best on bugs but are also more likely to clog spray nozzles and cause leaf burn or curling. Less concentrated ones are not effective insect controls. Used at a temperature of 85°F or over, soap sprays may burn African violet leaves. Heavy concentrations of soap spray leave a white residue, which most people find undesirable on ornamentals and houseplants. If left to cool overnight most mixtures will harden and gel, and will have to be shaken vigorously before using.

■ Liquid Soap Spray

2–4 tablespoons liquid soap
1 gallon water

Mix liquid soap into water and apply as directed above.

■ Powdered Soap Spray

¼ cup powdered soap
1 gallon warm water

Dissolve powdered soap in 2 cups of the water. Add remaining water and apply as directed above.

■ Bar Soap Spray

¼ cup grated bar soap
1 gallon water

Boil the water and add the soap to dissolve. Allow to cool to about room temperature and apply as directed above.

Here are some suggestions for making plant juice sprays. Look around for nonpoisonous weeds or tree leaves that are seldom bothered by insects. Clean, healthy-looking vegetation is the best indicator. Seek plants like pine and poplar and all edible herbs that are nontoxic and usually pest-free. Hairy-leafed plants that are free of insects do not necessarily indicate vegetation that contains repellent compounds; it is their irregular surface that keeps away many insects. Therefore, these plants are not good choices for plant juice sprays.

■ Plant Juice Spray

1 part chopped leaves of pine *or* poplar *or* edible herbs
1 part water

Mix leaves and water and blend for 30 seconds. Strain the liquid through several thicknesses of cheesecloth and pour into a sprayer. Spray on plants and reapply weekly and after each rain until infestation is reduced. For follow-up applications make a fresh solution. This spray can be stretched by diluting it with water, but no more than 5 times its original amount or it will lose effectiveness.

In informal tests at the Rodale Research Center, the staff has found certain sprays made from insect carcasses to be effective on over 20 insects. Among insects affected are cabbage loopers, grape skeletonizers, stinkbugs, armyworms, granular cutworms, ants, slugs, gnats, wireworms, and several species of caterpillar. The following formula makes a very strong extract that you can dilute up to 25 thousand times its volume without any loss of effectiveness.

■ Insect Juice Spray

½ cup insect carcasses of the pest to be sprayed
1 pint water

Blend the insects and water together until all is homogenized. Strain the liquid into a glass jar or plastic container. To use, pour a few drops of the concentrated solution into the sprayer, and then fill to the top with water. Spray on infested plants immediately. Freeze the remaining concentrate for weekly reapplications and after rain, until the infestation has lessened.

Caution: Do not collect houseflies, mosquitoes, fleas, or ticks for making insect juice spray solution. These insects harbor human disease, and using them in a spray can spread disease agents.

■ General All-Purpose Insect Spray

This spray makes use of the repellent qualities of garlic, onion, and hot peppers. The soap makes it cling to plant leaves.

1 garlic bulb
1 small onion
1 tablespoon cayenne pepper
1 quart water
1 tablespoon liquid soap detergent

Chop or grind garlic and onion, add cayenne, and mix with water. Let steep 1 hour, then add liquid soap detergent. Store in a tightly covered jar in the refrigerator up to 1 week.

■ Nicotine Spray

This spray helps control aphids, caterpillars, and destructive worms. Allow a handful of tobacco to stand in 1 gallon of water for 24 hours. Dilute solution to the color of weak tea.

Caution: Do not use this spray on tomato, pepper, eggplant, or any other plants that are members of the solanaceous family, since nicotine can kill them.

■ Garlic Spray

Garlic works well against wireworms, cutworms, slugs, and whiteflies.

6 tablespoons chopped garlic
2 teaspoons liquid paraffin
1 pint water
¼ cup liquid soap

Soak garlic in liquid paraffin for 24 hours. Add water and liquid soap. Mix well. Strain and store in a glass jar for no longer than 1 week.

■ Buttermilk/Flour Spray

For a heavy infestation of spider mites in the orchard, this spray works wonders. It is a sticky mixture that suffocates the bugs without hindering the tree's transpiration or respiration.

5 pounds white flour
1 pint buttermilk
25 gallons water

Mix ingredients together, siphon into sprayer, and apply weekly to orchard trees until the leaves are full grown and mite populations have decreased to about 3 per leaf.

■ Repellent Spray

This spray incorporates a number of different plants, all with repellent qualities.

½ cup fresh spearmint leaves
½ cup green onion tops
½ cup horseradish roots and leaves
½ cup red-hot peppers
water
2 tablespoons liquid detergent

Blend together spearmint leaves, onion tops, horseradish roots and leaves, and peppers with enough water to cover the mix. If the blend is too viscous, add more water and blend again. Strain the mixture, and add ½ gallon of water. Add liquid detergent. To use, dilute ½ cup of repellent in ½ gallon water in a sprayer. Store unused portion in a cool place for no longer than 3 days.

■ Alcohol Spray

A touch of alcohol is a deadly potent for mealybugs. An alcohol spray, used on a regular basis, is an excellent means of paring down this frequent visitor to greenhouses and houseplants.

½ cup alcohol
2 tablespoons soap flakes
1 quart warm water

Mix together the alcohol and soap flakes in water. There is no need to strain this solution. Make fresh batches each time you spray.

■ Salt Solution

It is a recorded fact that many fruit trees grown along coasts and constantly exposed to salt air are free of curculio. Light salt solutions are also useful against spider mites and cabbageworms in the greenhouse and in the garden.

2 tablespoons salt
1 gallon water

Put salt and water into a sprayer, shake, and use.

Dormant Oil Sprays

Dormant oils are petroleum-based formulations (97 percent petroleum, 3 percent inert ingredients) used in a spray form for controlling pests on hardy fruit trees. They must be applied in winter or very early spring, up until about ¼ inch of green is showing on the buds. If the trees are in leaf or are flowering, the spray can cause burn and heavy leaf and fruit damage. The flavor of the fruit may also be tainted.

Mechanical, not chemical, stranglers, these sprays encase the tree in a tight, continuous, oxygen-proof film that smothers eggs and the new offspring of insect species. Many people immediately assume such a barrier would also shut off oxygen to the tree, but at this particular time the tree is getting its oxygen and other sustenance from its roots.

Unlike most other mechanical insect traps, dormant oil sprays do have a residual effect that is actually advantageous. The residue is nontoxic, will not affect soil organisms, and does not bring about resistant insect species as chemicals so often do. It is particularly important in the control of mites and scale insects that are recurrent pests.

Dormant oil sprays control a host of sucking and chewing insects, such as aphids, thrips, mealybugs, whiteflies, pear psylla, red spiders, and various forms of scale. They also destroy the eggs of codling moths, oriental fruit moths, assorted leaf rollers, and cankerworms.

Apply dormant oil anytime from winter after all the leaves have fallen to late April before any buds develop beyond the ¼-inch-green stage. (Depending on locale and weather conditions, dates will vary.) Some orchardists prefer to spray closer to the spring date, because the shells of insects hatched the previous fall are more penetrable at that time. Spray the oil on a calm, sunny day with just-above-average temperatures. Cover the entire tree in one spraying. Do not work down one line of a grove of trees and up the other, since any overlapping of spray caused by such a practice can damage trees, especially citrus trees and those in arid areas.

If you purchase dormant oil, make certain it does not contain any combination of arsenate of lead, Bordeaux mixture, or lime sulfur. These are unnecessary additions that are dangerous both to you and to soil organisms.

■ Dormant Oil Formula

Although dormant oil is not expensive, you may wish to make your own.

½ cup fish oil
½ cup No. 10 mineral oil
1 cup liquid detergent
2 gallons water

Thoroughly mix together the fish oil, mineral oil, and liquid detergent. Disperse the oil mixture in tiny droplets in a bucket containing the water. Pour the liquid into the sprayer.

Botanical Sprays

Botanical poisons are plant derivatives with a rather all-encompassing "knock-down" effect on insects, injurious ones and beneficials as well. Before World War I, in advance of the manufacture of devastating nerve gases for militaristic purposes that later became the basic ingredients for synthetic pesticides, various homemade sprays and the botanical poisons—rotenone, pyrethrum, and ryania—were the order of the day. Pyrethrum, a dried form of a species of chrysanthemum flower, in fact, had been in use at that time for over one hundred years. Up to that period in history, these dusts and sprays supplied a relatively safe means for growers, particularly large-scale ones, to rid their fields of economically destructive pests. Because of their natural origins, they quickly degraded in the soil and, unless used improperly or to excess, affected humans and animals only negligibly.

Today botanical poisons continue to appear under trade names on garden suppliers' shelves. Rotenone is available in a pure state, while pyrethrum is usually mixed with a combination of rotenone and ryania. (See Appendix C, "Mail-Order Suppliers and Manufacturers," for sources.)

Pyrethrum has a good track record as an annihilator of leafhoppers, cabbage loopers, aphids, whitefly, corn earworms, lygus bugs, thrips, and cranberry fruitworms. It works less effectively on artichoke plum moths, imported cabbageworms, tomato fruitworms, and beet armyworms. It is nontoxic to beneficial bees, ladybug larvae, and warm-blooded animals (although some human allergic reactions have been reported). It does harm earthworms and adult ladybugs.

Certain pyrethrum flowers grow mainly in Kenya and Ecuador where they are rare and, as a result, extremely expensive. What we find readily available are commercial spray preparations that contain only a portion of the dried heads plus one or two other plant-derived bug killers (not to be confused with pyrethroids, which are untested and unregistered synthetic chemicals).

In recent years, botanists have discovered a species of pyrethrum, called cinerariifolium, that has higher concentrations of the resin than its powerful African or South American cousins. Unfortunately, this flower is still as yet largely unavailable to laypersons. Coccineum, on the other hand, although considerably lower in potency, is yet another species and one that many gardeners raise for making their own sprays. (See Appendix C, "Mail-Order Suppliers and Manufacturers," for a source for these seeds.)

■ Pyrethrum Spray from Homegrown Flowers

dried coccineum heads
3 quarts water

With a mortar and pestle or in a blender, grind a few dry coccineum heads to a fine powder. Make a paste of the powder and about 1 cup of the water. Whisk paste into the remaining water. Line a large funnel with several thicknesses of cheesecloth and insert the funnel in the spray opening. Filter the spray solution through the funnel. Agitate sprayer as you treat the crops.

We recommend that you spray during the evening and that you avoid applying spray within 3 to 7 days of harvesting. Do not keep leftover spray; dispose of it and clean the sprayer well.

Controlling Insects with Animals

The presence of beneficial insect-eating birds, toads, frogs, salamanders, and snakes in your garden is nature's gift about which you need do nothing but stand in awe and appreciation. Some gardeners and farmers, however, choose to go one step further by providing comfortable nesting places for some of these creatures, particularly for birds, who are perhaps the easiest of the group to encourage. In St. Matthew, South Carolina, for example, the local citizens hold an annual three-day festival in celebration of the vernal arrival of the purple martins. The town fathers of St. Matthew, which was once an area ridden with mosquitoes, came up with the idea of erecting a rather elaborate network of birdhouses on public and private buildings to draw these prodigious insect eaters. Now the birds have regular nesting grounds, and the mosquito population is under control.

■ Bird Seed

Because most birds have simple tastes, enticing them with a suitable feed is rather effortless. You can make this economical mix that draws a large variety of birds by buying both millet and sunflower seeds at a farm supply or feed mill.

1 part white millet
1 part high-oil sunflower seed

Mix millet and seeds together. Store any unused portion in a cool, dry place.

Bird field guides and certain ornithological works will help you find specific birds to seek out for particular insect infestations. In the meantime, we offer a brief list of the most common insect-feeding birds that deserve your most gracious welcome.

Common Insect-Feeding Birds

Baltimore orioles
bluebirds
bobolinks
brown creepers
brown thrashers
chickadees
cowbirds
doves
field sparrows
finches
flickers
goldfinches
gulls
house wrens
indigo buntings
juncoes
meadowlarks
mockingbirds
nuthatches
phoebes
purple martins
robins
swallows
woodpeckers
wrens
yellow-throated warblers

Other Insect Controls

For the most effective management of insect pests, many gardeners combine sound cultural practices with other methods of control, generally called mechanical controls. Various attractants that lure insects away from garden plants are one type of mechanical control, and include such things as appealing nesting places, attractive colors, pleasing sounds, food scraps, and sweets. Another type of mechanical control is traps, such as butterfly nets, canvas drop cloths to catch insects shaken from trees, and sticky barriers for insects moving in the air, through the trees, or on the ground. Two more sophisticated mechanical controls that have been notably successful are insect secretions called pheromones, which are used as attractants, and razor-sharp earth particles known as diatomaceous earth, which are lethal traps.

Pheromones are specific chemical secretions that insects emanate for various purposes, among them sex attraction. For thousands of years, gardeners and farmers have made use of this knowledge by using live insects to lure others of the same species, then trapping them in escape-proof containers. In more recent times, scientists have been working with synthesized forms of these natural elements to determine pest densities on a particular crop or area. Of late, pheromone traps for controlling pests within a defined space have become available to general consumers. The market is presently inundated with various brands of simply constructed pheromone traps that work well for Japanese beetles in a small-scale gardening operation. (See Appendix C, "Mail-Order Suppliers and Manufacturers," for some mail-order sources.)

Diatomaceous earth is a naturally occurring substance that mechanically kills insects. It is composed of fossilized, microscopic, one-celled organisms called diatoms. As these organisms die, their shells build up in deposits at the bottom of lakes and lagoons. When these water bodies dry up, over a period of millions of years, huge deposits of diatoms remain.

Scientists have been working with the idea of diatomaceous earth as an insect dust for more than 45 years. They have discovered that milling breaks down the diatom shells, each covered with a pattern of holes, into tiny razor-sharp needles. Scattered over sections of the garden floor or mixed with stored grains or seeds, these sharp edges attack the wax coating that covers a pest's external skeleton. Since this thin, hard frame is the only thing keeping in vital fluids, the insect gradually loses moisture and dies within about 12 hours.

Diatomaceous earth works on a long list of bugs, but only when they are in their pupal, maggot, or grub stage. At this point in development they must actually crawl through the stuff to become punctured by the sharp edges of the material. Among the insects that it effectively controls are slugs, Colorado potato beetles, squash and cucumber beetles, root maggots, aphids, and bean beetles. It also cuts into the bodies of cabbage loopers, tomato hornworms, various fruit flies and worms, Japanese beetles, pink boll weevils, lygus bugs, thrips, snails, ants, and cornworms.

If you decide to use diatomaceous earth, avoid commercial formulations that are mixed with piperonyl butoxide, a chemical synergist. This additional substance may be harmful to humans and animals. Also, wear a mask when applying diatomaceous earth. Although it is completely safe for humans in its pure form, the dust can irritate lungs. (See Appendix C, "Mail-Order Suppliers and Manufacturers," for mail-order sources of this substance.)

One other effective way to control insects that is worth mentioning is to put out jar lids filled with fermenting yeasts and carbohydrates. If you bury these lids to the rims in your garden and fill them with beer, honey, molasses, or corn syrup, insects such as the codling moth and the oriental fruit moth, fruit fly, and borer will eat these and die.

Keeping Fungi under Control

Fungi that harm other plants exhibit themselves in some very showy ways, and, therefore, we identify them by their appearance. Downy mildew (also fake mildew) surfaces as pale patches on the undersides of leaves. True or powdery mildew lives on the upper leaf surface and sucks out nutrients. Rust fungi imparts a distinct reddish color to leaves, while leaf-spot fungi causes round, yellow green marks that darken with time. Gray mold is the grayish downy circle that forms on berries, fruits, and flowers.

The best way to deter a fungal outbreak is to establish an inhospitable environment for these organisms. This involves pursuing good cultural practices; providing a clean, light, airy environment; and supplying proper nutrients in the soil. In addition, over the years, gardeners have expanded on these basic principles and have discovered a few tips which work well for them.

■ Plant Juice Remedy

Elements in certain plants inhibit fungal spore germination. *Cerespora*, a fungus which causes leaf spot, can be retarded with a spray made from clematis, corn leaves, and the papery outer leaves of garlic. Make a solution by blending the substances with water in a blender. Filter the liquid and spray it directly on plants until the condition subsides.

■ Baking Soda for Grapes

Grape fungi (especially black rot) live on the acid in the developing skin of the fruit. Baking soda, used in the correct proportions, alkalizes the condition while the grapes are developing and makes them unappealing for the fungi. Prepare a solution of 4 teaspoons baking soda dissolved in 1 gallon water, and spray the mixture evenly over the grapes and vines. Apply once when the fruit starts to appear and weekly thereafter for about 2 months. Also, reapply after each rain.

■ Spices to Preserve Stored Beans and Grains

Aspergillus flavus is a fungus that produces carcinogenic aflatoxin on storage beans, peanuts, and grains. A spice mixture is a natural preservative that combats this condition. Some grain storage firms have used this method successfully to replace chemical fungicides in storage elevators.

In individual cheesecloth bags, tie together cinnamon sticks, whole black peppercorns, ground black mustard, and some green garlic. Place one bag into each gallon container with beans and grains.

Controlling Animal Pests

In spite of the fact that animals wreak as much, or more, havoc in our garden as insects do, they are vital to a balanced ecology. For instance, redwing blackbirds may threaten your corn at the tender sprout age, but this bird also feeds on cutworms, aphids, and beet webworms, other dangers to your crops. Such complicated relationships among the flora and fauna are the rule, not the exception, in your garden. To guard your harvests, you must approach your crops' protection from animals on an individual basis rather than with some wholesale method.

Most safeguards against animals are physical, such as fences, steel posts, scarecrows for birds, lure crops, or overplanting to share the bounty. All of these methods are effective in their own right, but a few formulas do exist for substances that will deter some of your garden's animal pests.

Cats and Dogs

■ Cat and Dog Repellent

Buy hot cayenne pepper in bulk, and sprinkle it wherever the animals lounge or play. Once they have a taste of this hot stuff, they will go elsewhere.

Deer

A salt block hanging from a post in the garden or from a tree at the edge of the field sometimes causes deer to forget crops. Hanging human hair in cheesecloth bags from trees, at the height at which deer nibble, is also an excellent deterrent.

Blood meal is an effective, inexpensive nitrogen fertilizer and deer deterrent. Sprinkle it close to susceptible plants or all around the garden at least twice a season, or make the spray below.

■ Blood Spray Deer Repellent

1 tablespoon blood meal
2 gallons warm water

Mix blood meal into the warm water. Pour into a sprayer and coat plants and trees. Apply regularly when plants are most vulnerable. *Caution:* Excess application may burn plants, so be careful with amounts. This formula is also effective against rabbits and shrews.

■ Dr. Gouin's Deer Repellent Spray

Dr. Francis Gouin at the University of Maryland has achieved a fair amount of success in repelling deer with this spray.

1 tablespoon Tabasco sauce
1 tablespoon commercial adhesive (such as Vapo-Guard) *or* ½ cup nondetergent soap powder
1 gallon water

Mix the ingredients together, pour them into a sprayer, and thoroughly spray tops and undersides of leaves that you expect are most attractive to these forest creatures. This formula is also effective against mice.

Moles

Moles find castor beans and their by-products extremely repulsive. (See Appendix C, "Mail-Order Suppliers and Manufacturers," for sources.) *Caution:* Take care when using around children; ingestion of certain amounts can be toxic to humans.

Plant potatoes or other root crops with castor beans (about 4 to a 40-foot-square area). Or, make a spray from the oil.

■ Castor Bean Mole Repellent

¼ cup castor oil
2 tablespoons liquid detergent
6 tablespoons water

In a blender, whip together castor oil and liquid detergent until the resultant mixture is like shaving cream. Add the water and whip again. Take a regular garden sprinkling can, fill it with warm water, and add 2 tablespoons of the oil mixture. Stir and sprinkle the liquid immediately over the areas of the greatest damage. For best results, apply after a rain or a thorough watering.

Rabbits

Rabbits are strict vegetarians and shun any sort of animal products. Placed in the path of their favorite pickings, such substances often serve to repel them. To protect trees in the fall, paint them with old animal lard.

A sprinkling of rock phosphate around the border of a garden patch and around the base of tender plants also often deters rabbits, and Blood Spray Deer Repellent (above) deters rabbits as well.

■ Cow Manure Rabbit Repellent

Mix water with cow manure to a liquid consistency. Sprinkle the liquid on rows of tender vegetables with a broom or other sweep. Apply twice a month or after each rain. The mixture should last for about 1 month.

■ Talcum/Hot Pepper Rabbit Repellent

Rabbits love to eat young shoots of delphiniums, tulips, crocuses, dianthus, and numerous other flowers. The following sometimes discourages rabbits.

1 part talcum powder
1 part ground hot pepper

Mix and sprinkle regularly over the flower patch.

Chapter 16 Auto, Work Area, and Outdoor Equipment

Suzanne Ebbert and Deborah Wilson

Keeping a well-organized work area, such as your garage or workshop, can make the space and those things in it a real delight to use and maintain. It means being orderly in storing your possessions, but it also means making some judgments about what equipment you really need and want to store, and what objects are merely taking up space due to some hazy intentions you have for them off in some indeterminate future. This includes any half-obsolete sporting or camping equipment that you keep next to your newer models, just in case of some emergency.

The first step in caring for your garage or workshop and its contents is to assume Solomon's crown and divide your belongings into those you really use, need, or have definite plans for, and those you can part with. If you're having trouble making such decisions, one good way to determine if you'll ever get to some languishing project or use a particular extraneous item is to ask yourself if it's been sitting unused in your garage or workshop for two or three years; if so, find it a new home. It's helpful to perform this assessment on a yearly basis.

Traditional garage sales or tag sales, of course, are natural ways to remove these things from your work area. You can also donate many of these items to your local charitable institutions. As a last resort, detach usable parts before finally throwing irreparable objects away.

Ridding yourself of any excess paraphernalia is part of operating efficiently in your workplace, but another aspect is being sure that you have the proper tools to perform the tasks or projects you have in mind. Working with the right tools makes any job easier and quicker, so you're likely to finish more of those repair jobs. (It makes the yearly assessment of the goods in your garage easier, too.) Working without the right tools can lift you to the heights of frustration, and in many cases, it can be dangerous. This is especially true when servicing cars or working with power tools. Spend some time choosing and assembling the tools you need first, before tackling potentially dangerous activities. Safety goggles and gloves are almost always a good idea, too.

Auto Care

Maybe your car is one of your most cherished possessions—something you pamper. Or maybe your car is just a way to get around and nothing more. Regardless of how you feel about that hunk of metal, it needs a lot of tender, loving care to make it last and give you the most for your money. You may choose to pay someone else to provide that care, or you can do it yourself. Doing your own work can really save money. And you can formulate several of your own auto-care products and save even more.

A very basic part of auto care is keeping it clean. The exterior surfaces of most vehicles are subject to rust, so the surface must be kept as clean and free of dirt as possible. A protective coating of wax at least twice a year is a must.

Drive-through-type car washes may be convenient, but they use harsh detergents and abrasive brushes that can damage your car's finish in time. It's better to wash your car yourself, by hand. To do so, first make sure all of the car windows are tightly closed. Then hose off all loose dirt. Don't miss the undersurface areas of bumpers, fenders, and the chassis. Remove any tar deposits by rubbing with a little baking soda on a damp cloth. After these steps, rinse, then soap up with Car Wash (below). If your car is really dirty, you can use a mild liquid dishwashing detergent, but don't use this too often, or on a new wax job. Although mild, these detergents can dull the finish and remove the wax.

■ Car Wash

¼ cup soap flakes
2 gallons warm water

Add soap flakes to water. Mix to dissolve soap. Using a large sponge, a mitt, or a soft cloth, apply this solution to the car. Always start at the top and work down. Wash one section at a time and then rinse. Wash everything—including the undersurface of bumpers, fenders, and the chassis. Wash the wheels, wheel covers, and tires last. Unless you're really speedy, don't try to suds the entire car at once, especially in hot weather. The soap will dry and be difficult to rinse off, and the surface will streak. Rinse everything thoroughly. Dry the entire surface with a chamois or a very soft, absorbent, lint-free cloth. Do not use paper towels. They will leave tiny scratches in the finish.

If it has a good layer of wax on the finish, you can wash your car without any detergent or soap. Just hose off vigorously and thoroughly. Using a bucket of clear, warm water, wash all surfaces with a large sponge, a mitt, or a soft cloth. Rinse thoroughly and wipe dry with a chamois or a very soft absorbent cloth.

Chrome

Shining chrome can add that special glow to your car's appearance, if it is kept in good condition. It needs to be cleaned every time you wash the car, using the same cleaning product you use for the exterior painted surface or the Chrome Cleaner, below. Also, when waxing your car, be sure to apply wax to the chrome parts as well. This will help the chrome to hold up better against the elements.

■ Chrome Cleaner

Apply baking soda to the chrome surface, and make a paste by adding water. Rub with a sponge. Let the paste set for a few minutes, rinse, and wipe dry with a soft cloth. This formula will remove all of those tiny rust pittings that age chrome fast.

Tires

Wheels and tires require special care, since they collect so much dirt and grease. Use a brush to scrub the tires. A synthetic scouring pad with a mild liquid detergent works well on both the tires and whitewall trim. Soap-filled steel wool pads are also good for cleaning the whitewalls. If there's a lot of tar on the tires, use a little baking soda. Sprinkle it on, scour with a damp scouring pad, and rinse well. Dry with a soft cloth.

Vinyl and Convertible Tops

Vinyl and convertible tops can be washed as you wash the rest of the exterior, but they also require some additional care. You may need to scrub them with a soft-bristled brush. This helps to get the dirt out of the grained surface. Apply a protective dressing to the surface. (For additional suggestions for the care of vinyl upholstery, see Index.)

When cleaning convertible tops, do not scratch the rear window. They are often made from a plastic glazing material. If they are plastic, be careful of what you use to clean them. Do not use any formula containing alcohol, acetone (contained in fingernail polish remover), or ammonia. Vinegar is okay.

Windows and Windshields

Clean windows not only make the car look better, but also allow you to see better. Better visibility means a safer trip, so keep that windshield clean—that goes for headlights and taillights also. For quicker cleaning, wipe up and down on one side of the window and then left to right on the other side. This way you'll know which side needs more work.

■ Extra-Strength Windshield Cleaner

If your windshield is coated with a film of dead bugs, use this cleaner.

½ cup whiting
¼ cup baking soda
1 cup fuller's earth
water

Mix whiting, baking soda, and fuller's earth together, and slowly add water to make a paste. Apply mixture to the glass with a sponge. Polish with a dry, lint-free cloth.

■ Vinegar Window/Windshield Cleaner

2 tablespoons white vinegar *or* lemon juice
3 cups water

Mix together and store in a spray container. To use, spray solution across window surface and wipe until dry with a lint-free cloth, or shine with crumpled newspaper. This formula is good for both glass and plastic surfaces.

■ Borax Window/Windshield Cleaner

2 tablespoons borax *or* washing soda
3 cups water

Mix ingredients together and store in a spray container. To use, spray solution across window surface and wipe until dry with a lint-free cloth. This cleaner is safe for both glass and plastic surfaces.

■ Ammonia Window/Windshield Cleaner

1½ cups household ammonia
1½ cups water

Mix and store in a spray container. To use, spray surface with solution and dry with a lint-free soft cloth. *Caution:* Do not use on plastic surfaces.

Carpeting

It is difficult to keep the carpeting in a car clean. Always use mats, since they help to control the dirt and grease that accumulate. In spite of all precautions, though, the carpeting inevitably will become dirty. Vacuum the carpeting frequently—every time you wash the car, if possible. Frequent vacuuming picks up most of the dirt before it has a chance to be ground into the carpet fibers. For picking up heavy dirt without shampooing, you can sprinkle some absorbent material, such as cornmeal or fuller's earth, on the carpet. Allow to sit for several hours, then vacuum.

When spills occur, wipe them up immediately. Don't let water or rain soak through the carpeting even when cleaning. The carpet will be difficult to dry, and mildew may attack it. Occasionally, the carpeting may require shampooing. For carpet shampoos, see Index.

Floor Mats

Floor mats will protect the carpeting from wear and control dirt and grease. Make sure your car is fitted with the correct size. A floor mat that's too small won't offer much protection to the carpeting. Clean the mats every time you wash the car, more frequently if you really drag dirt in on your shoes. For those times when you can't avoid walking in dirty or muddy areas, you may want to put something else on top of the mats to collect that extra dirt. Large pieces of scrap cloth or newspaper can be used for this. Remove these carefully when you no longer need them, and discard, dirt and all.

Most mats are made from rubber or vinyl. Never use harsh chemicals, solvents, or abrasives like steel wool scouring pads to clean them. Certain chemicals can react with the rubber or vinyl, and strong abrasives can scratch the surface. To clean, use the following formula.

■ Car Floor Mat Cleaner

¼ cup mild dishwashing detergent
2 gallons warm water

Mix detergent and water together and gently scrub the mats with the solution and a stiff-bristled brush. For tar spots, rub with a little baking soda or some Scouring Cleanser (see Index). Rinse. Dry thoroughly on both sides. Occasionally, you may want to use a protective coating of petroleum jelly on the mats, which will also give them a nice shine.

Upholstery

Upholstery in cars is usually vinyl or cloth, although some luxury models may be outfitted with real leather. Car upholstery must be cared for as you would any fine furniture. It can be expensive to have it repaired or replaced professionally. Vacuum the creases and crevices on a routine basis. Be careful not to scratch or puncture the material. Wipe up any spills immediately. Periodically wipe vinyl or leather upholstery with a damp sponge, and apply a conditioner to keep it from drying out. For further suggestions for the care and cleaning of vinyl, cloth, or leather upholstery, see Index.

It's a good idea to invest in a set of seat covers, even if your car is new. The seat covers will protect the upholstery from spills, punctures, and rips. The upholstery will hold up longer and won't detract from the resale value of your car.

Garage and Workshop

These work areas are no longer the simple shops that they once were. Today there is an array of complex tools—electric and even electronic—and sophisticated chemical compounds to get various jobs done. The tools almost border on being instruments, and the paints and adhesives sound like something directly from an organic chemistry text.

In spite of the advances due to space age technology, there are many basic techniques that haven't changed, and many formulations that can work as well today as they did for Grandpa. Here are a few that will work well and keep you in touch with yesteryear.

Adhesives

An adhesive is any substance that bonds two other substances together. The choice of adhesive depends upon the nature of the materials to be bonded, the condition of the surfaces to be bonded, and the purpose for bonding.

Adhesives can be classified by their chemical characteristics. They can also be classified by the bonding mechanism. Some work by evaporation of moisture from the adhesive; others consist of two substances that, when mixed, work by chemically reacting to form an adhesive material that then forms the bond. This is known as "curing." Some silicone types "cure" by absorbing moisture to form a bond. Other types require heating by an iron, and the bond forms during the cooling process.

■ Gum Arabic Adhesive

This adhesive works for paper as well as for broken glass or porcelain.

6 tablespoons gum arabic
1 cup water
½ cup plus 2 tablespoons glycerin

Dissolve gum arabic in water and add glycerin. Mix well. Apply to both surfaces of broken object with a tongue depressor or wooden stick. Hold together for 5 minutes. If the area of the break will receive extra stress in its normal use, hold the pieces together for 15 minutes with a vise, clamp, or rubber bands. This adhesive works best if it's made fresh for each use, but it can be stored in an airtight container for a short period of time. Before using stored adhesive, test it first on scrap paper.

Painting

Painting may or may not be your thing, but no one likes to clean up. To make it easier on yourself, clean up immediately. In fact, to save some work, carry a dampened cloth with you as you paint—moistened with thinner or turpentine for oil-based paints and with water for latex-based ones. Wipe up any splatters immediately. Have trouble painting around the trim? Use a piece of cardboard as a guide to keep yourself on track.

Do you have some old paintbrushes around that you forgot or want to forget to clean? Before you throw them away, try this one.

■ Stiff Paintbrush Cleaner

Put enough white vinegar in an old saucepan just to cover the brush bristles, and bring to boil. Turn down to simmer a few minutes. Remove brushes from vinegar and wash in soap and warm water. Set out to dry.

When painting, always work in a well-ventilated area and never near an open flame. Many paints and solvents contain flammable petroleum distillates. Avoid breathing the fumes of the paint or of any cleaning solvent that you may use. If you are spray-painting, use a protective mask. This will limit the amount of fumes and particles that you inhale.

To clean paint applicators, first remove the excess paint by stroking the brush or roller over old newspaper or old rags immediately after you finish painting, then clean it with the proper solvent (see Table 16.1). Next, wash the brush or roller in a solution of detergent and warm water. Rinse thoroughly and shake to remove excess water. If you plan to use the same applicator within a day or two, wrap it in plastic wrap to keep it flexible. If you've finished the job and aren't going to be using the applicator for a while, allow it to dry out completely. Comb the bristles with a wire brush to straighten them. To store, wrap the bristles in paper and store flat.

Table 16.1 Solvents for Various Wall Coatings

Coating	Solvent
Lacquer	Lacquer thinner
Latex-based paint	Water
Oil-based paint	Turpentine or paint thinner
Shellac	Denatured alcohol

Don't get into the habit of soaking brushes in a container. You'll inevitably forget about them, and the bristles will loosen. If you must soak, don't let the bristles rest on the bottom of the jar or can. They will permanently lose their shape. Instead, suspend the brush in the container.

If you use a spray gun, clean the gun by running the proper solvent through the gun until only solvent sprays out. Also clean the spray gun can with solvent inside and out. Allow the entire unit to dry thoroughly. For information on making your own paints, read "Homemade Paints" (see Index).

Putty

Commercial types of putty, used to fill cracks in walls, usually contain calcium sulfate (plaster of paris), dextrin, and silica. Wood putty contains wood flour instead of silica. How do they work? As the moisture is released from the dextrin (a vegetable gum made from starch), the mixture hardens. You can easily make your own putty.

■ Plain Putty

linseed oil
whiting

Add enough oil to the whiting to make a paste. Apply to the cracks with a putty knife. Allow to dry. Sand surface if needed. It's now ready for painting.

For small nail holes in plaster or drywall, try the old toothpaste trick. Fill holes with white toothpaste and level with a putty knife. Allow to dry and touch up with paint. Or try Quick-Patch Putty (below).

■ Quick-Patch Putty

1 part salt
1 part powdered starch
water

Mix salt and starch, and add enough water to make a paste. Apply and allow to dry. Touch up with paint.

■ Woodwork Quick Fix

Mix a little dry instant coffee with spackling paste, Plain Putty (above), or equal parts starch and water. Fill in holes on woodwork—usually no staining is required.

Tools

To keep your tools working at their optimum level, you must keep them clean. They are under constant attack by dirt, grease, and rust. There's no secret to caring for tools. Keep them organized—have a place for all gardening, woodworking, and car-repair tools. Dust after each use if needed, rinsing off any mud and dirt. Dry thoroughly with a soft cloth to prevent rust formation. Periodically wipe all metal parts with a cloth that has been moistened with olive oil or lubricating oil. This is especially important if humidity is a problem. If they are really dirty, scrub with a soap-filled steel wool pad, and rinse. Apply a coat of oil, and rub off the excess. To remove rust, use fine-grade (No. 00) steel wool moistened with oil.

Keep the handles clean, too. Some small hand tools have plastic handles. To clean, use warm water and baking soda. Apply paste to the surface and rub. Rinse and dry the entire tool thoroughly. For wooden handles, periodically rub well with a soft cloth moistened with linseed oil.

Washing Up

Then there's clean-up time. For hands that never seem to get clean with ordinary soap, try this one.

■ Tough Hand Cleaner

¼ cup grated naphtha soap ends
1 cup water
2 tablespoons mason's sand *or* pumice

Place soap and water in a saucepan. Place over low heat, stirring until soap is melted. After mixture cools, add mason's sand or pumice and mix. Store in a wide-mouth container. Cottage cheese or margarine tubs are ideal. To use, dip fingers into soap mixture and lather hands. Rinse well. Repeat if necessary. This formula also works well on greasy tools. Be sure to rinse well and dry tools thoroughly.

If you're fortunate enough to have a washing area in your workshop, then you might occasionally have the problem of a clogged drain, with all that grease and dirt making their way into the sink. There are many commercial drain cleaners on the market, but most contain very caustic ingredients, such as lye, which requires extreme care when handling. The fact is, often these cleaners only function in preventive maintenance; that is, they keep the drain clean to prevent a real clog from forming. When you do have a large blockage, only a snake or disassembling the plumbing seems to work. For periodic cleaning of your workshop drain, you can use a very basic formula made from very basic ingredients. (For additional sink and drain cleaners, see Index.)

■ Vinegar Drain Cleaner

½ cup baking soda
½ cup white vinegar
water

Pour baking soda into the drain (remove the drain strainer if possible), followed by the vinegar. *Caution:* These 2 ingredients will react with foaming and fumes. Wait about 2 hours, then flush with water. Repeat if necessary. Use this periodically to keep the drain clean.

■ Salt Drain Cleaner

This one works for greasy drains.

½ cup salt
½ cup baking soda
6 cups boiling water

Pour the salt and baking soda directly into the drain. (Removing the drain strainer first may help.) Follow this with the boiling water. Allow to sit for several hours, overnight if possible. Then flush with water.

■ Grease Spot/Oil Spill Remover

In our world, grease is something we can't seem to get away from. If grease spots are making your work area look like the inside of an oil barge, you can easily clean up the excess. Sprinkle fuller's earth or cornmeal on the spots. Allow to sit for several hours. If necessary, add more for additional absorbing power. Then sweep up the remains. Clean surface with an appropriate cleaner. (See Index for cleaners for your particular surface.)

Outdoor Equipment

The popularity of outdoor sporting and camping equipment is phenomenal, and most of that equipment is expensive. Cleaning, polishing, and proper storage will ensure that you'll get many years of use from your investment.

■ All-Purpose Cleaner for Sporting Equipment

This cleaner will work well for a lot of sporting and camping equipment that is not made of very absorbent material. Use it for golf balls and clubs; fiberglass or plastic-coated skis; nonwooden ski poles; or vinyl-type foot-

balls, basketballs, and volleyballs. Use it even on your fiberglass canoe. Do not use it on wood or leather items or delicate wool, nylon, or down-filled items.

2 tablespoons mild liquid detergent
2 tablespoons borax
2 gallons warm water

Mix detergent and borax in water. With a sponge or soft cloth, wash surface. Rinse and dry thoroughly. When storing metal items, moisten a soft cloth with olive oil and rub over metal parts. Buff with a dry, soft cloth to remove excess oil. This will keep rust from forming.

■ Fabric Waterproofer

This can be used to make canvas tents and bags water-resistant. Use it only on articles that are reserved for outdoor use.

3 cups soybean oil
1½ cups turpentine

Mix and paint on outer surface. Allow to dry.

■ Flame Extinguisher

Cooking outdoors can be great fun, but don't forget to extinguish those flames when you break up camp. This extinguisher is more effective than water alone.

2 teaspoons baking soda
2 teaspoons salt
1 quart water

Mix all ingredients in a convenient spray bottle. To use, spray directly on the base of fire. (For additional fire extinguisher formulas, see Index.)

■ Flame Retardant

This formula will provide some flame-retardant characteristics to fabric. Always wash and rinse the article completely before applying this solution.

1 ounce water glass
9 ounces water

Mix well and soak fabric in solution. Hang article up to dry. It's now ready for wearing. *Caution:* Water glass is caustic to the skin and toxic upon ingestion. Wear gloves and handle carefully.

■ Heavy-Duty Golf Ball Cleaner

If your game has been in a slump, add a little sparkle.

2 tablespoons household ammonia
1 tablespoon whiting
1 cup warm water

Mix ammonia and whiting in water. Scrub golf balls with this mixture and a soft-bristled brush. Soak about 15 minutes, if needed. Rinse and dry.

Leather items, like saddles, good baseball gloves, and footballs, should be cleaned with Saddle Soap (see Index). Use a leather preservative (see Index) to replenish the oils and keep the items from drying out and cracking. Vinyl items need to be conditioned occasionally with petroleum jelly or the vinyl will dry out and crack.

Footwear

Many sports have their own footwear that has been specially designed for high performance under particular conditions. Some can be very expensive because of the special design or because high-quality materials have been used for extra durability. Here are some materials used for footwear and the best way to treat them.

Canvas Canvas shoes can be washed in mild detergent. Rinse well and dry.

Leather These items require cleaning, conditioning, and, often, waterproofing. For more information on leathers, see Index.

Plastics Some manufacturers are using certain plastics in their footwear. Many new ski boots have an outer shell of fiberglass. These only require cleaning with a little soap or mild detergent and warm water. Rinse and dry well. Never use alcohol, acetone (contained in fingernail polish remover), or ammonia on plastic or plasticized items. If there are spots to be removed, make a paste of baking soda and warm water, and rub on spots with a sponge or soft cloth. Wash with soap or a mild detergent. Rinse and dry.

Rubber Rubber needs only to be washed with warm water and a mild detergent and dried.

Suede Normally, suede only requires periodical brushing with a soft-bristled brush. When these items get really dirty, try Suede Cleaner (see Index).

Clothing

Sports clothing should be washed according to manufacturers' directions. Some items should only be dry cleaned. See Chapter 4, "Laundry," for additional suggestions for washing and spot removal.

Homemade Paints

Diana Branch McMasters

In this section, you'll discover the difficulties—and impracticalities—of making paints at home, the economy and simplicity of whitewash, and the charm of milk paint.

Oil Paint

It wasn't so very long ago that you could go into a local hardware store and come home with all the necessary ingredients for making your own interior and exterior paints at home. The basic ingredients included white lead as the base pigment, linseed oil as a binder, turpentine as a thinner, and powdered pigments for final tinting. Early in this century it was a common practice for painters to mix their own paint at home before going out on a job. That way they could be sure how well the paint would perform and could guarantee their work accordingly. Ready-mixed paints just weren't available, and painters mixed their own out of necessity.

Things have changed. The technology and chemical engineering involved in manufacturing ready-mixed paints have improved the quality and the convenience of using them at such a price as to make homemade paint obsolete. During this period of transition, white lead, the backbone of the homemade paint industry, was banned from the market, due to the risk of lead poisoning. In light of the dwindling demand for paints made at home, nothing took white lead's place on the retail shelf. In turn, powdered pigments disappeared from the shelf as well. Now only the most conscientious of sleuths can find sources for the materials.

We went out on a hunt and after many failures found a base pigment source through a friend at an old paint store. Our friend found a few dusty boxes of powdered tinting pigments tucked away in the basement—all shades no one else had wanted. (We thought we'd be safe with vermillion red. Were we ever fooled!)

The ingredients most commonly used in place of white lead are titanium dioxide and zinc. Artists buy them by the tube, but the cost would be outrageous for anyone planning to mix paint by the gallon. In its powdered form, titanium dioxide sometimes can be bought from paint or plastics companies by the 50-pound bag. We found a source that would sell 50 pounds for 85 cents per pound. They recommended that we use it at a rate of 6 to 7 pounds per gallon of paint. At that rate, homemade oil paint could cost $10 per gallon, compared to $10 to $25 for ready-mixed paint. However, the price could easily double if shipping charges for materials are involved.

A big problem in working with titanium dioxide powder is getting the lumps out. The process of mixing the powder with oil involves using very little oil at first to make a paste. In a paste, powder can be mashed and mixed to get rid of lumps that would escape your spoon in a more liquid suspension. Even so, it's hard to get a smooth pigment. To do it right you really need the help of a high-speed mixer or blender.

Unfortunately, there are two things wrong with this scheme. You aren't likely to save yourself any money, and you may be disappointed with the quality of your product. We've come to the sad conclusion that it just isn't practical to make your own oil-based paints at home anymore. Painters who used to make their own confirm this. They're sold on the quality, convenience, and price of ready-made paint. This is one of the rare things that can't be done better by hand.

Whitewash

Whitewash, of Tom Sawyer fame, still has a place around the home or farmstead. It's an economical alternative to paint, most appropriately used where appearance isn't crucial and for large expanses where the cost of paint might be hard to justify.

A simple mixture of garden lime, water, and salt, whitewash can be applied rapidly with a large paste brush, making light work of cleaning up basement walls, the inside or outside of outbuildings, or even a big old fence like Tom's. Though it isn't durable like paint, it is so inexpensive and easy to apply that doing the job over every few years isn't nearly the chore painting would be. Whitewash will do a good job of sealing pores in cement, though it's not a waterproofer, and its mildly germicidal quality makes it desirable for use inside barns.

■ Interior Whitewash

5 pounds hydrated (agricultural) lime
1 gallon water
1½ pounds salt
2 quarts warm water
powdered pigment (optional)

Stir lime into gallon of water. Let set overnight. The next morning, dissolve salt in 2 quarts warm water. Add pigment until you get the color you like. Gradually add the salt mixture to the lime water. Stir thoroughly, and stir again every 10 minutes or so while you are painting with the wash. Store leftover whitewash in a tightly closed can.

Be sure to add enough pigment to compensate for the dilution when the salt mixture is added to the lime water. Also, the paint will dry to a lighter color, so test a small area with the paint, allowing it to dry to be sure the color is correct.

Yield: about 2½ gallons

[*Continued on next page*]

■ Exterior Whitewash

Directions for rendering your own tallow can be found in "Homemade Soap" (see Index).

5 pounds hydrated (agricultural) lime
1 gallon water
1½ pounds salt
1 pound alum
3 quarts warm water
powdered pigment (optional)
1 pound tallow

Prepare as Interior Whitewash (above), adding alum along with the salt to be dissolved in the warm water. When all ingredients except tallow are mixed, place on stove to heat. Melt tallow on a separate burner. When both are hot, stir the tallow into the whitewash. Apply hot

Yield: about 3 gallons

Milk Paint

Back in the days when milk was a much cheaper commodity than it is now, folks sometimes used it to make paint for interior walls and furniture. Milk paint was especially good to use if members of the household were bothered by the smell of commercial paint, for it had no offensive odor.

Milk paint soaked deep into the grain of wood and, unless thickened to a more opaque finish with lime, left a transparent quality to its finish that resembled stain. Like stain, it was quite durable—it wouldn't chip or peel. For extra protection, it usually received a coat of varnish.

Today, milk paint is most often used in restoring antiques and old homes. Its unique transparency has never been captured by a commercial paint, so those who do restoration work have to mix their own.

■ Skim Milk Paint

The following formula was adapted from the original edition of Dick's Encyclopedia of Practical Receipts and Processes, *a volume of household recipes published in 1895. We prepared a test batch, substituting commercial whiting for the Spanish White called for in the original recipe. The test batch came out satisfactorily, but we cannot vouch for the paint's long-term performance.*

The original formula stated that sour milk should not be used, because it would combine with the lime to form an earthy salt which would be unable to resist dampness in the air.

6 ounces hydrated (agricultural) lime
½ gallon skimmed milk
4 ounces linseed oil
3 pounds finely powdered commercial whiting
powdered pigment (optional)

Put the lime into a clean bucket, and put on it enough milk to make it about the thickness of cream. Add the oil, a small amount at a time, stirring the mixture with a wooden spatula or spoon. Then stir in the rest of the milk. Strew the whiting gently over the surface of the mixture. The whiting will gradually sink to the bottom of the bucket; it should then be well stirred into the mixture. If you are making colored paint, stir in the powdered pigment last, a little at a time, until you get the desired hue.

Appendix A
Chemical Substances and Their Recommended Uses

The chart below lists the chemical properties of a variety of substances used in home and yard products, as well as the types of practical applications for which the substances are suited.

When reading across the chart for the information pertaining to any particular substance, please keep this in mind: A substance's chemical properties are based upon an evaluation of the 100 percent pure substance itself, while a certain application may use just a minute amount of that concentrated substance. For example, banana oil (amyl acetate), which is moderately toxic by inhalation and ingestion in its pure form, is not harmful to the body when used in a very minute amount as a flavoring agent.

For more information, you may wish to consult *The Condensed Chemical Dictionary*, 10th ed., revised by Gessner G. Hawley, New York: Van Nostrand Reinhold Co., 1981.

Substances and Their Chemical Properties	Internal Use	External Use (cosmetic/hygiene)	Household Use
Acacia (gum arabic) Thin flakes, powder, granules, or angular fragments with mucilaginous texture. Soluble in hot and cold water.	X	X	X
Alcohol, butyl Colorless crystals with camphorlike odor. Soluble in water. Miscible with alcohol and ether. *Cautions:* Moderately		X	X

Substances and Their Chemical Properties	Internal Use	External Use (cosmetic/hygiene)	Household Use
toxic. Irritant to eyes and skin. Flammable. Use in well-ventilated area.			
Alcohol, denatured Ethyl alcohol to which another liquid has been added to make it unfit to use as a beverage. *Cautions:* Highly toxic by ingestion. Flammable.			X
Alcohol, ethyl (grain alcohol) Colorless liquid. *Caution:* Flammable.	X	X	X
Alcohol, isopropyl (rubbing alcohol) Colorless liquid with pleasant odor. Miscible with water, alcohol, ether, and chloroform. *Cautions:* Moderately toxic by ingestion and inhalation. Flammable.		X	X
Alcohol, methyl (wood alcohol) Colorless liquid. Miscible with water, alcohol, ether, benzene, and most other organic solvents. *Cautions:* Toxic by ingestion. Flammable. Use in well-ventilated area.			X
Almond oil White to yellowish oil distilled from ground kernels of bitter almond. *Caution:* Toxic by inhalation.	X	X	X
Alum: *see* Aluminum sulfate			

Substances and Their Chemical Properties	Internal Use	External Use (cosmetic/hygiene)	Household Use
Aluminum potassium sulfate (potassium alum) White odorless crystals with an astringent taste. Soluble in water; insoluble in alcohol. Solutions in water are acidic.	X	X	X
Aluminum powder Silvery white, crystalline solid. *Caution:* Powder forms flammable, explosive mixture in air.			X
Aluminum stearate (aluminum tristearate) White powder. Insoluble in water, alcohol, and ether; soluble in petroleum and turpentine oil.		X	X
Aluminum sulfate (alum) Colorless crystals with saline, astringent taste. Soluble in water; insoluble in alcohol.	X	X	X
Aluminum tristearate: *see* Aluminum stearate			
Ambergris Irregular, gray, waxy, opaque masses with musky, sometimes unpleasant odor. Insoluble in water; soluble in alcohol, chloroform, ether, fats, and oils.		X	X
Ammonia, household Colorless liquid with intense, pungent, suffocating odor. *Cautions:* Irritant to eyes and skin. Use in well-ventilated room.			X
Ammonia soap: *see* Ammonium oleate			

Substances and Their Chemical Properties	Internal Use	External Use (cosmetic/hygiene)	Household Use
Ammonium carbonate Colorless white powder with strong odor of ammonia. *Caution:* Evolves irritant fumes when heated.	X	X	X
Ammonium chloride (sal ammoniac) White, somewhat hygroscopic crystals with a saline taste. *Caution:* Low toxicity.	X	X	X
Ammonium citrate White granules. Soluble in water. *Caution:* Low toxicity.	X	X	X
Ammonium oleate (ammonia soap) Brown, jellylike mass. Soluble in water and alcohol.		X	X
Ammonium phosphate White, mildly alkaline crystal powder. *Caution:* Low toxicity.	X	X	X
Ammonium selenate Colorless crystals. Soluble in water; insoluble in alcohol. *Caution:* Moderately toxic.			X
Ammonium stearate Tan, waxlike solid, free from ammonia odor. *Caution:* Low toxicity.		X	X
Ammonium sulfate Brownish gray to white crystals. Soluble in water; insoluble in alcohol and acetone. *Caution:* Low toxicity.	X		X

Substances and Their Chemical Properties	Internal Use	External Use (cosmetic/hygiene)	Household Use
Amyl acetate (banana oil) Colorless liquid with characteristic banana odor. *Cautions:* Moderately toxic by inhalation and ingestion. Flammable.	X	X	X
Anthracene oil A coal tar fraction. *Cautions:* Toxic and irritating.			X
Antimony chloride (antimony oxchloride) White powder. Soluble in hydrochloric acid and alkali tartrate solution. *Caution:* Highly toxic.			X
Antimony oxchloride: *see* Antimony chloride			
Asbestos powder Gray, fibrous powder. *Cautions:* Proven potent carcinogen. Toxic by inhalation of dust particles.	Not recommended for home use.		
Attar of roses (rose oil) Transparent, yellow to green or red essential oil with fragrant scent and sweet taste. *Caution:* Combustible.	X	X	X
Baking soda: *see* Sodium bicarbonate			
Balsam A resinous mixture of varying compositions. Obtained from several species of evergreen trees or shrubs. All types are insoluble in water; soluble in organic liquids.	X	X	X

Substances and Their Chemical Properties	Internal Use	External Use (cosmetic/hygiene)	Household Use
Banana oil: *see* Amyl acetate			
Bay rum A mixture of bay oil, orange peel oil, oil of pimento, and alcohol. Fragrant odor. *Caution:* Combustible.		X	X
Beeswax Wax from the honeycomb of the bee. Insoluble in water; soluble in hot alcohol and benzene, chloroform, ether, and carbon disulfide.	X	X	X
Benzene Colorless to light yellow liquid. Aromatic odor. *Cautions:* Highly toxic by inhalation, ingestion, and skin absorption. Flammable and explosive (dangerous fire risk).			X
Benzoic acid White sealer or needle crystals with odor of benzoin or benzaldehyde. *Cautions:* Combustible. Possible allergic reaction.	X	X	X
Benzoin, tincture of Benzoin dissolved in alcohol. Alcohol content 75 to 83 percent by volume. *Cautions:* Low toxicity. Combustible.		X	X
Bergamot oil Essential oil. Brownish yellow to green liquid with agreeable odor and bitter taste.	X	X	X

Substances and Their Chemical Properties	Internal Use	External Use (cosmetic/hygiene)	Household Use
Bleach, household: *see* Sodium hypochlorite			
Bleaching powder: *see* Chlorinated lime			
Blue vitriol: *see* Copper sulfate			
Borax: *see* Sodium borate			
Boric acid Colorless, odorless scales of white powder. Stable in air. *Caution:* Moderately toxic in large doses.		X (water solution only)	X
Brazil wax (carnauba wax) Hard, amorphous, light yellow to greenish brown lumps with slight odor. *Caution:* Combustible.	X	X	X
Calcium carbonate (chalk, powdered or precipitated; whiting) White or off-white powder. Soluble in water and acids.		X	X
Calcium chloride White, deliquescent crystals, granules, lumps, or flakes. *Caution:* Low toxicity.	X	X	X
Calcium hydroxide (lime, agricultural) Soft white crystalline powder with alkaline, slightly bitter taste. *Cautions:* Skin irritant. Hazard from dust inhalation.	X	X	X
Calcium sulfate (gypsum; plaster of paris) White odorless powder or crystals.	X	X	X

Substances and Their Chemical Properties	Internal Use	External Use (cosmetic/hygiene)	Household Use
Calgon: *see* Sodium hexametaphosphate			
Camphor Colorless or white crystals. Slightly soluble in water; soluble in alcohol. *Cautions:* Moderately toxic. Flammable.		X	X
Camphor oil Colorless natural oil with a strong odor. Soluble in alcohol, ether, and chloroform. *Cautions:* Moderately toxic. Flammable.		X	X
Canaga oil (ilang-ilang oil; ylang-ylang oil) Essential oil from the flowers of the tree *Canangium odorata.*		X	X
Carbolic acid: *see* Phenol			
Carbon, activated: *see* Charcoal, activated			
Carnauba wax: *see* Brazil wax			
Cassia oil (cinnamon, oil of) Yellowish or brownish liquid which darkens and thickens on exposure to air. Slightly soluble in water; soluble in equal volume of alcohol.	X	X	X
Castile soap A white, odorless hard soap made from sodium hydroxide and olive oil.		X	X
Castor oil (ricinus oil) Pale yellowish or almost colorless, transparent, vis-		X	X

Substances and Their Chemical Properties	Internal Use	External Use (cosmetic/hygiene)	Household Use
Castor oil *(continued)* cous liquid with faint, mild odor and nauseating taste. *Cautions:* Low toxicity. Develops heat spontaneously.			
Cedar wood oil Colorless crystals with cedar wood odor. *Caution:* Combustible.		X	X
Cement, hydraulic (portland cement) Finely divided gray powder composed of lime, alumina, silica, and iron oxide.			X
Ceresin wax White or yellow waxy cake. White is odorless; yellow has slight odor. Soluble in alcohol, benzene, and chloroform; insoluble in water. *Caution:* Combustible.		X	X
Chalk, powdered or precipitated: *see* Calcium carbonate			
Charcoal, activated (carbon, activated) Black, highly absorptive powder. *Cautions:* Moderate hazard by inhalation. Flammable.			X
Chinese white: *see* Zinc oxide			
Chlorinated lime (bleaching powder) White powder with chlorine odor. *Caution:* Evolves chlorine with moisture at room temperature.			X

Substances and Their Chemical Properties	Internal Use	External Use (cosmetic/hygiene)	Household Use
Cinnamon, oil of: *see* Cassia oil			
Citric acid Odorless, colorless, translucent crystals or powder with strong acid taste. *Caution:* Combustible.	X	X	X
Citronella oil Light yellowish essential oil with rather pungent citrus-type odor. *Caution:* Moderately toxic.		X	X
Coal oil (petroleum) Dark yellow to brown or greenish black, oily liquid. Insoluble in water; slightly soluble in alcohol; soluble in benzene and chloroform. *Caution:* Flammable (moderate fire risk).			X
Coal tar: *see* Creosote			
Coal tar pitch: *see* Pitch			
Cocoa butter Yellowish white solid with chocolatelike taste and odor.	X	X	X
Cocoa powder Powder prepared from roasted, cured cocoa beans.	X	X	X
Coconut oil White semisolid fat. *Caution:* Combustible.	X	X	X
Copper naphthenate Green blue solid. Soluble in gasoline, benzene, and mineral oil distillates. *Cautions:* Moderately toxic by ingestion. Flammable (moderate fire risk).			X

Substances and Their Chemical Properties	Internal Use	External Use (cosmetic/hygiene)	Household Use
Copper sulfate (blue vitriol) Blue crystals or blue crystalline granules or powder. Soluble in water. *Caution:* Highly toxic by ingestion.			X
Corn oil Pale yellow liquid with a characteristic taste and odor. *Caution:* Combustible.	X	X	X
Cornstarch White amorphous powder.	X	X	X
Corn syrup (glucose) Sweet, colorless, viscous liquid.	X	X	X
Corundum (emery powder) Natural aluminum oxide with small amount of iron, magnesium, silica, and other substances. *Cautions:* Slight hazard by inhalation. A nuisance dust.			X
Cream of tartar: *see* Potassium bitartrate			
Creosote (coal tar; tar oil) Colorless or faintly yellow, oily liquid with characteristic odor and caustic, burning taste. *Cautions:* Moderately toxic. Skin and eye irritant.			X
Cresol Colorless, yellowish, or pinkish liquid with a strong odor. *Cautions:* Moderate to highly toxic irritant. Corrosive to			X

Substances and Their Chemical Properties	Internal Use	External Use (cosmetic/hygiene)	Household Use
skin and mucous membrane. Can be absorbed through the skin.			
Cresylic acids A commercial mixture of phenolic materials made from petroleum or coal tar. *Caution:* Corrosive to skin.			X
Dextrin A yellow or white powder that is water soluble.	X	X	X
Diatomaceous earth A bulky, light material containing 88 percent silica. *Caution:* Moderate risk from dust inhalation.		X	X
Diglycol laurate Light, odorless, straw-colored, oily liquid		X	X
Diglycol stearate White waxlike solid with faint fatty odor. Dispenses in hot water. *Caution:* Combustible.		X	X
Dimethyl morpholine Liquid. Soluble in water. *Cautions:* Moderately toxic. Flammable (moderate fire risk).			X
Emery powder: *see* Corundum			
Epsom salt: *see* Magnesium sulfate			
Ethylene chloride (ethylene dichloride)	Not recommended for home use.		

Substances and Their Chemical Properties	Internal Use	External Use (cosmetic/hygiene)	Household Use
Ethylene chloride *(continued)* Colorless, oily liquid with chloroformlike odor and sweet taste. *Cautions:* Highly toxic by ingestion, inhalation, and skin absorption. Strong irritant to eyes and skin. Flammable (dangerous fire risk).			
Ethylene dichloride: *see* Ethylene chloride			
Ethylene glycol Clear, colorless, syrupy liquid with sweet taste. *Cautions:* Toxic by ingestion. Combustible.		X	X
Ethylene glycol monethyl ether Colorless, practically odorless, liquid. *Cautions:* Moderately toxic. Flammable (moderate fire risk).		X	X
Eucalyptus oil Oil with camphorlike, pungent odor and cool, spicy taste. *Cautions:* Moderately toxic. Combustible.	X	X	X
Ferric chloride Black brown solid. Soluble in water and alcohol. *Caution:* Low toxicity.	X	X	X
Flaxseed oil: *see* Linseed oil, boiled and raw			
Formaldehyde Colorless, pungent, irritating		X	X

Substances and Their Chemical Properties	Internal Use	External Use (cosmetic/hygiene)	Household Use
gas. Soluble in water and alcohol. *Cautions:* Highly toxic by inhalation or skin contact. Flammable (moderate fire risk).			
French chalk Soft, white granular variety of steatite.			X
Fuel oil Oil used in home heating furnaces.			X
Fuller's earth A porous, powdered, highly absorptive clay.		X	X
Furfural: *see* Furfuraldehyde			
Furfuraldehyde (furfural) Colorless liquid which becomes reddish brown when exposed to air and light. *Cautions:* Highly toxic irritant to eyes, skin, and mucous membrane. Can be absorbed by skin.			X
Gasoline A mixture of volatile hydrocarbons. *Caution:* Highly flammable (dangerous fire and explosion risk).	Not recommended for home use.		
Gelatin White to yellow powder. Soluble in hot water. *Caution:* Combustible in dry form.	X	X	X
Glucose: *see* Corn syrup			

Substances and Their Chemical Properties	Internal Use	External Use (cosmetic/hygiene)	Household Use
Glycerin (glycerol) Clear, colorless, odorless, sweet-tasting, syrupy liquid. Soluble in water and alcohol. *Caution:* Low toxicity.	X	X	X
Glycerol: *see* Glycerin			
Gum arabic: *see* Acacia			
Hamamelis water (witch hazel) Colorless liquid. A 14 percent alcohol with 1 percent witch hazel extract is commonly known as witch hazel.		X	X
Hydrogen peroxide Colorless, heavy liquid, sold in aqueous solution of various strengths. *Cautions:* Concentrated solutions are highly toxic and strong irritants. Flammable (dangerous fire and explosion risk).		X	X
Ilang-ilang oil: *see* Canaga oil			
Iodine Grayish black granules having a metallic luster and characteristic odor. Soluble in alcohol; insoluble in water. *Cautions:* Highly toxic by ingestion and inhalation. Intensely irritating to eyes, skin, and mucous membrane.	X	X	X
Iron oxide red (jeweler's rouge) Dense dark red powder or lumps. Soluble in acids; insoluble in water.		X	X

Substances and Their Chemical Properties	Internal Use	External Use (cosmetic/hygiene)	Household Use
Jeweler's rouge: *see* Iron oxide red			
Kaolin (clay; clay, China or white) White to yellowish or grayish fine powder.	X	X	X
Kerosene Water white, oily liquid with strong odor. *Cautions:* Moderately toxic by ingestion and inhalation Flammable (moderate fire risk).			X
Lactic acid (milk acid) Colorless or yellowish, odor-less, hygroscopic, syrupy liquid. *Cautions:* Moderately toxic by ingestion. Irritant.		X	X
Lamp black Black or gray pigment. Not compatible with water. *Caution:* Dust may be fire risk.			X
Lanolin (wool fat) Yellowish to light gray semi-solid. Soluble in ether; insoluble in water.		X	X
Lard Soft white, fatty mass with faint odor and bland taste *Caution:* Combustible.	X	X	X
Latex A white, free-flowing liquid obtained from small species of shrubs or trees. *Caution:* Toxic by ingestion			X

Substances and Their Chemical Properties	Internal Use	External Use (cosmetic/hygiene)	Household Use
Lauryl pyridinium chloride Mottled tan semisolid. Soluble in water and organic solvents. *Cautions:* Toxicity is unknown. Combustible.			X
Lavender oil Colorless, yellowish, essential oil with sweet odor and slightly bitter taste.	X	X	X
Lead Heavy, ductile, soft gray solid. *Caution:* A cumulative poison, highly toxic by inhalation of dust or fumes.	Not recommended for home use.		
Lemon oil (oil of lemon) Color, odor, taste characteristic of lemon. *Caution:* Combustible.	X	X	X
Licorice Plant root or extract of *Glycyrrhiza glabra* or *G. glandulifera.* Characteristic sweet taste. Yields a brown powder when pulverized.	X	X	X
Lignite wax: *see* Montan wax			
Linseed oil, boiled and raw (flaxseed oil) Golden yellow oil which thickens, hardens, and darkens on exposure to air.		X	X
Lubricating oil A fraction of refined mineral used for lubrication of moving surfaces.			X

Substances and Their Chemical Properties	Internal Use	External Use (cosmetic/hygiene)	Household Use
Lye: *see* Potassium hydroxide			
Magnesium silicate (talcum powder) White, apple green, or gray powder with a pearly or greasy luster and feel. *Caution:* Moderate hazard by inhalation.		X	X
Magnesium sulfate (epsom salt) Colorless crystals with a saline, bitter taste. *Caution:* Moderately toxic by ingestion.	X	X	X
Menthol (peppermint camphor) White crystals with cooling odor and taste. *Cautions:* Mildly toxic. Moderate irritant to mucous membranes on inhalation. Combustible.	X	X	X
Mercuric chloride White odorless crystals or powder. Soluble in water and alcohol. *Cautions:* Highly toxic by ingestion, inhalation, and skin absorption (may be fatal).	Not recommended for home use.		
Methyl salicylate (wintergreen oil) Colorless, yellowish, or reddish liquid oil, with odor of wintergreen. *Cautions:* Highly toxic by ingestion. Irritant. Use in foods restricted. Combustible.	X	X	X

Substances and Their Chemical Properties	Internal Use	External Use (cosmetic/hygiene)	Household Use
Milk acid: *see* Lactic acid			
Mineral oil: *see* Petrolatum liquid			
Mineral spirits: *see* Naphtha			
Monocalcium phosphate (superphosphate) Colorless, pearly scales or powder, deliquescent in air.	X	X	X
Montan wax (lignite wax) White, hard-earth wax. Soluble in benzene and chloroform.		X	X
Moth balls: *see* Naphthalene			
Myrrh Plant resin. Soluble in part water and part alcohol. *Cautions:* Low toxicity. Combustible.	X	X	X
Naphtha (mineral spirits) Colorless liquid from refined petroleum distillate. *Caution:* Flammable (dangerous fire risk).			X
Naphthalene (moth balls) White crystalline, volatile flakes with strong coal tar odor. *Cautions:* Moderately toxic. Poisoning can result from ingestion of large doses, inhalation, or skin absorption.			X
Neat's-foot oil A pale yellow oil with a peculiar odor. *Cautions:* Low toxicity. Combustible.			X

Substances and Their Chemical Properties	Internal Use	External Use (cosmetic/hygiene)	Household Use
Neroli oil (orange flower oil) Pale yellow essential oil with a pleasant odor and bitter taste. *Caution:* Combustible.	X	X	X
Oil of lemon: *see* Lemon oil			
Oleic acid Yellow to red oily liquid with lardlike odor. *Caution:* Combustible.	X	X	X
Olive oil Pale yellow or greenish yellow liquid with slight odor and taste. *Caution:* Combustible.	X	X	X
Orange flower oil: *see* Neroli oil			
Orris root (white flag) Yellowish, fragrant powder from root of the flag plant.	X	X	X
Oxalic acid Transparent, colorless crystals. *Cautions:* Highly toxic by inhalation and ingestion. Strong irritant.			X
Oxyquinoline sulfate Pale yellow with slight saffron odor and burning taste. *Caution:* Moderately toxic.		X	X
Paraffin White, translucent, tasteless, odorless solid. *Caution:* Combustible.		X	X
Peanut oil Yellow to greenish yellow oil. *Caution:* Combustible.	X	X	X

Substances and Their Chemical Properties	Internal Use	External Use (cosmetic/hygiene)	Household Use
Peppermint camphor: *see* Menthol			
Peppermint extract Colorless or slightly yellowish, volatile, essential oil with strongly aromatic odor and taste.	X	X	X
Petrolatum liquid (mineral oil) Colorless, transparent, oily liquid, almost tasteless and odorless. A mixture of liquid hydrocarbons. *Caution:* Combustible.	X	X	X
Petroleum: *see* Coal oil			
Petroleum distillate Volatile, colorless liquid, miscible with most organic solvents. *Caution:* Flammable.		X	X
Petroleum jelly Colorless or pale yellow, translucent, fattylike mass. *Caution:* Combustible.		X	X
Phenol (carbolic acid) Colorless, crystalline mass. Soluble in alcohol and water. *Cautions:* Highly toxic by ingestion, inhalation, and skin absorption. Do not handle with bare hands. Keep tightly closed and protected from light.			X
Pine oil Colorless to light amber liquid having a strong, piney odor. *Cautions:* Low toxicity. Combustible.			X

Substances and Their Chemical Properties	Internal Use	External Use (cosmetic/hygiene)	Household Use
Pine tar pitch: *see* Pitch			
Pitch (coal tar pitch; pine tar pitch) Sticky, viscous, dark brown to black liquid or semisolid with strong odor and sharp taste. *Caution:* Flammable (moderate fire risk).			X
Portland cement: *see* Cement, hydraulic			
Potash: *see* Potassium carbonate			
Potassium bitartrate (cream of tartar) White crystals or powder with slightly acid taste. Soluble in water; insoluble in alcohol.	X	X	X
Potassium carbonate (potash) White deliquescent, granular, translucent powder with alkaline reaction. *Cautions:* Toxic by ingestion. Strong irritant.	X	X	X
Potassium chlorate Transparent, colorless crystals or white powder, soluble in water or alcohol. *Cautions:* Moderately toxic. Flammable (forms explosive mixtures with sulfuric acid, sugar, phosphorus, sulfite, and other oxidizing agents)			X
Potassium hydroxide (lye) White, deliquescent pieces, lumps, sticks, pellets, or flakes. [*Continued*]			X

Substances and Their Chemical Properties	Internal Use	External Use (cosmetic/hygiene)	Household Use
Potassium hydroxide *(continued)* *Cautions:* Highly toxic by ingestion and inhalation. Strong irritant.			
Potassium nitrate (saltpeter) Transparent colorless or white crystalline powder with pungent saline taste. *Caution:* Dangerous fire and explosion risk when shocked or heated.	X	X	X
Potassium oleate Gray tan paste. Soluble in water and alcohol. *Caution:* Combustible.		X	X
Potassium persulfate White crystals. Soluble in water; insoluble in alcohol. *Cautions:* Moderately toxic. Strong irritant. Flammable (dangerous fire risk).			X
Propylene glycol Colorless, viscous, stable hygroscopic liquid, practically odorless and tasteless. *Cautions:* Mildly toxic. Combustible.	X	X	X
Pumice Highly porous igneous rock. Insoluble in water.		X	X
Pyrethrin Viscous liquid. Insoluble in water; soluble in other common solvents such as alcohol and benzene. *Caution:* Moderately toxic by ingestion and inhalation.			X

Substances and Their Chemical Properties	Internal Use	External Use (cosmetic/hygiene)	Household Use
Rape seed oil Dark brown (when crude) or pale yellow (when refined) viscous liquid with unpleasant taste and odor. *Cautions:* Low toxicity. Flammable (possible fire risk).	X	X	X
Resin Essential oils from bark of many trees. Soft and sticky at room temperature. *Caution:* Combustible.			X
Rhubarb, tincture of Roots and stalks of rhubarb treated with a 10 percent alcohol solution.	X	X	X
Ricinus oil: *see* Castor oil			
Rose oil: *see* Attar of roses			
Rose water Steamed distilled product of fresh flowers.	X	X	X
Rosin Angular, translucent, amber colored fragments. Insoluble in water; soluble in alcohol and benzene. *Caution:* Flammable (may ignite spontaneously in air).			X
Rottenstone A soft, decomposed limestone; light gray to olive in color.			X
Sal ammoniac: *see* Ammonium chloride			

Substances and Their Chemical Properties	Internal Use	External Use (cosmetic/hygiene)	Household Use
Salicylic acid White powder with acrid taste. *Cautions:* Low toxicity. Combustible.	X	X	X
Sal soda: *see* Sodium carbonate			
Salt: *see* Sodium chloride			
Salt cake: *see* Sodium sulfate			
Saltpeter: *see* Potassium nitrate			
Sassafras bark and root Bark and root of plant *Sassafras albidum* contain only 6 to 9 percent oil; therefore they are not nearly so toxic as the oil. *Caution:* Some people choose to avoid this plant for food consumption because of the toxicity in high concentrations of the oil (*see* Sassafras oil).		X	X
Sassafras oil Yellowish or reddish yellow volatile liquid oil from the leaves, bark, and root of the plant *Sassafras albidum.* *Caution:* Toxic by ingestion (not to be used in food or beverages).		X	X
Senna leaves Dried leaves of several species of cassia. *Caution:* Laxative and stimulant which may be habit forming.	X	X	X

Substances and Their Chemical Properties	Internal Use	External Use (cosmetic/hygiene)	Household Use
Shellac Insect resin. Soluble in alcohol; insoluble in water. *Caution:* Flammable (dangerous fire risk).			X
Shortening, hydrogenated (animal or vegetable) Solidified vegetable or animal fat created by process of hydrogenation.	X	X	X
Silica gel A regenerative absorbent consisting of amorphous silica.		X	X
Silicone Liquid, semisolid, or solid, depending on molecular weight and degree of polymerization. Soluble in most organic solvents. *Caution:* Unhalogenated types are combustible.		X	X
Soda ash: *see* Sodium carbonate			
Sodium alginate Colorless or slightly yellow solid occurring in granular and powdered forms. Becomes a viscous collodial solution with water. *Caution:* Combustible.	X	X	X
Sodium aluminate White powder. Soluble in water; insoluble in alcohol. *Cautions:* Toxic. Strong irritant to tissue.			X
Sodium bicarbonate (baking soda)	X	X	X

Substances and Their Chemical Properties	Internal Use	External Use (cosmetic/hygiene)	Household Use
Sodium bicarbonate *(continued)* White powder or crystalline lumps with slightly alkaline taste. Soluble in water; insoluble in alcohol.			
Sodium bisulfate Colorless crystals or white, fused lumps. Strongly acid in water solution. *Cautions:* Highly toxic. Strong irritant.			X
Sodium borate (borax) Odorless crystals becoming opaque on exposure to air. Slowly soluble in water. *Caution:* Highly toxic if ingested.			X
Sodium carbonate (sal soda; soda ash; washing soda) White crystals. Soluble in water; insoluble in alcohol. *Cautions:* Moderately toxic. Irritant to mucous membrane.		X	X
Sodium chloride (salt) Colorless, transparent crystals or white crystalline powder. *Caution:* Low toxicity.	X	X	X
Sodium citrate White crystals or granular powder. Odorless, stable in air, pleasant acid taste. Soluble in water; insoluble in alcohol. *Caution:* Combustible.	X		X
Sodium dodecylbenzenesulfonate		X	X

Substances and Their Chemical Properties	Internal Use	External Use (cosmetic/hygiene)	Household Use
White to light yellow biodegradable flakes, granules, or powder. *Cautions:* Moderately toxic by ingestion. Combustible.			
Sodium hexametaphosphate (Calgon) White powder. Completely soluble in water	X	X	X
Sodium hydroxide (lye) White, deliquescent pieces, lumps, sticks, pellets, or flakes. *Cautions:* Highly toxic by ingestion and inhalation. Strong irritant.			X
Sodium hypochlorite (bleach, household) Liquid with disagreeable, sweetish odor and pale greenish color. *Cautions:* Toxic by ingestion and inhalation. Avoid prolonged contact with skin.			X
Sodium lauryl sulfate Small white or light yellow crystals with slight characteristic odor. Soluble in water. *Cautions:* Low toxicity. Combustible.	X	X	X
Sodium metaphosphate White powder. Soluble in water.	X	X	X
Sodium metasilicate (water glass) Lumps of greenish glass. Soluble in steam under pressure. *Caution:* Low toxicity.			X

Substances and Their Chemical Properties	Internal Use	External Use (cosmetic/hygiene)	Household Use
Sodium pentachlorophenate White or tan powder. Soluble in water, alcohol, and acetone. *Cautions:* Highly toxic by ingestion and inhalation. Irritant to skin and eyes.			X
Sodium perborate White odorless crystals or powder with salty taste. *Cautions:* Toxic by ingestion. Fire risk.		X	X
Sodium phosphate, dibasic Colorless, translucent crystals or white powder with cooling, saline taste. *Caution:* Low toxicity.	X	X	X
Sodium sesquicarbonate White needle-shaped crystals. *Caution:* Low toxicity.	X	X	X
Sodium sulfate (salt cake) White, odorless crystals or powder with bitter, saline taste.	X	X	X
Sodium sulfite White crystals or powder with saline, sulfurous taste. *Caution:* Prohibited in meats and other sources of vitamin B_1.		X	X
Sodium thiosulfate White, translucent crystals or powder with cooling taste and bitter aftertaste.		X	X
Sodium tripolyphosphate White powder. *Caution:* Low toxicity.	X	X	X

Substances and Their Chemical Properties	Internal Use	External Use (cosmetic/hygiene)	Household Use
Soybean oil Pale yellow oil. Soluble in alcohol. *Caution:* Combustible.	X	X	X
Spermaceti White, semitransparent, waxy solid which becomes rancid on exposure to air. *Cautions:* Low toxicity. Combustible.		X	X
Stearic acid Colorless, odorless, waxlike solid with slight odor and taste. *Caution:* Combustible.	X	X	X
Stearomide Colorless flakes. Slightly soluble in alcohol.			X
Stoddard solvent Colorless solvent. *Cautions:* Moderately toxic by ingestion. Flammable (moderate fire risk).			X
Sucrose (sugar) White, granular crystals.	X	X	X
Sugar: *see* Sucrose			
Sulfite liquor Waste liquor produced in the sulfite paper process.		X	X
Sulfonated castor oil (turkey red oil) Red, oily liquid, soluble in water. *Cautions:* Low toxicity. Combustible.			X

Substances and Their Chemical Properties	Internal Use	External Use (cosmetic/hygiene)	Household Use
Superphosphate: *see* Monocalcium phosphate			
Talcum powder: *see* Magnesium silicate			
Tallow Extracted from solid fat or suet of cattle, sheep, or horses. *Caution:* Combustible.	X	X	X
Tannic acid Lustrous, faintly yellowish, amorphous powder. *Cautions:* Moderately toxic by ingestion and inhalation. Combustible.	X	X	X
Tar oil: *see* Creosote			
Thymol White crystals with aromatic odor and taste. *Caution:* Moderately toxic by ingestion and inhalation.		X	X
Tin Silver white, ductile solid. *Caution:* Elemental tin has low toxicity but most tin compounds are toxic.			X
Titanium dioxide White to black powder depending on purity.		X	X
Tragacanth gum Dull white, translucent plates or yellowish powder. *Caution:* Combustible.	X	X	X
Trichlor: *see* Trichloroethylene			

Substances and Their Chemical Properties	Internal Use	External Use (cosmetic/hygiene)	Household Use
Trichloroethylene (trichlor) Stable, low-boiling, colorless, heavy liquid with chloroform-like odor. *Cautions:* Highly toxic by inhalation, moderately by ingestion and skin absorption. Flammable (moderate fire risk).	Not recommended for home use.		
Triethanolamine Colorless, viscous, hygroscopic liquid with slight ammonia odor. *Cautions:* Low toxicity. Combustible.			X
Trisodium phosphate Color crystals. Soluble in water. *Cautions:* Moderately toxic by ingestion. Irritant to tissue.	X	X	X
Turkey red oil: *see* Sulfonated castor oil			
Turpentine gum Viscous balsamic liquid with strong piney odor. *Caution:* Flammable.			X
Turpentine oil Colorless, liquid with penetrating odor. *Cautions:* Flammable (moderate fire risk). Highly toxic by ingestion, moderately toxic by inhalation and skin absorption.			X
Ultramarine blue Blue, powdered pigment. *Caution:* Low toxicity.		X	X

Substances and Their Chemical Properties	Internal Use	External Use (cosmetic/hygiene)	Household Use
Urea White crystals or powder with almost odorless, saline taste. *Caution:* Low toxicity.		X	X
Vermiculite Platelet-type crystalline structure with high porosity.		X	X
Vinegar White to brownish liquid containing from 4 to 8 percent acetic acid.	X	X	X
Washing soda: *see* Sodium carbonate			
Water glass: *see* Sodium metasilicate			
White flag: *see* Orris root			
White vitriol: *see* Zinc sulfate			
Whiting: *see* Calcium carbonate			
Witch hazel: *see* Hamamelis water			
Wood alcohol: *see* Alcohol, methyl			
Wool fat: *see* Lanolin			
Ylang-ylang oil: *see* Canaga oil			
Zinc bromide White, hygroscopic, crystalline powder. *Caution:* Low toxicity.		X	X

Substances and Their Chemical Properties	Internal Use	External Use (cosmetic/hygiene)	Household Use
Zinc chloride White, granular, deliquescent crystals or crystalline powder, soluble in water. *Caution:* Severe skin and tissue irritant when in solution; moderate skin irritant in solid form.	X	X	X
Zinc oxide (Chinese white) Coarse white or grayish odorless powder with bitter taste. *Caution:* Fumes harmful by inhalation but nontoxic.	X	X	X
Zinc sulfate (white vitriol) Colorless crystals, small needles, or granular crystalline powder, without odor. Astringent metallic taste. *Caution:* Low toxicity.	X	X	X

Appendix B
Sources of Ingredients

Ingredients	Sources
Acetone	Drugstore or chemical supply house
Alcohol, denatured or isopropyl	Drugstore, hardware store, or chemical supply house
Alkanet root	Herbal shop
Alum, powdered	Drugstore or chemical supply house
Aluminum stearate	Chemical supply house
Ammonia, household	Grocery store or chemical supply house
Ammonium hydroxide	Chemical supply house
Ammonium sulfate	Garden supply house or chemical supply house
Amyl acetate	Drugstore or chemical supply house
Artist's gum eraser	Stationery store or hobby shop
Beeswax, white or yellow	Hardware store, hobby shop, or chemical supply house
Blood meal	Garden supply house
Borax	Grocery store or drugstore
Camphor oil	Drugstore or chemical supply house
Carnauba wax	Chemical supply house
Castile soap	Drugstore
Castor oil	Drugstore
Ceresin wax	Hobby shop or paint store
Chalk	Hardware store or paint store
Charcoal, activated	Hardware store, hobby shop, or chemical supply house

Ingredients	Sources
Chlorinated lime	Hardware store
Clay	Health food store
Coconut oil	Health food store
Diatomaceous earth	Swimming pool supply house or garden supply house
Dyes, candle	Hobby shop
Essential oils	Drugstore or health food store
French chalk	Fabric store or sewing center
Fuller's earth	Drugstore or building supply center
Glycerin	Drugstore
Graphite, powdered	Hardware store
Gum arabic	Drugstore or chemical supply house
Herbal tea	Health food store
Hydrated lime	Hardware store or garden supply house
Hydrogen peroxide	Drugstore
Iodine	Drugstore
Ipecac	Drugstore
Jeweler's rouge	Hardware store or chemical supply house
Kerosene, deodorized	Hardware store, paint store, gas station, or oil distributor
Lacquer	Hardware store or paint store
Lacquer thinner	Hardware store or paint store
Lanolin	Drugstore or chemical supply house
Lard	Butcher or grocery store
Lauryl pyridinium chloride	Chemical supply house
Lemon oil	Drugstore or chemical supply house
Lemon peel, powdered	Health food store
Linseed oil, raw or boiled	Hardware store or paint store
Lye	Grocery store
Magnesium carbonate	Chemical supply house
Mineral oil	Drugstore
Mineral spirits	Hardware store or paint store
Montan wax	Chemical supply house

Ingredients	Sources
Mustard, dry	Grocery store
Naphtha bar soap	Grocery store or hardware store
Neat's-foot oil	Hardware store
Oleic acid	Chemical supply house
Olive oil	Grocery store
Orange peel, powdered	Health food store
Paraffin	Grocery store, hobby shop, or hardware store
Peppermint oil	Drugstore
Petroleum jelly, white	Drugstore
Petroleum naphtha	Hardware store or paint store
Pigments, powdered	Hardware store or paint store
Pine oil	Drugstore, hardware store, or chemical supply house
Portland cement	Building supply center
Potash	Chemical supply house
Potassium alum	Drugstore or chemical supply house
Pumice, powdered	Hardware store or paint store
Rottenstone	Hardware store or paint store
Salicylic acid	Drugstore or chemical supply house
Sand, builder's or mason's	Building supply center
Sandpaper	Hardware store or paint store
Shellac	Hardware store or paint store
Shellac wax stick	Hardware store or paint store
Silica gel	Hardware store, hobby shop, or chemical supply house
Silicone oil	Drugstore, foundry, or foundry supply house
Soap flakes	Grocery store or restaurant supply house
Sodium citrate	Drugstore or chemical supply house
Sodium hypochlorite	Chemical supply house
Sodium perborate	Drugstore

Ingredients	Sources
Soft water	Rainwater or water from a water softener
Soybean oil	Health food store
Steel wool	Grocery store or hardware store
Sweet oil (sweet oil is a highly pure form of olive oil and the less expensive olive oil can be substituted for use in formulas)	Drugstore
Talcum powder	Drugstore
Tallow (must be rendered at home)	Butcher or grocery store
Tincture of benzoin	Drugstore
Tincture of green soap	Drugstore
Trisodium phosphate	Hardware store or chemical supply house
Turpentine	Hardware store or paint store
Vermiculite	Building supply house or garden supply house
Vinegar, apple cider or white	Grocery store
Vitamin E oil	Drugstore or health food store
Washing soda	Grocery store
Water-based color	Hardware store or paint store
Water glass	Drugstore or chemical supply house
Whiting	Hardware store or paint store

Appendix C
Mail-Order Suppliers and Manufacturers

Chemical Supply Houses

Fisher Scientific Co.
Corporate Headquarters
711 Forbes Avenue
Pittsburgh, PA 15219

Stevenson Bro. & Co., Inc.
1039 West Venango Street
Philadelphia, PA 19140

VWR Scientific, Inc.
P.O. Box 8188
Philadelphia, PA 19101

Ward's Natural Science
Establishment, Inc.
P.O. Box 1712
Rochester, NY 14603
or
P.O. Box 1749
Monterey, CA 93940

For a recent listing of chemical supply houses and availability of specific chemicals, consult the *OPD Chemical Buyers Directory*, which is available at your local library, or write to:

Schnell Publishing Co., Inc.
100 Church Street
New York, NY 10007

Natural Hygiene and Remedies

Aphrodisia
28 Carmine Street
New York, NY 10014
(Herbs, spices, oils. Catalog: $2.50)

Borchelt Herb Gardens*
474 Carriage Shop Road
East Falmouth, MA 02536
(Seed listing: send first-class postage)

*Sources which list organically grown herbs.

W. Atlee Burpee Co.
300 Park Avenue
Warminster, PA 18974
(Seeds, plants)

Caprilands Herb Farm
Silver Street
North Coventry, CT 06238
(Catalog: send self-addressed, stamped envelope)

Casa Yerba*
Star Route 2, Box 21
Days Creek, OR 97429
(Herb seeds, plants. Catalog: $1.00)

Caswell-Massey Co., Ltd.
575 Lexington Avenue
New York, NY 10022
(Herbs, dried flowers, spices, potpourris, botanicals, oils. Catalog: $1.00)

Cedarbrook Herb Farm*
Don and Karman McReynolds
986 Sequim Avenue South
Sequim, WA 98382
(They do not ship. Farm and gift shop open April–October. Specialize in large bay trees and elephant garlic. 150 varieties of kitchen, tea, rockery herbs. Catalog: 25¢)

The Dutch Mill Herb Farm*
Route 2, Box 190
Forest Grove, OR 97116
(Herb plants, dried herbs, herb wreaths)

Greene Herb Gardens*
Greene, RI 02872
(Herbs, herb plants, seeds)

Haussmann's Pharmacy
534–536 West Girard Avenue
Philadelphia, PA 19123
(Unusual botanicals. Catalog available.)

Herbal Bodyworks
219 Carl Street
San Francisco, CA 94117
(Natural ingredients. Catalog: 50¢)

Herbarium, Inc
Route 2, Box 620
Kenosha, WI 53140
(Botanical drugs, spices)

Herbs 'N' Honey Nursery
c/o Mrs. Chester Fisher, Jr.
16085 Airlie Road, P.O. Box 124
Monmouth, OR 97361
(Over 350 varieties of culinary, fragrance, and tea herb plants)

Herbst Brothers Seedsmen, Inc.
1000 North Main Street
Brewster, NY 10509
(Catalog: free)

Hickory Hollow*
Route 1, Box 52
Peterstown, WV 24963
(Seeds, teas, products. Send self-addressed, stamped envelope for brochure.)

Indiana Botanic Gardens, Inc.*
P.O. Box 5
Hammond, IN 46325
(Wide variety of botanicals, herbal products. Catalog: 60¢)

*Sources which list organically grown herbs.

Natural Hygiene and Remedies ***(continued)***

Johnny's Selected Seeds
Albion, ME 04910
(Herb seeds. Catalog: free)

Meadowbrook Herb Garden*
Wyoming, RI 02898
(Seeds, plants, herbal products. Catalog: 50¢)

Misty Morning Farm*
2220 West Sisson Road
Hastings, MI 49058
(Herb plants, seeds, teas, dried herbs, herb products, lectures, garden tours, classes. Catalog: send self-addressed, stamped envelope)

Nature's Herb Co.
281 Ellis Street
San Francisco, CA 94102
(Herbs, spices. Catalog: 50¢)

Nichols Garden Nursery*
1190 North Pacific Highway
Albany, OR 97321
(Herbs, plants, seeds, teas, dried herbs, spices, botanicals. Catalog: free)

Old-Fashioned Herb Co.
P.O. Box 1000-G
Springville, UT 84663
(Full line of herbal products, including capsules, tablets, extracts, ointments, syrups, bulk herbs)

George W. Park Seed Co.
P.O. Box 31
Greenwood, SC 29647
(Flower and vegetable seeds, perennial and annual herbs. Catalog available.)

Penn Herb Co.
603 North Second Street
Philadelphia, PA 19123
(Dried herbs, seeds, herb products, essential oils. Catalog: free)

Otto Richter & Sons Ltd.
Goodwood, ON
Canada L0C 1A0
(Herb seeds, books. Catalog: $1.00)

Sandy Mush Herbs
Route 2, Surrett Cove Road
Leicester, NC 28748
(Catalog: $1.00, refundable with first order)

Taylor's Garden, Inc.
1535 Lone Oak Road
Vista, CA 92083
(Herbs, scented geraniums. Catalog: free)

Weleda, Inc.
841 South Main Street
Spring Valley, NY 10977
(All-natural body-care products, dried herbs, books. Catalog: free)

*Sources which list organically grown herbs.

Well-Sweep Herb Farm*
317 Mount Bethel Road
Port Murray, NJ 07865
(Price lists available for seeds, plants, and products. Catalog: 50¢)

Western Comfrey, Inc.
P.O. Box 45
Canby, OR 97013
(Comfrey root cuttings, comfrey products such as tea, skin cream, tablets, capsules, gel. Quarterly publication, *Comfrey Digest*. Brochure: free)

White Mountain Herb Farm*
P.O. Box 64
Jefferson, NH 03583
(Dried herbs and live plants sold on a mail-order basis. Complete list available containing 68 different varieties.)

Wide World of Herbs, Ltd.
United States:
P.O. Box 266
Rouses Point, NY 12979

Canada:
11 Sainte Catherine Street East
Montreal, PQ
Canada H2X 1K3
(Botanicals)

Paintmaking Suppliers

Powdered pigments are available to your hardware or paint retailer in 1-pound boxes under the Rainbow label, from:

Empire White Products Co.
45 Hermon Street
Newark, NJ 07105

You may also wish to consult the *Thomas Register* for the names of companies listed under Paint, Pigment, and Plastics Manufacturers that are closest to you, since you'll not want to get involved with shipping.

*Sources which list organically grown herbs.

Appendix D
Further Reading

Adamson, Helen L. *Grandmother's Household Hints: As Good Today as Yesterday.* New York: Paperback Library, 1963.

Bacon, Richard. *The Yankee Magazine Book of Forgotten Arts.* New York: Simon and Schuster, 1978.

Bairacli-Levy, Juliette de. *The Complete Herbal Book for the Dog.* New York: Arco, 1973.

——. *Herbal Handbook for Farm and Stable.* Emmaus, Pa.: Rodale Press, 1976.

Bingham, Joan, and Riccio, Dolores. *Make It Yourself.* Radnor, Pa.: Chilton Book Co., 1978.

Bracken, Peg. *The I Hate to Housekeep Book.* Greenwich, Conn.: Fawcett World Library, 1970.

Buchman, Dian Dincin. *The Complete Herbal Guide to Natural Health and Beauty.* New York: Doubleday & Co., 1973.

"Built-In Dishwashers." *Consumer Reports,* June 1980. pp. 366–70.

Candee, Richard. "Preparing and Mixing Colors in 1812." *Antiques,* April 1978, pp 849–53.

Consumer Guide. *The Faster, Cheapest, Best Way to Clean Everything.* New York: Simon and Schuster, 1981.

——. *Helpful Household Formulas.* New York: Beekman House, 1981.

Consumer Guide Handbook of Helpful Hints. Publications International. Distributed by Los Angeles Times Syndicate. Excerpt in *Sunday Call-Chronicle,* Allentown, Pa., 6 April 1980.

Deis, Robert. "The Candle That Grows on Trees." *Down East Magazine,* December 1978, pp. 23-25.

Detergents—In Depth, '80. New York: The Soap and Detergent Association.

Dick, William B. *Dick's Encyclopedia of Practical Receipts and Processes.* 5th ed. New York: Dick and Fitzgerald Publishers, 1895.

"Dishwasher Detergents: Does It Really Matter Which One You Use?" *Consumer Reports,* June 1980, pp. 371-73.

Editors of *Organic Gardening. Getting the Most from Your Garaen.* Emmaus, Pa.: Rodale Press, 1980.

Editors of Rodale Press. *The Organic Gardener's Complete Guide to Vegetables and Fruits.* Emmaus, Pa.: Rodale Press, 1982.

Farmer, Fannie Merritt. *The Boston Cooking School Cook Book.* New York: Gordon Press, 1982.

"Floor Waxes and Finishes," *Consumer's Research Magazine,* January 1978, pp. 12-16.

"Glass Cleaners." *Consumer Reports,* September 1980, pp. 570-71.

Goldschmiedt, Henry. *Practical Formulas for Hobby or Profit.* New York: Chemical Publishing Co., 1973.

Halpin, Anne M., ed. *Rodale's Encyclopedia of Indoor Gardening.* Emmaus, Pa.: Rodale Press, 1980.

Handbook of Industry Terms. 2d ed. New York: The Soap and Detergent Association, 1981.

Handsfield, Leicester, and Handsfield, Harriet, eds. *Dick's Encyclopedia of Practical Receipts and Processes: How They Did It in the 1870's.* New York: Funk and Wagnalls Co., 1975.

Heinerman, John. *Healing Animals with Herbs.* Orem, Utah: BiWorld Industries, 1979.

Heloise. *Heloise's Housekeeping Hints.* New York: Pocket Books, 1971

——. *Heloise's Kitchen Hints.* New York: Pocket Books, 1971.

——. *Heloise's Work and Money Savers.* New York: Pocket Books, 1971.

High Detergency Modified Soap. Philadelphia, Pa.: Eastern Regional Research Center, Agricultural Research Service, U.S. Department of Agriculture, April 1977.

Hirst-Smith, Ann. *The Complete Candlemaker.* New York: Van Nostrand Reinhold Co., 1974.

Hiscox, Gardner D., ed. *Henley's Twentieth Century Book of Formulas, Processes and Trade Secrets.* Rev. ed. Cornwells Heights, Pa.: Publishers Agency, 1981.

"How to Care for Gold and Silver." *Better Homes and Gardens,* May 1981, p. 234.

"How to Get Stains Out of Anything." *Family Circle,* 1 July 1981, pp. 53–54. (Excerpted from Grunfeld, N., and Thomas, M. *Spot Check.* Los Angeles: Price/Stern/Sloan Publishers, 1980.)

"How to Take Ring Marks off Furniture and 24 Other Furniture-Care Tips." *Family Circle,* 19 May 1978, p. 172.

Hylton, William H., ed. *The Rodale Herb Book.* Emmaus, Pa.: Rodale Press, 1974.

Instant Kitchen Tricks. New York: Dell Publishing Co., 1966.

Jensen, Bernard. *Nature Has a Remedy.* Santa Cruz, Calif.: Unity Press, 1978.

Keely, Jane. "Around the House." *Good Housekeeping,* January 1981, p. 45.

Kirk and Othmer. *Enamels.* Encyclopedia of Chemical Technology, vol. 9, 3d ed. New York: John Wiley and Sons, 1978–80.

Lawson, Donna. *Mother Nature's Beauty Cupboard.* New York: Bantam Books, 1974.

Libien, L., and Strong, M. *Home Care. Special Report H. C. 401.* New York: Chicago Tribune/New York News Syndicate.

Linfield, W. M. "Soap and Lime Soap Dispersants." *Journal of the American Oil Chemists' Society,* January 1978, pp. 87–92.

Mager, Nathan H., and Mager, Sylvia K., eds. *The Household Encyclopedia: What to Do—How to Do It.* Rev. ed. New York: Pocket Books, 1966.

Mohr, Merilyn. *The Art of Soap Making.* Ontario, Can.: Camden House, 1979.

Moore, Alma C. *How to Clean Everything.* New York: Simon and Schuster, 1971.

Painting and Decorating Contractors of America. *Painting and Decorating Craftsman's Manual and Textbook.* Binghamton, N.Y.: Vail-Ballou Press, 1957.

Percivall, Julia, and Burger, Pixie. *Household Ecology.* Englewood Cliffs, N.J.: Prentice-Hall, 1972.

Pinkham, Mary E. *Mary Ellen's Best of Helpful Kitchen Hints.* New York: Warner Books, 1980.

Pinkham, Mary E., and Higgenbotham, Pearl. *Mary Ellen's Best of Helpful Hints.* New York: Warner Books, 1979.

Plummer, Beverly. *Fragrance: A Recipe Book.* New York: Atheneum, 1975.

Rinzler, Carol Ann. *The Consumer's Brand-Name Guide to Household Products.* New York: Lippincott and Crowell, 1980.

Rose, Jeanne. *Herbs and Things: Jeanne Rose's Herbal.* New York: Grosset & Dunlap, 1972.

——. *The Herbal Body Book.* New York: Grosset & Dunlap, 1976.

——. *The Herbal Guide to Living.* New York: Bantam Books, 1982.

"Rug Shampoos." *Consumer Reports,* March 1980, pp. 160–61.

Schneck, Stephen, and Norris, Nigel. *Complete Home Medical Guide for Cats.* New York: Stein and Day, 1975.

Singer and Gordon. *The Dictionary of Household Hints and Helps.* Edited by Allan T. Hirsh, Jr. New York: Grosset & Dunlap, 1974.

Staff of *Organic Gardening. The Encyclopedia of Organic Gardening.* Emmaus, Pa.: Rodale Press, 1978.

Stark, Norman. *The Formula Book.* Fairway, Kans.: Andrews and McMeel, 1975.

——. *Formula Book Two.* Fairway, Kans.: Andrews and McMeel, 1976.

Thomas, Virginia C. *My Secrets of Natural Beauty.* New Canaan, Conn.: Keats Publishing, 1972.

Tierra, Michael. *The Way of Herbs.* Santa Cruz, Calif.: Unity Press, 1980.

"213 Ways to Do It Better." *Family Circle,* July 1979, pp. 100–144.

"Understanding Automatic Dishwashing." New York: Pamphlet prepared by the Consumer Affairs Committee, The Soap and Detergent Association.

Vanderwalker, F. N. *The Mixing of Colors and Paints.* Chicago, Ill.: Frederick J. Drake and Co., 1935.

Vivian, John. *Wood Heat.* Emmaus, Pa.: Rodale Press, 1978.

Weakley, Tom. *How to Make Candles.* Brattleboro, Vt.: The Stephen Greene Press, 1971.

Webster, William E., and McMullen, Claire. *Contemporary Candlemaking.* New York: Doubleday & Co., 1972.

Wigginton, Eliot, ed. *The Foxfire Book.* New York: Anchor Press-Doubleday & Co., 1972.

Woman's Almanac and Book of Facts. New York: Dell Publishing, 1965.

Yepsen, Roger B., Jr., ed. *Organic Plant Protection.* Emmaus, Pa.: Rodale Press, 1976.

Index

Note: Formula titles appear in italics.

D